Eccentric Lives

The Daily Telegraph

BOOK OF 21st CENTURY OBITUARIES

Eccentric Lives

𝕿𝖍𝖊 𝕯𝖆𝖎𝖑𝖞 𝕿𝖊𝖑𝖊𝖌𝖗𝖆𝖕𝖍

BOOK OF 21st CENTURY OBITUARIES

Edited by
Andrew M. Brown

UNICORN

Published in 2022 by
Unicorn, an imprint of Unicorn Publishing Group
Charleston Studio
Meadow Business Centre
Lewes BN8 5RW
www.unicornpublishing.org

ISBN 978 1 914414 87 9
10 9 8 7 6 5 4 3 2 1

Design by newtonworks.uk

Jacket illustration (also on page ii) by Jonathan Bentley

Printed by Gutenberg Press, Malta

Eccentric Lives

Introduction

Over the past 36 years, *Daily Telegraph* obituaries have become a sort of cult, devoured with relish every day by thousands of readers of all ages and backgrounds. And the sort of *Telegraph* obit that people think of first – alongside those tales of wartime derring-do which fill many separate books of their own – is the eccentric.

The inventor of the *Telegraph* obituary as we know it was Hugh Massingberd. He was an eccentric himself, although 'like most true eccentrics', as his friend Craig Brown recalled, he 'did his best to appear conventional'. Two days after his death on Christmas Day 2007, the paper treated Massingberd to a full-page obituary (a masterly piece of writing, which is reprinted here for the first time complete and unedited). His vision of obituaries was that they could be essentially a comic form, and that it was our peculiarities, foibles and eccentricities that made us really human.

Many people are surprised to discover that a daily obits section is not something that goes back to the earliest days of *The Telegraph*. In fact, obituaries used to be done in an ad hoc way, and the most common type of obit was a short and stodgy list of honours with no sense of a pulsating human being.

Massingberd changed all that. Although in general a modest man, he was soon referring to the introduction of the new section in September 1986 as the 'big bang', and putting on record the creation story of *Telegraph* obits. He 'eagerly publicised', his obit relates, 'his pride in the column both in the prints and on wireless and television'.

Nearly 30 years later, in 2014, when I was given the job of looking after the section, one of the questions that nagged at me was: will the well dry up? Are eccentrics still arriving on the slab of 21st century history?

Are we not living in an age of conformity? Once, the Church, academia and other walks of life provided a safe harbour for the oddball or the prophet. Now, these institutions screen out any hint of unorthodox tendencies. They have selection committees who choose candidates in their own image: a recipe for drab uniformity – for managers, not thinkers. Definitely not for eccentrics.

And yet we do find some quirky clerics clinging on to the lower rungs of the ecclesiastical ladder, and several feature in these pages. The Reverend David Johnson is one. Though 'keen of mind and sharp of wit', he was possessed of an eccentricity 'which led some to revere him as an institution and others to opine that he ought to be confined to one'.

Even among the aristocracy, once fertile mulch for wacky behaviour, you might think the pressure to join the ranks of corporate Britain would militate against distinctiveness in thought and action. But in places eccentricity still wins through.

Take Margot (Marchioness of) Reading. In her later years she expressed opinions that were 'diametrically opposed to most sane people', insisting, for example, that football hooligans were keeping up Britain's 'historic spirit' in the face of 'milksops, and Left-wing liberals and wetties'.

After making my shortlist – the idea being that this would be a new collection of lives we have celebrated in the recent past – I found that some characteristics were disproportionately represented. Notably, obsessiveness: a quality that's found in collectors like Gerry Wells, 'whose life was dominated by his fascination with radio apparatus' and who turned his Edwardian house in Dulwich into a museum of vintage wireless technology.

Anthony Carter built a vast collection of bayonets and detailed them in learned books ('slender cruciform blade ... capable of killing even the most thickly clad enemy'); the Oxford philosophy don John Simopoulos was obsessed with telephones and spent his summer holidays working at the Rome telephone exchange; and the rocket scientist Roy Dommett, guardian of Britain's nuclear deterrent, was in his spare time a devoted practitioner of morris dancing.

Unlike the collectors, however, Viv Nicholson struggled to hold on to anything. After her husband's pools win she kept her promise to the tabloids to 'spend, spend, spend' – on a '£4,000 luxury bungalow' and 'a pink Cadillac', among other delights.

Retaining the formal obit structure, deadpan and coolly factual, serves to point up any comedy in the subject-matter. A case in point is the Italian lothario 'Zanza'. He died *in flagrante* with a female companion, 'at around two in the morning in his Mitsubishi Pajero 4x4, parked in a small peach grove owned by his family'. The story of this Latin lover, a legend in his home town of Rimini, had been covered in some news pages, but given the full-dress obit treatment it went 'viral' in Italy as well as in Britain.

There is sadness in these stories, too. Nothing is funny about the life of Anne Naysmith, the concert pianist who had worked with Sir Adrian Boult and ended her days sleeping in a car on the streets of West London. But the story of her life is mysterious and poignant.

We are not in the business of making moral judgments. If we were, I doubt whether we would have found space for the 'gentleman adventurer', 'Dandy Kim' Waterfield, boyfriend of Diana Dors and founder of the original Ann Summers sex shop, who spent time in a French jail after stealing from the film mogul Jack Warner's house on the riviera.

Similarly, there's nothing especially admirable about Eileen Fox, film extra and self-described 'Queen of Soho'. She once unsuccessfully sued British Airways, claiming that during a flight to the Seychelles she had been bitten on the bottom by a flea. 'It was a jumbo jet and they must have been elephant fleas,' she said.

To me, though, 'Foxy' Fox seems to demonstrate a core quality of eccentrics, which is a kind of vitality. She was willing to jump on to the spinning wheel of life, not caring that it might throw her off.

Compiling this personal selection was a bit like being one of those cheese testers who pushes a hollow probe deep into a round of Stilton to see the microflora threading their way through. It's inevitably slightly random. I have tried to choose the unfamiliar and avoid the famous – an exception being Jeremy Thorpe, because the obit is such a rollicking good read – and concentrate mostly on homegrown subjects or those with connections to Britain.

Obits is the most collaborative of journalistic exercises, so I pay warm tribute to my predecessors in the obits chair after Hugh Massingberd: David (Lewis) Jones, Kate Summerscale, Christopher Howse, Andrew McKie and Harry de Quetteville. I am grateful to Chris Evans, the editor of *The Telegraph*, for entrusting me with the job, and I owe a particular debt of gratitude to my early colleague on the desk Jay Iliff, who guided me and is a model of that rare quality Hemingway called grace under pressure.

Lord (Ian) Strathcarron at Unicorn publishers, with his enthusiasm convinced me that it was time to compile a new obits collection and Lucy Duckworth tolerated my chronic procrastination. I offer my thanks for their kindness and their moral and practical support to my colleagues on the desk over the years, the writer-editors Chris Maume (esteemed former obits editor at *The Independent*) and Georgia Powell (now Beaufort), the outstandingly gifted chief obits writer Katharine Ramsay, Kate Moore, Christian House, and our newest recruit Iona McLaren, and to all the specialists who contributed to this volume, in anonymity, in addition to the names already mentioned. They include Lynn Barber, Andrew Barrow, Trevor Beeson, Mick Brown, Tim Bullamore, Robert Chalmers, Nicholas Farrell, Edward Fox, Robert Gray, George Ireland, Jake Kerridge, Alexander Lucie-Smith, John and J. R. H. McEwen, James Owen, Harry Phibbs, Dai Prichard, Iain Thornber, the late David Twiston Davies, Martin Vander Weyer, Hugo Vickers, Geoffrey Wheatcroft, Roger Wilkes and A. N. Wilson.

Andrew M. Brown
June 2022

Anthony Carter

Internationally respected author of works on bayonets and belt frogs

Carter with part of his unsurpassed collection of 19th and 20th century bayonets

ANTHONY CARTER, who has died aged 58, spent his whole life in singleminded devotion to the study, promotion and sale of late 19th and 20th century bayonets.

These well-documented weapons were mass-produced in a rich variety of models which could serve not only as lances, cutlasses and knives but also as saws, trowels, and even wire cutters. When Carter became fascinated by them as a boy, they commanded less interest among collectors than swords or muskets. Nevertheless, there was sufficient demand for him to be able to set up as a dealer. He found ample stocks in junk shops and army surplus stores at home and abroad, as armies recognised the declining importance of hand-to-hand fighting in modern warfare.

In time Carter became the leading British authority. He produced a series of learned books, and had a long running column in *Guns Review*, in which he examined such knotty questions as the existence of the legendary Nepalese *kukri* bayonet. He was particularly admired for his four volumes on German bayonets; even German collectors admitted that he left all other writers on the subject standing.

A typical Carter entry, on the British Rifle No 4 Mark 1, records that it had a slender cruciform blade which tapered to a sharp point and could be used only for thrusting. 'In this respect it was adequate,' he recorded with John Walter, in their book *The Bayonet, 1850–1970*, 'since tests held in 1922–4 had convinced the authorities that the short blade was capable of killing even the most thickly clad enemy – who was taken to be a Russian in winter clothing. The spike was never popular with the troops, but it had the great advantage of simplicity that made it easy to make; it was also very cheap, in terms of money, material and labour.'

In addition, Carter wrote, and sometimes published for others, specialist works in allied fields. His three-volume *Bayonet Belt Frogs*, meticulously illustrated with his own drawings, is the only work on these accoutrements, which are used to hang scabbards from belts. As such it is known to collectors worldwide simply as 'BBF'.

John Anthony Carter was born on September 21 1943 at Loughton, Essex. His father, a surgeon, was a dogged patriot who stored weapons against the possibility of a German invasion; his mother was a keen collector of antiques.

Anthony spent his pocket money on a pair of First World War bayonets at the age of eight. He went to Uppingham, then read English and Philosophy at King's College, London, while running a bayonet stall in Portobello Road. He joined Christie's in London, where he worked in the fine art department; then, in 1969, he became deputy manager at the auction house's branch in Montreal.

Slipping easily into the persona of the Englishman Abroad, Tony Carter (or 'TC', as he was known) found many bayonet bargains, and spent his lunchtimes at the Sir Winston Churchill pub. The customers never tired of military talk, to which the American draft-dodger behind the bar would contribute, and

Carter would amuse the company by producing from his pocket an American trench knuckleduster which he carried in case his girlfriend's husband appeared.

When Christie's closed its operation in Montreal in 1971, Carter returned to England. Three years later he married Evelyn Palmer, with whom he was to have two daughters. For some years he produced catalogues, and later ran a website, for enthusiasts around the world. It was his misfortune that, when his marriage broke up, much of his collection had to be sold.

A man of great charm and elegance, he lived at Morton on the Hill, Norfolk, on the estate of his sister, who had been married to a descendant of a bayonet manufacturing family. He was a fanatical viewer of *Coronation Street* and enjoyed walking his dogs and talking to a peacock called Fred, whom he named after *The Daily Telegraph*'s Toronto correspondent, Fred Langan; Carter's only association with violence was his appearance as a murderous bayonet expert in Langan's novel, *The Stringer*.

Anthony Carter was working on a book about the the 1866 French Chassepot bayonet, which has a brass handle and wavy blade, and was completing his ground-breaking second volume on the German cutlery industry of Solingen when he died, after a hernia operation.

Anthony Carter, born September 21 1943, died June 22 2002

Graham Mason

Denizen of Soho who became noted for his bibulous misbehaviour

Graham Mason (2001), painted by the artist Rupert Shrive

GRAHAM MASON, the journalist who has died aged 59, was in the 1980s the drunkest man in the Coach and Horses, the pub in Soho where, in the half century after the Second World War, a tragicomedy was played out nightly by its regulars.

His claim to a title in bibulous misbehaviour was staked against stiff competition from Jeffrey Bernard and a dedicated cast of less celebrated but formidable drinkers. Mason was a fearsome sight at his most drunkenly irascible. Seated at the bar, his thin shanks wrapped around the legs of a high stool, he would swivel his reptilian stare round behind him to any unfortunate stranger attempting to be served, and snap: 'Who the f--- are you?' Sometimes this prompted a reaction, and on one occasion a powerful blow to the head sent Mason flying, with his stool, across the carpet. Painfully clawing himself upright, he set the stool in its place, reseated himself and, twisting his head round again, growled: 'Don't you *ever* do that again.'

Unlike his friend Jeffrey Bernard, though, Graham Mason did not make himself the hero of his own tragedy. His speciality was the extreme. In one drinking binge he went for nine days without food. At the height of his consumption, before he was frightened by epileptic fits into cutting back, he was managing two bottles of vodka a day. His face became, in his own description, that of a 'rotten choirboy'. At lunchtime he would walk through the door of the Coach and Horses still trembling with hangover, his nose and ears blue, whatever the weather. On one cold day he complained of the *noise* that the snow made as it landed on his bald head.

His practice of 'boozer's economics' meant dressing in the shabbiest of clothes, many of them inherited from the late husband of the woman with whom he lived. He wore a threadbare duffel coat with broken toggles. One day it was inexplicably stolen from the pub coathook.

Jeffrey Bernard took the opportunity to combine kindness with condescension by buying a replacement of much grander design and cloth.

From the 1960s on, Mason was a friend of many of the painters as well as the writers, actors, layabouts, retired prostitutes, stagehands and hopeless cases that then gave Soho its flavour. He enjoyed talking to Francis Bacon in the Colony Room Club because Bacon was very funny; and, until they finally had a row, Bacon enjoyed talking to him.

Mason had a gift for contriving very telling nicknames. A failed actress who rode a bicycle and was addicted to tittle-tattle became 'The Village Postmistress'. Gordon Smith, a stage-door keeper of fussy temperament, was 'Granny Gordon'. One barman was 'Princess Michael'.

In a couple of hours one evening in February 1988 he had loud altercations with John Hurt ('You're just a bad actor'); with a law writer nicknamed The Red Baron, who was later murdered

('You know I don't like you. Go away and leave me alone.'); and
with Jeffrey Bernard (who stood up and shook him by the lapels).
Michael Heath often featured Mason in his strip-cartoon *The
Regulars.* In one episode he is shown apologising for being so
rude the night before: 'You see, I was sober.'

Amid the violence of Soho arguments he became a friend of
Elizabeth Smart, the Canadian author of *By Grand Central Station
I Sat Down and Wept,* a book about her lover George Barker, the
poet, who became another friend. Mason succeeded in liking
Francis Bacon's final close friend, John Edwards, which some
people did not; and the poet John Heath-Stubbs took a shine to him.

One of his first friends in Soho was John Deakin, the
photographer, whom he defended against the charge, put about
by Daniel Farson, of being cruel to everyone. 'The only man John
Deakin was unkind to was David Archer,' Mason asserted. David
Archer, who ran a bookshop at a loss, was the man Deakin lived
with.

Mason felt at home in the Colony in the years before
homosexuality was decriminalised because no one minded one
way or the other.

Mason's own closest friendship was with Marsh Dunbar, the
widow of an admired art director at *The Economist.* He lodged
with her at first in a fine early 19th century house in Canonbury
Square, Islington, where she was bringing up three sons. She
had herself fallen into Soho after the War, knowing everyone
from John Minton to Lucian Freud. Though enthusiastically
heterosexual, she lived with Mason until her death.

In the days before licensing liberalisation, he resorted in
the afternoon when pubs were closed to drinking clubs such as
the Kismet, a damp basement with a smell that wits identified
as 'failure'; it was known as The Iron Lung and Death in the
Afternoon. Mason admired the diminutive but firm presence
behind the bar, known as Maltese Mary. But his favourite resort
remained the Colony.

Graham Edward Mason was born on July 19 1942 in Cape
Town, South Africa. He had been conceived on a sand dune, and

to this, as a devotee of Laurence Sterne's *Tristram Shandy*, he sometimes attributed his abrasive character. He was educated at Chingola, Northern Rhodesia (now Zambia), and then joined a local newspaper. From there, as a bright and promising 18-year-old, he was recruited for the American news agency UPI by its bureau chief in Salisbury, Southern Rhodesia (now Harare, Zimbabwe).

He learned fast as a reporter of the civil war in Congo, finding the veterans from the Algerian war among his colleagues both kind and helpful. He witnessed a line of prisoners executed with pistol shots to the head, and was himself injured in the thigh and chin by a mortar shell. Among those he interviewed in a Rhodesia moving towards UDI (Unilateral Declaration of Independence) were Joshua Nkomo and Robert Mugabe; he did not take to the latter.

Posted to the UPI office in London in 1963, he set off in a Land Rover with three friends and no proper map, through Tanganyika, Kenya, Ethiopia and Sudan to Port Sudan on the Red Sea, and thence on an East German ship via Trieste to Hull.

From UPI's London office in Bouverie Street, Mason soon discovered Soho, and, like many before him, felt he had come home. He continued as a foreign correspondent, taking a year out in 1968 to work for 20th Century Fox on feature films, which he hated. With BBC Television News he reported from the Northern Ireland troubles, and in 1975 took another year out to run a bar in Nicosia. It happened to coincide with civil war, and he and Marsh Dunbar were lucky to be evacuated by the RAF. From then until 1980 he worked for ITN. One day he was found asleep under his desk, drunk. It was something of a low point.

He was living with Marsh Dunbar in a flat in Berwick Street, Soho. A fire there sent them, fleeing bills, to a run down council tower block on the Isle of Dogs. The compensation was a view of a sweep of the Thames towards Greenwich. He worked while he still could, managing Bobby Hunt's photographic library.

Graham Mason cooked Mediterranean food well, liked Piero della Francesca and *Fidelio*, choral evensong on the Third

11

Programme and fireworks. After Marsh Dunbar's death in 2001, with almost all his friends dead, he sat imprisoned by emphysema in his flat, with a cylinder of oxygen by his armchair and bottles of white wine by his elbow, looking out over the Thames, still very angry.

Graham Mason, born July 19 1942, died April 2002

Eileen Fox

Self-styled 'Queen of Soho' who sued British Airways, claiming to have been bitten on the bottom by a flea

EILEEN FOX, who has died aged 79, was a peripatetic bohemian and film extra, given to calling herself the 'Queen of Soho' in the 1960s and 1970s.

As talkative as she was rotund, 'Foxy', as she was invariably known, was certainly hard to miss in the small knot of streets just to the north of London's Shaftesbury Avenue. If she felt that she was receiving insufficient attention she would remove her clothes in public view.

'Foxy': she loosened her bra-straps on hearing *Rule Britannia*

Whether lunching at Jimmy the Greek's or devouring other customers' part-consumed cream buns at Patisserie Valerie, she made everyone else's business her own, often to their intense irritation.

The daughter of a prostitute and a father she never met, Eileen Daphne Fox was born of Jewish stock and brought up in east London in the 1920s. She was known from her early years simply as 'Foxy', a name that acknowledged both her easy informality and a natural cunning.

It was not an easy childhood. Her mother had little money, and Foxy received a basic education, managing to master only capital letters.

A flair for acting became apparent when she discarded her native Cockney accent in favour of something more refined. She worked as a telephone receptionist at a West End law firm and impressed clients who, on being connected to the senior partner, would compliment him on employing such a high standard of switchboard operator. The object of their esteem, however, was not a pearled daughter of the shires but a plump, untidy woman who was seldom seen without several plastic bags full of possessions.

In Soho, Eileen Fox became acquainted with the set that included Francis Bacon and Jeffrey Bernard, though she disapproved of their heavy drinking and always refused to buy alcohol for friends. She herself preferred fizzy, soft drinks which soon rotted away her teeth.

Eileen Fox was a stranger to reticence. At the drop of a good polka she would seize the nearest man to give him a dance to remember. When short of money, which was often, she would approach strangers with the suggestion that she read their fortunes. Task done, she would insist that they cross her own palm with silver – preferably of a high denomination.

She liked to strip, be it to enliven a party or to celebrate a rousing tune. A patriot, she could seldom hear *Rule Britannia* without loosening her bra straps. In the late 1970s she became a regular visitor to Ibiza, though curiously she ignored the island's nudist beaches.

As well as being a nude model for artists, Eileen Fox undertook work as a film extra, specialising in crowd scenes that called for gummy medieval serfs. One of her last appearances was in Kevin Costner's *Robin Hood: Prince of Thieves* (1991).

In 1980 she took British Airways to the Court of Appeal, alleging that she had been bitten on the bottom while travelling on one of the company's Boeing 747s to the Seychelles. 'It was a jumbo jet and they must have been elephant fleas,' she told reporters afterwards. She claimed that the unsightly bites cost her professional earnings as a nude model. Lord Justice Megaw and his colleagues were not convinced.

It transpired that Eileen Fox had earlier bounced a £500 cheque on British Airways and took exception when the airline sought recovery of the funds.

After that case she refused to pay for air travel. Instead, she worked for an international courier firm, delivering parcels around the globe and frequently selling the return stub of her free ticket in order to explore countries at greater leisure. From Nepal to Nigeria, Peru to Ukraine, Eileen Fox could be found hitch-hiking well into her old age. British drivers, stopping to pick up a gnarled old peasant, were astonished to be addressed with a very English 'Cheers!'

In Athens she spent several months working as a dishwasher, sleeping on the roof of a hotel near the airport while she earned her fare home. She was a frequent menace to British diplomats, who would find her on their embassy doorstep, demanding safe passage back to London.

Although always claiming penury, she was a generous woman, fond of the young and earnest in her desire to help.

In the 1980s she took advantage of the Conservatives' right-to-buy policy and took a mortgage on her council house in Elspeth Road, Battersea. She later sold the house for a profit of £80,000 and used the money to become a landlord in the Balearics.

She died in a nursing home on Ibiza, after a stroke. At her Anglican funeral the priest forwent traditional liturgy and instead invited congregants to tell their favourite Foxy memories.

To her own regret, she never married.

Eileen Fox, born *c.*1923, died 2002

Viscount Mountgarret

Landowner with a passion for cricket and shooting who took ill-advised pot shots at a hot-air balloon

THE 17th VISCOUNT MOUNTGARRET, who has died aged 67, was a Yorkshire landowner with an autocratic streak which occasionally got him into trouble with the authorities and attracted the amused attention of the press.

The 'exploit' for which he became most famous happened in 1982, when he took pot shots at a hot-air balloon flying over his grouse moor near Appletreewick in Yorkshire. The yellow-and-blue-striped balloon – owned by the Skipton Building Society – had drifted over Hardcastle Moor as Mountgarret's party

Mountgarret: a man of strong opinions, he believed in castrating rapists

was preparing for a drive. Its pilot, Graham Turnbull, was taking two passengers – an aircraft technician and a fish fryer – on a pleasure flight.

Turnbull later told a court: 'There was quite a few people below with guns. Suddenly shots struck the basket and the balloon itself, and I was covered with lead shot.'

A six-foot split was later found in the nylon canopy, as well as 20 holes in the protective 'scoop' covering the gas burner.

In court it was said that Mountgarret had fired twice at the balloon, hitting the pilot in the neck; the two passengers had ducked. Mountgarret, who denied recklessly damaging a hot-air balloon, and acting recklessly in a manner likely to endanger an aircraft, claimed that he had fired 'deliberate and calculated' warning shots because the balloon and its occupants were in 'extreme danger' from the guns. The magistrates, however, found him guilty and fined him £1,000 with £600 costs. The next year he had his shotgun licence temporarily withdrawn.

In 1999 Mountgarret was taken to an industrial tribunal, which ordered him to pay £19,484 compensation after his former gamekeeper won a claim for unfair dismissal.

The tribunal heard that Mountgarret was prone to 'unpredictable, irrational and intolerable rages'. The gamekeeper, Michael Rushby, claimed that Mountgarret had called him a 'bloody idiot' and a 'bloody imbecile' in front of guests and beaters at shooting parties.

But for these skirmishes, Mountgarret might have lived out his life in comparative obscurity, managing his estate and pursuing his interests of shooting, stalking, cricket and golf. His friends in Yorkshire viewed him as a good host and an entertaining character who had probably been born in the wrong century; they knew him fondly as 'Garry' or 'Mount Ararat'.

At the end of a day's shooting, his guests would retire to his house near Harrogate, where they might be invited to participate in one of their host's favourite pastimes, indoor golf. Mountgarret would appoint a certain feature – his double bed, for example – as the 'hole'. The players would then chip their golf balls through the house (up the stairs, if necessary), occasionally damaging the contents as they did so.

Richard Henry Piers Butler was born at Knaresborough on November 8 1936, and was educated at Eton and Sandhurst. He was commissioned in the Irish Guards in 1957, retiring in the rank of captain in 1964. Two years later he succeeded his father in the viscountcy, which had been created in 1550.

In 1968 he sold his family's house, Nidd Hall, at Ripley, Yorkshire, and devoted himself to managing his 2,000-acre estate at South Stainley, near Harrogate.

Among Mountgarret's passions was cricket and, although he described himself as a 'pretty indifferent' cricketer, he turned out for the Household Brigade, the Ramblers, I Zingari and the Yorkshire Gentlemen. He was elected president of Yorkshire County Cricket Club in 1984. At the time the club was riven by internal arguments, particularly over whether Geoffrey Boycott should be allowed to serve on the committee at the same time as being a player; but when Mountgarret proposed new rules for the club in 1986, 92 per cent of the membership supported him. Two years later, however, Mountgarret's position as president was threatened by a splinter group which wanted to remove him in favour of the Duke of York. Finally, in 1990, Mountgarret was not re-nominated for the post, and was succeeded by Sir Len Hutton.

On assuming the post, Mountgarret had announced his intention of 'banging a few heads together in the interests of common sense'. Some committee members did not warm to this approach, preferring their president to act more in the manner of a figurehead. However, he presided over the founding of the Cricket Academy and the appointment of a team manager.

Mountgarret was a man of forceful personality and strong opinions. In the House of Lords he opposed the introduction of compulsory seatbelts, on the ground that it infringed individual liberty. In 1980 he proposed that motorists should be allowed to pass through a red light, when the road was clear, if they wished to turn left.

In 1983 – after the siege at the Libyan embassy in St James's Square during which a young woman police constable was shot dead – Mountgarret floated an idea for embassies in London to be moved to the suburbs. He also introduced a bill proposing that England, Wales and Northern Ireland should convert to Central European time.

But it was Mountgarret's excursion into the field of crime and punishment that excited most interest. In 1987 he supported the reintroduction of the death penalty – by lethal injection – for certain types of murder; he also proposed deportation to 'islands sovereign to the United Kingdom' for offenders serving sentences of more than 25 years, and castration for rapists who re-offended.

18

Those convicted of assault should be liable for 24 strokes of the birch.

In 1985 he was one of five Conservative peers who voted against the government's decision to give large salary increases to senior members of the Civil Service, the Armed Forces and the judiciary; and in 1990 he compared the poll tax to 'the monster created by Baron Frankenstein'. He was a supporter of John Redwood MP. Mountgarret lost his seat in the Lords under the reforms of 1999.

Mountgarret had recently moved out of Stainley House and was planning to live at a farmhouse on the estate.

He married first, in 1960, Gillian Margaret Buckley, with whom he had two sons and a daughter. The marriage was dissolved in 1970, and in that year he married Jennifer Fattorini (née Wills). After that marriage was dissolved in 1983, he married, thirdly, Ruth Waddington (née Porter), who had modelled Silvikrin shampoo in the 1960s.

His son, Piers James Richard Butler, born in 1961, succeeds in the viscountcy.

Viscount Mountgarret, born November 8 1936, died February 7 2004

Portland Mason

Film star's daughter said to have smoked when she was three and to have had a couture dress at four

Portland Mason carried shoulder-high on location for her St Trinian's film

PORTLAND MASON, who has died aged 55, was the daughter of the film star James Mason, and used to be routinely described in the press as 'the world's most precocious child'.

Born in Los Angeles on November 26 1948, Portland Mason's early years were spent in Hollywood, where her parents' house, built in the 1920s by Buster Keaton, was appointed with every luxury. When she was two she was allowed to go to bed at midnight. She was presented with her first couture evening gown when she was four. At six she appeared on television dressed in furs, diamonds and stiletto heels.

In 1956, when she was seven, she accompanied her parents on a visit to London, prompting the *Daily Express* to observe that she already owned a mink coat and that she had a 'Mamie Eisenhower fringe to her coiffured hair'. James Mason himself remarked at the time: 'We want Portland to be able to do what she likes, how she likes, and when she likes. That way we feel she will achieve a personality of her own.'

The child's mother, Pamela (Kellino) Mason, added that their daughter was already working on her memoirs: 'We are doing it by just letting her talk into a tape recorder. I am prompting her with questions like, "What do you think of divorce?"'

When Portland was only three, her father had introduced her to cigarettes. His master plan was that they would cause her to cough, thus encouraging her to avoid smoking in her later years. When, a short time afterwards, a friend asked Mason for a progress report, the screen star replied: 'Well, she's now up to two packs a day.'

In December 1958, it was reported that Portland had celebrated her 10th birthday by going shopping in Los Angeles for bras and a girdle.

Meanwhile, she attended the El Rodeo School in Beverly Hills, being delivered every morning by a Rolls-Royce and collected in the afternoon by a white Cadillac. Her favourite scent was Arpège.

Whether all this added up to an accurate impression of Portland Mason's character is doubtful. She went on to drama school and then tried modelling, and by the time she was 18, and living in London, a journalist who interviewed her found her 'surprisingly unspoilt, somewhat shy and unassuming'.

And by now she was already a veteran of a number of films. Aged seven she had starred in a picture called *The Child* (1954), directed by her father. She had appeared on television; played Gregory Peck's daughter in *The Man in the Gray Flannel Suit* (1956); and had had parts in two films starring her father, *Bigger Than Life* (1956) and *Cry Terror!* (1958). At one stage it looked as though she might even secure the part of Lolita in Stanley Kubrick's 1962 film of Nabokov's novel, but the role was taken by Sue Lyon.

In 1966 Portland Mason was in *The Great St Trinian's Train Robbery*, and two years later had a part in *Sebastian*, which starred Dirk Bogarde. She also appeared on the British stage: in 1967 she was at the Vaudeville in London, playing Hester in *A Woman of No Importance*. She later became a scriptwriter, and made her home in California.

In 1964 Portland Mason's parents' marriage was dissolved after 22 years. Her father died 20 years later, leaving a second wife, the actress Clarissa Kaye. There then began a bitter dispute over his estate between Clarissa and Mason's two children, Portland and her younger brother Morgan (the film producer, married to the singer Belinda Carlisle).

Mason had left everything to Clarissa, leaving his children to, as he put it, 'stand in line' for their inheritance. They decided to contest the will.

Even the disposal of James Mason's ashes became a matter of dispute. Clarissa had refused to hand them over to the children, preferring to keep them in an urn on the mantelpiece at the house she had shared with Mason at Vevey, overlooking Lake Geneva. After her death in 1994, it was discovered that the ashes had been transferred to a safety deposit box.

In 1999 a Swiss court finally ruled that the ashes should be given to Portland and Morgan. In November 2000 brother and sister were finally able to scatter their father's ashes beneath his marble monument in the cemetery at Vevey. A few months after this ceremony, Portland Mason suffered a serious stroke.

Recently she had been working on a book about her father. She is survived by her husband, Rob Schuyler.

Portland Mason, born November 26 1948, died May 10 2004

Maurice Flitcroft

Crane operator and aspiring golfer whose efforts to gatecrash the Open embarrassed the Royal & Ancient

MAURICE FLITCROFT, who has died aged 77, was a chain-smoking shipyard crane operator from Barrow-in-Furness whose persistent attempts to gatecrash the British Open golf championship produced a sense of humour failure among members of the golfing establishment.

In 1976 the 46-year-old Flitcroft bought a half-set of mail order clubs and set his sights on finding 'fame and fortune' by

Flitcroft: 'Golf's just a game and I tried my best. What did they need to get so uptight about?'

applying to play in the Birkdale Open 'with Jack Nicklaus and all that lot'. He prepared by studying a Peter Alliss instruction manual borrowed from the local library and instructional articles by the 1966 PGA Championship winner Al Geiberger, honing his skills by hitting a ball about on a nearby beach.

He obtained an entry form from an unsuspecting Royal and Ancient, which organises the championship, and, having no handicap to declare as an amateur, he picked the other option on the form: professional.

Invited to play in the qualifier at Formby, he put in a performance which one witness described as a 'blizzard of triple

and quadruple bogeys ruined by a solitary par', achieving a total
of 121: 49 over par, the worst score recorded in the tournament's
141-year history. In fact, this was only a rough estimate, his
marker having lost count on a couple of holes.

His playing partner, Jim Howard, recalled his suspicions being
aroused almost from the word go: 'After gripping the club like he
was intent on murdering someone, Flitcroft hoisted it straight up,
came down vertically and the ball travelled precisely four feet,'
he said. 'We put that one down to nerves, but after he shanked
a second one we called the R&A officials.' Under the rules of the
tournament, however, nothing could be done. 'It wasn't funny at
the time,' Howard recalled.

Others demurred, and Flitcroft's performance dominated the
next day's sports pages, while stars such as Jack Nicklaus found
themselves relegated to the small print. Flitcroft was interviewed
endlessly. The score, he maintained, 'weren't a fair reflection' of
his play. He had been suffering from 'lumbago and fibrositis, but
I don't want to make excuses', and he blamed the fact that he had
left his four-wood in the car: 'I was an expert with the four-wood,
deadly accurate.'

When an enterprising journalist visited Flitcroft's mother and
told her about her son's record-breaking performance, she asked:
'Does that mean he's won?' When informed of the true state of
affairs, she replied: 'Well, he's got to start somewhere, hasn't he?'

Furious that their game had been held up to ridicule, the R&A
tightened the entry rules. The following year, when Flitcroft
applied to play in the qualifying tournament, he received a letter
from the R&A's secretary, Keith Mackenzie, informing him that
he had been turned down on the grounds that he had provided no
proof of an improvement in his game.

The letter sparked a prolonged correspondence, in the course
of which Flitcroft challenged Mackenzie to a match at the Old
Course to settle the debate about his golfing talents. Subsequently
Flitcroft was banned from R&A tournaments for life.

Refusing to be beaten, in 1978 he posed as an American
professional named Gene Pacecki ('as in pay cheque', he

explained helpfully) and blagged his way into the qualifier
at South Herts, where he was detected after a few holes and
bundled unceremoniously off the course. At a qualifier at
Pleasington in 1983, he tried disguise, dyeing his hair, donning
a false moustache and masquerading as Gerald Hoppy, a
professional golfer from Switzerland. He fared rather better this
time, playing nine holes and 63 strokes before officials realised
that they had 'another Maurice Flitcroft' on their hands. 'Imagine
their surprise when they discovered they had the actual Maurice
Flitcroft,' he said.

In 1990 he entered the qualifier at Ormskirk as James Beau
Jolley (as in Beaujolais), an American golf professional. He hit
a double bogey at the first hole and a bogey at the second; he
claimed to be 'looking at a par' at the third before he was rudely
interrupted by an R&A golf buggy which screeched to a halt
in front of him. He remonstrated with the driver, asking to be
allowed to finish the hole, but officials were not in the mood to
show mercy. Nor did they return his £60 entry fee.

Flitcroft never understood why the R&A was so upset: 'I never
set out to belittle them. Golf's just a game and I tried my best.
What did they need to get so uptight about?'

Maurice Gerald Flitcroft was born in Manchester on November
23 1929, and claimed to have been a talented schoolboy athlete.
After leaving school he joined the Merchant Navy, then made
a living as a high-diving comedy stunt man with a travelling
theatre group. After his marriage he moved to Barrow-in-
Furness, where he became a crane operator at the Vickers
Armstrong shipyard. He retired in the 1970s.

Flitcroft's entryist assaults on the Open made him a cult figure
in some golfing circles. He received mail from around the world
addressed simply to Maurice Flitcroft, Golfer, England.

A club in New York state named a trophy after him, and
another in Michigan named a member-guest tournament in his
honour, the event featuring a green with two holes to give the
truly hopeless a sporting chance. In 1988, when Flitcroft was
flown in as an honorary competitor at the event, he explained

that it was the first time he and his wife had been out of the house together 'since our gas oven exploded'. His game seemed to have improved somewhat and he completed the course with a score in the low 90s. 'I hit a lot of good shots,' he claimed proudly.

Though he was banned from playing on almost every course in Britain, in 1993 Flitcroft was permitted to play a round at a course at Windermere with *The Daily Telegraph*'s golf correspondent Lewine Mair. Later he invoiced the newspaper for 12 lost balls. He enjoyed hitting a golf ball about on the beach until he broke his hip in 2001.

Maurice Flitcroft's wife, Jean, died in 2002, and he is survived by their two sons and by two stepsons. The R&A declined to comment on his death, explaining that Flitcroft had 'only played in qualifiers'.

Maurice Flitcroft, born November 23 1929, died March 24 2007

Hugh Massingberd

Genealogist who reinvented the obituary in *The Daily Telegraph*, and wrote brilliantly on everything from country houses to musicals, cricket and soap opera

Massingberd in 2000, with genealogical reference books on the shelves

HUGH MASSINGBERD, who has died aged 60, always used to insist, during his time as obituaries editor of *The Daily Telegraph*, that understatement was the key to the form.

It is by no means an infringement of that principle to begin his own obituary with the declaration that those who worked for him – and indeed everyone who came to know him properly – considered him one of the most extraordinary and lovable Englishmen of his time.

He was also one of the most complex. A gentleman to his roots, he was nevertheless delighted to be guyed as 'Massivesnob' in *Private Eye*. The supreme master of fact, he revelled in daydreams. Shy and diffident, he at the same time exhibited a strong theatrical streak, holding forth masterfully as public speaker or broadcaster.

Above all, the man seemingly content to be taken as a Woosterish bumbler and *bon vivant* possessed a prodigious capacity for hard work. This professed amateur of journalism – he would type with two fingers – matched any professional in practice. Consistently excellent articles poured forth from him; business was dispatched with military address and efficiency; challenges to his editorial vision were resisted with steely resolve.

No wonder that he was judged an eccentric. The term, however, does no justice to Hugh Massingberd's gigantic brain. His ability to absorb and retain information was as astonishing as his ability to recall it at will. No one of his generation knew more about England and English life.

This was not just a matter of his having edited *Burke's Landed Gentry* (Volumes II and III, 1969 and 1972) or the *Peerage, Baronetage & Knightage* (1970 edition), though sometimes it appeared that he knew those weighty volumes almost by heart. As remarkable as the depth and accuracy of his knowledge was its range – from country houses to television soap operas, from the works of Anthony Powell to the odds at Wincanton, from the royal family to West End musicals. Unlike so many autodidacts, Massingberd never paraded his encyclopaedic mind; more likely, he would listen politely as some bore regaled him with anecdotes which he already knew. Many left his company completely unaware of the phenomenon they had encountered.

Equally, he never sought a heavyweight reputation as a journalist. On the contrary, he developed an easy and conversational style which drew on the infinite stores of his brain in the lightest and most readable vein.

It was as obituaries editor of *The Daily Telegraph* from 1986 to 1994 that he found the perfect fulfilment for his gifts. First, though, he had to reinvent the whole concept of the form, substituting for the grave and ceremonious tribute the sparkling celebration of life.

Before his arrival at *The Telegraph*, obituaries had been regarded as an inferior branch of News, and afforded minimal space. As far back as 1969, however, Massingberd had discerned the immense potential that lay in this disregarded cranny of journalism. The moment of illumination had come when he went to see Roy Dotrice's rendering of John Aubrey's *Brief Lives* at the Criterion Theatre.

Picking up a dusty tome, Dotrice/Aubrey read out a dreary entry about a barrister (Recorder of this, Bencher of that, and so on). Suddenly he snapped shut the volume with a 'Tchah!' and turned to the audience: 'He got more by his prick than his practice.'

There and then, Massingberd later wrote, 'I determined to dedicate myself to chronicling what people were really like through informal anecdote, description and character sketch.' Laughter, he added, would be by no means out of place.

His ambition took many years to come to fruition. When, in 1979, during the strike at *The Times*, Massingberd sought to convince *The Telegraph*'s editor, Bill Deedes, to venture upon a more expansive obituaries section, he was given to understand that it would be rather poor form to exploit the difficulties of a rival publication.

Finally, in 1986, Max Hastings gave Massingberd his opportunity. Immediately, *Telegraph* readers found themselves regaled by such characters as Canon Edward Young, the first chaplain of a striptease club; the last Wali of Swat, who had a fondness for brown Windsor soup; and Judge Melford Stevenson, who considered that 'a lot of my colleagues are just constipated Methodists'.

The column also made a speciality of tales of derring-do from the Second World War. The foibles of aristocrats proved another fertile source. The 6th Earl of Carnarvon appeared as a 'relentless raconteur and most uncompromisingly direct ladies' man'. The 9th Earl of St Germans listed his recreations as 'huntin' the slipper, shootin' a line, fishin' for compliments'. The 12th Marquess of Huntly married a nurse 40 years his junior: 'I still have my own teeth. Why should I marry some dried up old bag?' Part of the fun lay in the style which Massingberd evolved to pin down the specimens on display. Liberace, readers were gravely informed, 'never married'. Hopeless drunks were 'convivial'. Total shits 'did not suffer fools gladly'. Financial fraudsters seemed 'not to have upheld the highest ethical standards of the City'.

These were Massingberd's glory years. Shaking off restraint, he eagerly publicised his pride in the column both in the prints and on wireless and television. On the desk, he was the perfect boss. The soul of laughter and camaraderie, he allowed colleagues inflated credit when praise was flying, and nobly assumed the blame for their errors. 'Excellent obituary,' he would tell the malefactor. 'Just one small thing ...' – and some hideous mistake would be apologetically revealed. He preferred to regard all his geese as swans.

In the material sense, too, Massingberd pushed generosity well beyond the bounds of sanity. Invariably strapped for cash, he conducted himself as a *grand seigneur*. It was literally impossible to buy a ticket or to pay for lunch or dinner when he was present; and those who resisted beyond the bounds of seemliness were liable to discover that Massingberd had squared the waiters beforehand.

Wholly resistant to routine social life, he loved the gossip and jokes of journalism as much as he recoiled from the self-seeking graft of the profession. With like-minded companions, his imagination would take wing, chasing the comic possibilities of a person or a situation into the realms of surrealistic ecstasy. Indeed, Massingberd preferred to present himself in caricature. His gourmandism, for instance, was treated in 18th century mode, as the heroic exploits of a valiant trencherman. By way of variation, he was once photographed as a Roman emperor, garlanded with sausages.

The inevitable consequence of his bingeing proved another triumph of style, as Massingberd, a tall, slim and notably handsome youth with hollowed-out cheeks, transmogrified into an impressively corpulent presence whose moon face lit up with

Pickwickian benevolence. But this man, who delighted so many people, never satisfied himself. Supersensitive, he registered every slight, however effectively his feelings were concealed. Just occasionally hints of vulnerability would slip through the guard, in a waspish review, or an uncharacteristically sharp aside.

As Massingberd made clear in his courageously self-revealing autobiography, *Daydream Believer* (2001), fantasy and hero-worship afforded him far more secure and accessible satisfactions than he found in reason and reality.

In particular the theatre provided inexhaustible delight. His obsession with the stage appeared rather that of an acolyte attending a rite than that of a boulevardier seeking an evening's entertainment.

As a matter of course, the programme would be committed to memory in every detail. When he found a performance that answered to his needs – in general a lushly romantic musical such as *The Phantom of the Opera*, though Alan Bennett's *Forty Years On* also claimed his intense loyalty as an exercise in comic nostalgia – he would attend scores of times, long after he knew the show off by heart.

Afterwards he loved to hang about the stage door, too shy to beard the departing actors himself, but eager, if possible, to push forward a companion to obtain autographs, and perhaps to deliver a rehearsed remark. Very occasionally, he would close in to speak for himself. 'I just want to say how deeply I have admired you,' he would begin, before proceeding, to the mounting alarm of the victim, to list every performance the thespian had given over the previous 40 years.

Cricketers (especially Surrey's Monty Lynch and Alistair Brown), journalists (Auberon Waugh) and comedians (Peter Cook and Harry Enfield) were likewise unknowing recipients of his unstinting devotion. If there was a common characteristic among his heroes, it lay in their willingness to take risks and to flout convention.

Among writers, Massingberd loved the works of P. G. Wodehouse, Anthony Powell and James Lees-Milne, whose interest in the intricacies of class he shared. His genealogical expertise, however, had taught him that the common man plays a leading role in every family. If Massingberd once characterised his youthful self as a 'howling snob', this fault did not survive his journalistic contacts with the more arrogant and ignorant country-house owners. In fact, no one was ever less snobbish than Massingberd in the corrupting sense of the term; that of disdaining merit outside rank. He had, though, been a thwarted and insecure young man, whose early history inclined him towards a romantic view of aristocracy.

He was born Hugh John Montgomery at Cookham Dean, in Berkshire, on December 30 1946. His father was in the Colonial Service and later worked for the BBC; his mother was a 'Leftward-leaning schoolmistress'.

His remoter background, however, was distinctly grand, even if it promised a great deal more than it delivered. The Montgomerys, seated at Blessingbourne in Co Tyrone, were a Protestant Ascendancy family, albeit exceptionally conscious of the need to right the wrongs suffered by Roman Catholics. In his youth Hugh stayed at the Montgomerys' pseudo-Elizabethan (actually 1870) pile in the full expectation that one day it would be his.

There was a strong military tradition in the family. Hugh's paternal grandfather was Major-General Hugh Montgomery, while his great-uncle, the major-general's younger brother, ended his career as Field Marshal Sir Archibald Montgomery-Massingberd, Chief of the Imperial General Staff from 1933 to 1936. The two brothers had married Massingberd sisters, and the field marshal became Montgomery-Massingberd after 1926, when his wife inherited Gunby, a fine red-brick William and Mary house in Lincolnshire.

The Massingberds had owned land at Gunby since 1495. In 1802 a Miss Massingberd married Peregrine Langton, second son of Bennet Langton, a friend of Dr Johnson's. Bennet Langton had once, with a friend, knocked up the Doctor at 3am. 'What, is it you, you dogs!' Johnson shouted: 'I'll have a frisk with you.' Peregrine Langton's and Elizabeth Massingberd's grand-daughter

Emily Massingberd (1847–97), a militant feminist and temperance campaigner who favoured male attire, was Hugh's great-grandmother. She married another Langton, Edmund, whose mother Charlotte was a cousin and sister-in-law of Charles Darwin, and whose grandfather was Josiah Wedgwood, founder of the pottery.

These were connections with the heart of the English intellectual elite; the composer Ralph Vaughan Williams, for instance, was a cousin of Hugh's. Their world, though, was far removed from the rambling, pebble-dashed Edwardian villa in which Hugh grew up at Cookham Dean. The house belonged to his maternal grandfather, a stock jobber named Seal, whose fortune had been much diminished in the Crash of 1929.

Seal's daughter Marsali, Hugh's mother, had been to Newnham College, Cambridge, and developed a clear-eyed view of the English class system that propelled her into teaching. On the other hand she had married, *en premières noces*, Roger de Winton Kelsall Winlaw, a Cambridge cricket Blue who played for Surrey and captained Bedfordshire before being killed in 1942 while serving with the RAF. They had two boys and a girl.

Hugh was the elder child – there would be a younger sister, Mary – of Marsali de Winlaw's second marriage, to John Montgomery. He thus grew up at Cookham Dean with hearty, cricket-mad half-brothers. His relative mediocrity as a games-player inspired the first of his fantasy creations, that of Sir John Julian Bruce, Bt, MA, OBE, VC, the great all-rounder – 'As England's opening bowler, I found that wickets fell like apples from a tree' – universally adored for his good looks, modesty and charm. Hugh filled countless exercise books with accounts of his prowess.

Life, however, stubbornly resisted the promptings of art. In the late 1950s, after the death of Hugh's maternal grandparents, the family was obliged to move downmarket at Cookham Dean, into a suburban bungalow. When Hugh came home from prep school he was so shocked that he tried to run away to the family's former house.

He had grown up a reclusive and lonely boy, whose best friend was the housekeeper, 'Biddo'. She adored him so wholeheartedly that she gave up her annual holiday to take him to the Scarborough cricket festival.

He also enjoyed the cruder, more open life he encountered when staying with his mother's sister Daisy, who had married a Somerset farmer called Joe Dinham. The Dinhams were addicted to steeplechasing, a passion which Hugh soon shared. Henceforth jockeys – especially, in those early days, Terry Biddlecombe – featured prominently among his heroes. Wincanton, which he had first visited with the Dinhams, always remained a favourite racecourse.

Over the years he would pull off some lucrative betting coups. Triumph, however, turned to disaster on one occasion when, having succeeded with compound bets on the first three races, he plunged on the last, with the prospect of a fortune at stake. His horse came to the last in the lead, but failed to clear the fence. Apparently it had been put off by the shock of Hugh's yellow 'trouserings'.

As a teenager, Hugh seemed to add substance to his dreams when he went to stay with his Uncle Peter at Blessingbourne. Peter Montgomery was something of a figure in Ulster, to such a degree that his homosexuality, at that date unknown to Hugh, did not prevent him from becoming Vice-Lord Lieutenant of Tyrone. Hugh, swept up suddenly into the jollifications of Irish country-house life, became enchanted by the prospect of one day being the master of Blessingbourne. Like Cyril Connolly before him, he found himself an aristocrat in Ireland, and middle class in England.

It was, therefore, a shattering blow to be told in his mid-teens that a cousin who intended to be a farmer would inherit Blessingbourne; this youth, it was judged, would be better qualified than Hugh to return the estate to order after years of benign neglect under Peter Montgomery. By way of compensation, Hugh was informed that he might one day live at Gunby as a tenant of the National Trust, to which the field marshal and his wife, who were childless, had given the house in 1944.

Meanwhile, Hugh's life at school brought little joy. As a day boy at Crosfield, the junior branch of the Quaker Leighton Park, and as a boarder at Port Regis in Dorset, he made no real mark, beyond narrowly scraping his cricket colours at Port Regis.

By the time he went to Harrow his fantasies were already set on Eton, which failed to endear him to his comrades on the Hill. 'Do you know, Monty,' his housemaster observed, 'I don't think you're shy at all. You're just bloody rude.' His form master was no more impressed. 'Most of the time,' he wrote, 'it seems that Montgomery is somewhere far, far away in his own thoughts.' Unexpectedly, though, this remote and diffident boy did briefly come into his own when yelling out drill commands in the Corps.

Hugh left Harrow a year early, in 1964. The only promise in his life at this period was his discovery of the satire boom. In no time he had the sketches from *Beyond the Fringe*, which opened at the Fortune Theatre in 1961, off by heart; and he was also an early aficionado of *Private Eye*, first published in the same year. 'At last,' wrote his form master after Hugh had written an essay on Satire, 'you have found a subject which really interests you.'

In 1963 the field marshal's widow died, and Hugh and his father adopted the surname Montgomery-Massingberd in order to qualify for the tenancy of Gunby. 'Well now, Master Hughie,' the housekeeper, clearly a clone of Mrs Danvers, told him on his first visit, 'coming as you do from the suburbs, I don't expect you've ever stayed in such a large house before, have you?' Hugh displayed a Betjeman-like relish for recording such social humiliations.

He seemed in particularly self-destructive mode at this time, rejecting any notion of Oxford or Cambridge on the grounds that he could bear neither the student radicals nor the Brideshead poseurs with their teddy bears. 'Above all,' he wrote in *Daydream Believer*, 'I didn't want to be young any more: I wanted to be middle-aged, even old – a quiet, comfortable recluse with my books and my pipe dreams.'

And so, masochistically, he chose the Law. Still only 17, he
began to commute from Cookham to solicitors in Lincoln's Inn.
By the afternoon on the first day, having been condemned to
a windowless cell and instructed to add up the assets of some
peeress, he was shaking with silent sobs.

Matters improved somewhat, due to the comradeship of a
fellow articled clerk who turned out to be something of a blood.
Hugh enjoyed entertaining this exquisite at Gunby, where
for the first and only time in his life he was able to play the
squirearchical role of which he always dreamed.

He lasted three dreary years in the Law, before snapping one
afternoon and walking out of the office for good. At much the
same time his father decided that he could no longer afford to
keep up the tenancy at Gunby. For the rest of his life Massingberd
maintained extremely friendly relations with new tenants, and
sometimes stayed at Gunby; nevertheless, another door had
slammed.

He had, however, turned the daily commute to Lincoln's Inn
to account by devouring hundreds of books. Now he further
extended his horizons by undertaking a Grand Tour with his
uncle, Mgr Hugh Montgomery.

Under the pressure of travel, their relations proved stormy,
not least when the Monsignor presented Hugh to his old friend
Giovanni Battista Montini, now Pope Paul VI. 'I stuck out my
hand in my best English country-house manner,' remembered
Massingberd, 'before Uncle Hugh thrust me violently to the floor
by the neck. "Get down!" he hissed, "Kiss St Peter's ring."'

Massingberd was now considering the option of taking up a
place at Selwyn College, Cambridge, in the autumn of 1968, and
that summer attended a crammer at Oxford to gain the necessary
qualifications. Fate intervened, however, when he heard about a
job as an assistant at *Burke's Peerage*.

He obtained the post, and for the first time in his life found
himself totally focused and committed. Thoughts of Cambridge
were dismissed as he applied himself with astounding industry

and grasp to the genealogies of the *Landed Gentry*, and then moved on to produce, single-handedly, a new edition of the *Peerage, Baronetage and Knightage*. The standards he set have never been matched since.

Suddenly, in 1971, as a result of an office coup organised by Christine Martinoni, whom he would marry the next year, Massingberd found himself appointed editor of all the firm's publications. As he later observed, for the first time in his life fantasy had collided with reality.

He drew up a list of projects, some of which came to fruition: *Burke's Guide to The Royal Family* (1973); *Presidential Families of the USA* (1975); *Burke's Irish Family Records* (1976); *Burke's Family Index* (1976); *Burke's Royal Families of the World* (two volumes, 1977 and 1980); and *Burke's Guide to Country Houses* (three volumes, 1978, 1980 and 1981).

He also made the most of the opportunity which his position conferred to meet some of his heroes, such as James Lees-Milne and Anthony Powell, while discovering another object of worship in Sir Iain Moncreiffe of that Ilk. (*Lord of the Dance: A Moncreiffe Miscellany*, which Massingberd edited, appeared in 1986.) There was even an encounter with Earl Mountbatten of Burma, very definitely not a hero, who wanted to enlist the help of Burke's in changing the name of the royal family to Mountbatten-Windsor.

Financial support for Massingberd's schemes, however, soon withered, although he did not finally resign from Burke's until 1983. He now sought to build another career as a freelance writer and columnist. *The Spectator* and *The Field* proved particularly amenable, the latter commissioning a series on 'Family Seats' and in 1984 putting him on contract. Within two years he had found fulfilment at *The Telegraph*.

Eventually, however, Massingberd became a victim of his own success. The *réclame* of his obituaries' page gave him the opportunity to write other pieces for the paper – a Heritage column on country houses, continuing his work for *The Field*; interviews with stars (in one of which he confessed to a desire to kiss Hugh Laurie); scores of book reviews; and – not conducive to good health – articles as restaurant critic.

The pressure of work was already feverish when, in 1992, he accepted an invitation to add the editorship of the Peterborough column to that of obituaries. This proved a step too far, and even after he had given up the post, he found his confidence drained. The obsessiveness which had powered his frantic workload now turned in upon itself, causing Massingberd agonies of self-doubt. As if in acknowledgment of his fall, which, in truth, hardly existed outside his own mind, he now reduced his by-line from the efflorescent Hugh Montgomery-Massingberd to plain Hugh Massingberd. Early in 1994 he suffered a near-fatal heart attack.

'It was quite salutary, really,' he later reflected. 'One felt that nothing mattered beyond kindness, good manners and humour.'

After a quadruple by-pass operation he recovered a measure of health, wrote a superb article on his brush with death, and for two years worked from home as *The Daily Telegraph*'s television critic. Again, though, the insecurities surfaced, and in 1996, as the pressure became intolerable, he wisely resigned the post.

He continued to write both books and book reviews, as authoritative and sparkling as ever. At last, though, he had some spare time to enjoy.

In particular he loved watching cricket at Lord's and (especially) the Oval, where in 2002 he enjoyed one of the best days of his life, as Alistair Brown hit a record 268 in a one-day game.

Best of all, Massingberd was finally able to turn his theatrical reveries into reality, when, from 2002, his skilfully chosen selection from the writings of James Lees-Milne, *Ancestral Voices*, was played with great success at venues throughout the country. In 2005 he devised another entertainment, *Love and Art*, based on Anthony Powell's *Dance to the Music of Time*. (He was president of the Anthony Powell Society.)

When this piece was produced at the Wallace Collection he enjoyed the supreme satisfaction of playing some of the parts himself. In his dreams he had always fantasised about being in the back row of the chorus during a long run of a musical. His performance of Anthony Powell's characters made it plain that he might have succeeded on stage at a far higher level than that.

What could he not have done? His books alone, something of a sideline notwithstanding their excellence, might have constituted a lifetime's work for an ordinary mortal.

They were: *The Monarchy* (1979); *The British Aristocracy* (with Mark Bence-Jones, 1979); *The London Ritz* (with David Watkin, 1980); *The Country Life Book of Royal Palaces, Castles and Homes* (with Patrick Montague-Smith, 1981); *Diana – The Princess of Wales* (1982); *Heritage of Royal Britain* (1983); *Royal Palaces of Europe* (1984); *Blenheim Revisited* (1985); *Her Majesty The Queen* (1986); *Debrett's Great British Families* (1987); *The Field Book of Country Houses and their Owners: Family Seats of the British Isles* (1988); four books with photographs by Christopher Simon Sykes – *Great Houses of England and Wales* (1994), *Great Houses of Scotland* (1997), *Great Houses of Ireland* (1999) and *English Manor Houses* (2001); *Queen Elizabeth The Queen Mother* (1999); and the autobiographical *Daydream Believer: Confessions of a Hero-Worshipper* (2001).

To the list of the publications which he edited should be added *The Daily Telegraph Record of the Second World War* (1989); *A Guide to the Country Houses of the North-West* (1991); *The Disintegration of a Heritage: Country Houses and their Collections 1979–1992* (1993); and six books of *Telegraph* obituaries.

After being diagnosed with cancer in 2004 he bore the treatments with courage, resignation and mordant wit.

Hugh Massingberd married first, in 1972 (dissolved 1979), Christine Martinoni; they had a daughter and a son. He married secondly, in 1983, Caroline Ripley.

Hugh Massingberd, born December 30 1946, died December 25 2007

John Michell

Merlin-like magus of the hippie underground who put Glastonbury on the New Age map

JOHN MICHELL, who has died aged 76, was a charismatic Old Etonian mystic often championed as a counter-culture seer for his fascination with alien life, geomancy, the countryside and crop circles; his most famous book, *The View Over Atlantis* (1969), is arguably the most influential tome in the hippie underground movement, and is credited with placing the Somerset town of Glastonbury as the capital of the New Age.

His wide knowledge and intellect was enhanced by a kind and inquiring nature, which brought him the status of a Merlin-like magus among his many followers and friends. These included the Rolling Stones, whom he took to Stonehenge on a UFO-hunting expedition. Mick Jagger's former wife Jerry Hall was a guest at his 70th birthday party.

At a summer solstice festival in the Somerset town of Glastonbury in 1971, he was the influence behind the 75 x 48ft stage – a scale model of the pyramid of Cheops, which Michell claimed was an example of the 'spiritual engineering' known in the ancient world. David Bowie was among the performers.

'In the mid-60s the Underground lacked a voice,' noted the *Fortean Times* (a magazine devoted to 'strange phenomena') in 2007. 'A figurehead was needed [and] came in the form of

John Michell, whose influence on the Underground cannot be overestimated.' For Michell, UFOs were not simply alien spacecraft, but machines intimately intertwined with forces derived from the alignment of the British landscape – forces particularly in evidence at Glastonbury.

'It was, I think, in 1966 that I first went,' Michell said, indicating that his excitement with the town was to do with 'strange lights in the sky, new music, and our conviction that the world was about to flip over on its axis so that heresy would become orthodoxy and an entirely new world order would shortly be revealed.' For some, such visions were more to do with the arrival of LSD in London in the same period. But though Michell was never far from rolled cigarettes, some of which even contained tobacco, his appreciation of the world was considered and far more substantial than mere drugs-driven musing.

His first book, *The Flying Saucer Vision: The Holy Grail Restored*, was published in 1967. Almost 30 years later he received significant acclaim for *Who Wrote Shakespeare?* (1996), received by *The Washington Post* as 'the best overview' of the enduring debate over the plays' true authorship.

That book was symptomatic of Michell's refusal to accept received wisdom on any subject. 'He hated authority,' said one friend.

John Frederick Carden Michell was born in London on February 9 1933, the eldest of three children. He was brought up at Stargroves, his family's Victorian estate near Newbury, which was later bought by his friend Mick Jagger. Michell's father, Alfred, was a man of property of Cornish descent. At Stargroves, John learned about birds, flowers and moths from a neighbouring naturalist, and acquired his lifelong love of the countryside.

He was educated at Cheam preparatory school, where he was head boy and won the high jump, and at Eton. Contemporaries included Lord Moyne, with whom as a child Michell would take tea at Biddesden House, and Ian Cameron, father of the current leader of the Opposition.

Michell went up to Trinity College, Cambridge, reading Russian and German, and put his linguistic talents to use as an interpreter during National Service.

On his arrival in London in the 1960s, he was divested of much of his inheritance by property speculators. Thereafter, he immersed himself in Bohemian London, around which he was to build his life.

A regular at Muriel's in Soho and at the Jermyn Street Turkish baths, Michell was drawn to rogues and waifs. To his friends the door of his Notting Hill house was always open, his kitchen supplied with shepherds' pie from Lidgate's. His desk-cum-dining table was covered in a jumble of letters which he would lift with elegant long fingers to read out to guests. Somehow he always knew where everything was.

His loathing for authority was best expressed in his campaign against metric measures, to which he frequently gave voice in his regular column in *The Oldie*. An anthology of these pieces was published in 2005 as *Confessions of a Radical Traditionalist*.

Among the best of his many other books was *Eccentric Lives and Peculiar Notions* (1984), a compendium of the lives of weird and wonderful folk, from flat-earthers to auto-trepanners. He was also a popular speaker at the Port Eliot Lit Fest on his favourite subject of crop circles, even starting a magazine on the phenomenon, *The Cerealogist*, and holding 'cornferences' to discuss the latest news on the subject.

'He just loved ideas and the possibility of another spiritual universe waiting to be discovered,' said one who knew him well. But it was for his wit, original mind and capacity for friendship that he will be best remembered.

Michell was brought to his last resting place in Stoke Abbott church by a Welsh cob, Ruby, on a gipsy flat cart which bore the painted words 'General Dealer'.

In 2007, Michell was briefly married to Denise Price, the Archdruidess of the Glastonbury Order of Druids. He is survived by his son, the writer Jason Goodwin.

John Michell, born February 9 1933, died April 24 2009

Sathya Sai Baba

India's most celebrated Swami, revered as a living
god by millions, but dismissed as a charlatan by some

SATHYA SAI BABA,
who has died, probably
aged 84, was India's
most famous, and most
controversial, Swami
or holy man, and one of
the most enigmatic and
remarkable religious
figures of the recent
past.

To his followers,
Sai Baba was a living
god; a claim he did
nothing to disavow. He
would frequently liken
himself to such figures
as Christ, Krishna, and
the Buddha, claiming
that he was the avatara
of the age – an avatara being a living incarnation of the divine.
To his detractors he was a charlatan, albeit one of considerable
ingenuity and enormous personal charisma.

From humble beginnings, his following grew until by the end
of the 20th century it was estimated to number more than three
million people around the world.

This made him a powerful and influential figure in Indian
social and political life, and several presidents and prime
ministers, including Deva Gowda and Narasimha Rao, found it
politically expedient to make their way to his ashram in the town
of Puttaparthi in southern India to be photographed paying their
respects.

Sai Baba's reputation was founded largely on claims of his miraculous powers. These included the apparent ability to materialise various tokens of devotion, such as amulets, rings and pendants, out of thin air; to produce 'vibhuti', or 'holy' ash in prodigious amounts from his fingertips; and to manifest fully formed lingams (ellipsoids made of crystal or quartz) from his stomach by regurgitation.

These feats made him the target of numerous sceptics and debunkers, who claimed that the 'materialisations' were little more than legerdemain which could be replicated by any competent Indian street magician. Sai Baba consistently refused to have his powers scientifically scrutinised, explaining that they were 'part of the unlimited power of God. You call them miracles, but for me they are just my way.'

Such is the mixture of myth, fabulation and hagiography that grew up around Sathya Sai Baba that the facts of his life are hard to establish. He is thought to have been born, as Sathya Narayana Raju, on November 23 1926, into a poor farming family in the village of Puttaparthi, in the arid state of Andhra Pradesh.

According to legend, as a child he would avoid places where animals were slaughtered, and bring beggars home to be fed. At the age of 14, after apparently being bitten by a scorpion, he began to display signs of delirium and hallucinations. Convinced that he was possessed, his parents summoned a local exorcist who shaved the boy's head, scored four Xs into his scalp, and poured the juice of garlic and lime into the wounds.

Shortly afterwards, he declared himself to be a reincarnation of Shirdi Sai Baba, one of southern India's most revered saints, who died in 1918. Challenged to prove his claim, he is said to have thrown some jasmine flowers on the floor; in falling the flowers arranged themselves to spell out the name 'Sai Baba' in Telugu.

Leaving his family, he travelled throughout southern India, gathering followers around him, and in 1950 he inaugurated his first ashram in Puttaparthi.

Sai Baba professed that his mission was ecumenical: the emblem of his organisation included symbols of all the world's great faiths, but his message was essentially drawn from Hindu teachings about man and God being inseparable by virtue of the atman, or eternal soul – the 'universal divine spark' present in all beings. The atman, he declared, 'can be known only through love' – a philosophy that he distilled in the maxim: 'Love all, serve all. All men then are God.'

But to his devotees Sai Baba seemed to be more God than most. One of his closest disciples, Professor N. Kasturi, the author of a four-volume biography, described him as 'a multi-faced avatar' – the embodiment of Rama, Christ, Krishna, Buddha and Zoroaster. Perhaps his most unlikely champion was a Vatican priest, Don Mario Mazzoleni, who in 1990 published a book, *A Catholic Priest Meets Sai Baba*, in which he declared that Christ and Sai Baba were the same manifestation of God on earth. After refusing an invitation from the Vatican to 'retreat from his heretical doctrinal positions', Mazzoleni was excommunicated in 1993.

Sai Baba frequently talked of himself as being 'the Supra-worldly Divinity in Human Form', and the World Saviour. When the American devotee and biographer, Dr John Hislop, asked him directly whether he claimed to be God, Sathya Sai is said to have replied: 'Let us say, I am the switch.'

Sathya Sai's message and his alleged miraculous powers brought him an enormous following not only in India, but also in the West. This went far beyond the hippies and spiritual seekers who had made their way to India in the Sixties in search of enlightenment. The numerous Sai groups that proliferated in Europe, America and Australia were liberally peopled with physicians, psychologists and teachers. By the 1990s the tiny village of Puttaparthi had swollen to the size of a town and an airport was built to accommodate the growing numbers of pilgrims.

Twice a day Sai Baba, a stocky figure in a red, floor-length robe, his head crowned in a dense halo of black hair, would appear for 'darshan' in the ashram's main temple. He would move among the adoring crowds, sometimes 'materialising' vibhuti into outstretched hands and summoning favoured devotees for private audiences.

His followers would frequently talk of miraculous healings, of being 'called' to him in dreams and visions, and of Sai Baba being able to read their minds – powers that were widely held among the faithful to be evidence of his 'omniscience', and which sceptics dismissed as either self-delusion or an expert use of the technique of 'cold reading', whereby facts are drawn out of a subject and fed back to them later without them realising it.

An Icelandic researcher, Professor Erlendur Haraldsson, conducted interviews with 29 subjects on Sathya Sai's mind-reading abilities. Of these, 19 reported that he had done so correctly, and five only partially correctly. One woman, whom Sathya Sai advised 'should get married', was married already.

As his organisation grew, Sai Baba established an extensive network of schools and colleges throughout India, and his programme of Education in Human Values (EHV) was adopted by schools in Europe and America. The most extravagant display of his largesse was the Rayalaseema water project, inaugurated on his 70th birthday, which provided water to more than 750 villages and several towns in Andhra Pradesh.

In 1991 he inaugurated the Sathya Sai Super-Speciality Hospital, which provided a range of medical services, up to major heart surgery, free of charge to local villagers, and was largely funded by an American follower.

Sai Baba always maintained a cloak of secrecy over his financial activities and the affairs of the ashram. In 1993 he was the victim of an apparent assassination attempt, when four armed men broke into his private rooms. His chauffeur and cook were murdered, but Sai Baba managed to escape unscathed. The intruders were shot dead by the police. Thereafter, pilgrims entering the ashram had to pass through metal detectors.

According to ashram officials, the assassination attempt was the result of a struggle between rival factions of devotees who had been denied positions of influence in the ashram. But the attempt on Sai Baba's life hinted at other, darker currents that had begun to eddy around his mission. Not least of these were allegations that young male devotees had been sexually abused by their guru in the course of private audiences.

These allegations were given wider currency with the advent of the internet, and an international campaign by devotees in Europe and America calling for his prosecution. But Sai Baba seemed impervious to criticism. He was never investigated by the Indian authorities, and pilgrims continued to flock to his ashram in their hundreds of thousands.

Sathya Sai Baba was certainly wrong about one thing, having, in 1963, announced that he would live until 2020. It remains to be seen whether another prediction is closer to the mark – that in 2028 his 'third incarnation', Prema Sai, will be born in the village of Gunaparthy in Karnataka state. 'With his [Prema Sai's] efforts, love, goodwill, brotherhood and peace will abound throughout the world,' Sai Baba declared. 'He will receive universal recognition from mankind.'

Sathya Sai Baba, born November 23 1926, died April 24 2011

Camille Wolff

Book dealer who crammed her house in Old Chelsea with biographies of mafiosi and serial killers

CAMILLE WOLFF, who has died aged 102, belied her appearance as a grey-haired great-grandmother by becoming one of Britain's pre-eminent dealers in the literature of true crime, a business she ran from her home, where biographies of mafiosi and studies of poisoners, torturers, axe-murderers and serial killers competed for space with accounts of famous capital trials.

To 'Cam', as she was universally known to her customers, the true crime genre was a congenial means of meeting a motley assortment of writers, lawyers, medics, police officers and even the occasional criminal. Her home, from where she bought and sold as Grey House Books, became a kind of trading post and social centre for murder fanciers not only from Britain but around the world.

Her 18th century house in Old Chelsea was crammed with thousands of true crime titles, one of the largest collections of its kind in the world ('You'll find the Mafia in the loo,' she would advise visitors); and when in 1990 she moved to an ivy-clad cottage in the Portobello Road, they spiralled up the stairs and into the bedrooms.

While most of her business was conducted by mail order, customers could telephone for an appointment to visit in person.

She would often offer them tea and biscuits, with instructions not to sit on the dozing cat while browsing the stock.

Those who signed her visitors' book included a gravedigger, a mystery-loving milkman and an American attorney who described himself as 'formerly racketbuster'. Most of her clients were men, many of them lawyers and judges, others coroners, pathologists, retired and serving detectives, even penal reformers. She used to deal in detective fiction as well as true crime, but wearied of the excesses of some niche devotees ('the Sherlock Holmes collectors are nuts') and decided to concentrate on real-life villainy.

While tracking the changing trends and fads in true crime, she quickly discovered the perennial appeal of books about Jack the Ripper. The business of finally nailing the infamous Victorian killer's identity worried her, at least to the extent that he may turn out to have been Jewish like her. She also hoped that he would not prove to have been American. 'The Americans have enough serial killers of their own,' she declared, 'and the English should be allowed to keep their first notable example.'

She personally recoiled from knifewielding psychopaths, her own tastes being more decorous, and centred on what some crime buffs call Malice Domestic – murders occurring within the family circle, such as the Victorian cases of Florence Maybrick and Adelaide Bartlett or Edwardian classics like Dr Crippen.

Wearing an air of delightful dottiness, she would use her early mail order catalogues to riff on the themes of some of her wares. Describing a book on murder by witchcraft, for example, she threw in the additional information that Warwickshire, the setting for one particularly gruesome case, had been notorious as the 'land of the covens', an area said to suffer from a 'superfluity of witches'.

Camille Joan Muriel Cohen was born on May 23 1912 at Didsbury, south Manchester, where her father was a textile trader. Her mother was a Sieff from the Marks and Spencer family. After a few years in Cairo, the Cohens returned to England, where Camille attended Manchester High School for

Girls, only to be expelled for teaching her school friends the facts of life.

Although she trained as a doctor she never practised, and joined Marks and Spencer in London, working in the occupational health department, treating staff in need of medical attention and inspecting kitchens to see that they complied with health and safety legislation.

It was only in retirement that she went into the book trade, running a general (mainly second-hand) dealership from her tiny Queen Anne house in Lawrence Street, Chelsea, eventually specialising in detective fiction and, from about 1980, true crime. When one early enthusiastic but impecunious customer told her he was a roofer by trade, she persuaded him to mend her leaking roof in return for books.

Her clientele soon expanded to include true-crime aficionados such as the television personality Jeremy Beadle, the Australian rock star Nick Cave and the Great Train Robbery mastermind Bruce Reynolds ('my favourite ex-criminal'). All became personal friends.

A lifelong libertarian, as a young woman she was at various times a member of the Fabian Society and the British Communist Party.

In 1995 she published *Who Was Jack The Ripper?*, a compendium of theories about the identity of the Victorian serial killer by some 50 experts and devotees, and which has since become a collectors' item. The book was launched at one of her regular literary lunches to which she invited a hand-picked group of enthusiasts for the true-crime genre to a causerie at which she would serve a selection of Marks and Spencer ready meals.

Camille Wolff married, in 1934, the solicitor Eric Wolff, who died in 1978. Their elder daughter, Miriam, also predeceased her, and she is survived by their younger daughter, Susan, who married the anti-apartheid activist Ronald Segal.

Camille Wolff, born May 23 1912, died September 4 2014

Canon John Andrew

Anglican priest in New York with a penchant for silver-buckled shoes, porcelain and high society

CANON JOHN ANDREW, who has died aged 83, was a notable rector of St Thomas's, Fifth Avenue, New York's most fashionable church, from 1972 to 1996 and chaplain to the Archbishop of Canterbury from 1961 to 1969.

The appointment of the team rector of Preston, Lancashire, to St Thomas's caused a few eyebrows to be raised at the time, but the touch of Englishness that he brought to Fifth Avenue proved to be a remarkable success.

Andrew was, in fact, a very able priest. His preaching was memorable and he had a dramatic talent for creating worship that was, in his own words, 'grand without being intimidating, precise without being precious'. The high quality of the music was sustained by the only choir school in North America. Allied to this was his considerable administrative ability, essential for a church with staff of 32, plus four other priests, serving a membership of more than 1,700, and with an annual budget of $700,000.

Although Andrew once described himself as 'the luckiest priest in the Anglican Communion', he was among those who were surprised that he did not become a bishop or a dean. There were a number of reasons for this. The fact that he was English stood in the way of further American appointments; and at that time the Church of England was notoriously reluctant to reclaim those who had ventured across the Atlantic.

More significant, however, was the resentment aroused by the style and influence of his ministry while chaplain at Lambeth in the 1960s. Archbishop Geoffrey Fisher, like most of his predecessors, employed two chaplains, one of whom was always a senior priest who handled the more important people and subjects and was himself being groomed for a bishopric. But when Michael Ramsey was translated from York to Canterbury he dispensed with the services of a senior man and brought with him 30-year-old John Andrew, who had been his chaplain at York for just over a year.

This move was related to Ramsey's inability to relate closely to men of his own age. Without children of his own, he tended to regard his chaplains as surrogate sons; and Andrew, who stayed with him for eight years, exercised a strong influence over the Lambeth household which became far from helpful. Senior bishops found it difficult to obtain access to the Archbishop without the approval of a young man who had never previously been more than a curate. Some stayed away, and one who tried to make personal contact with Ramsey was told by Andrew: 'You must remember that the Archbishop always discusses things very thoroughly with me.'

The lifestyle of the young chaplain also provoked comment, for he had a penchant for silver-buckled shoes, owned a fine collection of porcelain and enjoyed the company of high society. It was therefore something of a shock to him that, when the time eventually came for him to leave Lambeth, the only available appointment was the less than prestigious team rectory of Preston.

This did not suit him – or Preston – and after only three years relief came, largely through the influence of certain wealthy American ladies who had come to know him in London and recommended him to St Thomas's, Fifth Avenue.

John Gerald Barton Andrew was born at Scarborough on January 10 1931. He spent his childhood at nearby Anlaby, and after two years as a flying officer in the RAF won a scholarship to Keble College, Oxford, where he read Theology. In 1956 he was ordained by Ramsey to a curacy in the lively Cleveland parish of Redcar, and after three good years there spent the next 18 months very happily assisting in a parish in New Jersey before returning to York diocese as the Archbishop's chaplain.

In New York his generous hospitality was much appreciated, and invitations to intimate dinner parties in his huge Park Avenue apartment were greatly coveted. Minor royalty and other notables visiting New York were apt to dine with him, and their visits were always faithfully recorded in the parish newsletter. His capacity for hard work was also valued by the Americans and, without in any way compromising the conservative Anglo-Catholic tradition of St Thomas's, he modified the worship in such a way that it appealed to a very wide variety of people.

Andrew never severed his links with his native land. After the major Church festivals he would return to London, often visiting All Saints, Margaret Street – the nearest counterpart to St Thomas's – before travelling to Whitby to see his mother and sister. Later he acquired an apartment in Bath, and although he declined the Crown's offer of Tewkesbury Abbey no 'appropriate' English preferment came his way.

He was considerably affected by a violent mugging in 1988 which fractured his skull and left him comatose in a Manhattan street. He was proud to return to his pulpit less than a month later, though stooped and drawn, but while his enthusiasm remained firm his creative energy was never quite the same again. None the less, he continued to preside over the American branches of the order of St John of Jerusalem and the Royal School of Church Music.

He was appointed OBE in 1995 and in the same year was made an honorary canon of the Cathedral of St John the Divine in New York.

John Andrew retired to England for a time but in 1999 returned to New York, where he took on the role of rector emeritus at St Thomas's and continued to be involved in its liturgy, social activities and fundraising. He had been having dinner with Bishop John O'Hara of the Roman Catholic Archdiocese of New York when he collapsed, having suffered a major cardiac event.

He never married.

Canon John Andrew, born January 10 1931, died October 17 2014

Jeremy Thorpe

Charismatic leader of the Liberal Party who
fell from grace in one of the most spectacular
political scandals of the 20th century

JEREMY THORPE, the
former leader of the
Liberal Party who has
died aged 85, suffered
a fall unparalleled
in British political
history when a long-
drawn-out chain of
scandal dragged him
into the dock at the
Old Bailey, charged
with conspiracy and
incitement to murder.

For once the
cliché 'trial of the
century' did not seem
misplaced. Thorpe had
been a sparkling and
successful politician
who had come
tantalisingly close to

Thorpe: 'It never occurred to him that anybody
might not be glad to see him,' his mother said

realising the Liberals' dream of holding the balance of power.
In 1974, indeed, he was invited by the prime minister, Edward
Heath – whom he had once described as 'a plum pudding around
whom no one knew how to light the brandy' – to lead his party
into coalition with the Conservatives; he himself was offered the
post of foreign secretary.

It was understandable, therefore, that five years later, at
Thorpe's trial, even prosecuting counsel should have spoken
of a 'tragedy of truly Greek and Shakespearean proportions'.

Tragedy, however, is a large word, implying the destruction, if not necessarily of virtue, at least of some outstanding merit. Only in the context of a man's entire life can its just application be decided.

John Jeremy Thorpe was born on April 29 1929 into a highly political family. He would claim descent from Sir Robert de Thorpe, who was Chief Justice of the Court of Common Pleas in 1356 and Chancellor in 1371.

More to the point, both of Thorpe's parents were staunch Conservatives. His father John Thorpe, born in Cork, was a KC and, for a few years after the First World War, MP for Rusholme in Manchester. His mother was the daughter of Sir John Norton-Griffiths, 1st Baronet, another Conservative MP and one who gloried in the epithet 'Empire Jack' – even if he owed his baronetcy to Lloyd George.

Jeremy Thorpe, however, thought of himself as 'three-quarters Celt'; and in keeping with this bias, it was from his mother's friend Lady Megan Lloyd George that, rather to Mrs Thorpe's disapproval, he imbibed a romantic attachment to Liberalism.

The boy had two sisters, both older; he was brought up as the cynosure of his parents' eyes. 'It never occurred to him,' his mother remarked of his early days in Kensington, 'that anybody might not be glad to see him.'

Young Jeremy adored his father, but it was his mother who exerted the most powerful influence. A formidable woman, who affected an eyeglass, Ursula Thorpe nursed the highest ambitions for her son. 'That monocle!' Thorpe recalled in later life. 'We were all frightened of her. I have overcome the domination, and I am damn well not going to be dominated again.'

Thorpe was only six when tubercular glands were diagnosed in his stomach. For seven months he had to lie on his back in a spinal carriage; he suffered back pains for the rest of his life.

The Second World War caused a hiatus in what promised to be a conventional English education. In 1940 Thorpe and the younger of his sisters were sent to stay with an aunt in

America, where he attended the Rectory School in Connecticut, by contemporary English standards a decidedly easy-going establishment.

Thorpe loved it. His histrionic gifts – and in particular his talent for mimicry – began to flourish. He played Miranda in *The Tempest*, became an accomplished violinist, and showed precocious assurance as a public speaker.

In 1943 he returned to England to go to Eton, where the more rigorous discipline proved less agreeable. He was also greatly upset by the death of his father, after a stroke, in 1944. This misfortune left the family in dire financial straits, so that an uncle had to stump up the funds to keep the boy at Eton. It also, inevitably, increased the sway of Mrs Thorpe.

After Eton, Thorpe joined the Rifle Brigade for his National Service, only to be invalided out of the Army after six weeks as 'psychologically unsuitable'. It has been alleged that he became a bed-wetter to prove the point.

At Trinity College, Oxford, by contrast, the military reject flourished outrageously. His flamboyant dress – frock coats, stove-pipe trousers, brocade waistcoats, buckled shoes, and even spats – received all the attention they demanded; his penchant for Chinese vases suggested aesthetic sensibility; his witty persiflage kept the mockers at a distance.

Theoretically, Thorpe was reading Law; in reality he was laying the foundations of his political career. But though he became in turn president of the Liberal Club, the Law Society and the Union, he attracted criticism from contemporaries for the ruthlessness he showed in the pursuit of these offices.

Thorpe scraped a Third in his Finals. Afterwards, in 1954, he was called to the Bar by the Inner Temple, and built up a modest practice on the Western Circuit. He also, later in the 1950s, worked for commercial television, appearing regularly on current affairs programmes such as *This Week*, and sending back reports from Africa and the Middle East.

But politics was always his master passion. In 1952, with the help of Dingle Foot, whom he had befriended when at Oxford, he was adopted as Liberal candidate at North Devon which, though it had been a Liberal seat in the early 1930s, had a 12,000 Tory majority in the 1951 General Election.

Thorpe, at his very best on the stump, had no rival as a vote-gatherer. He could put any argument with skill and panache; his astonishing memory for faces persuaded voters that they were intimate friends; his brilliant gifts as a mimic kept the audience in stitches; his resourceful mind afforded quips and stunts for every occasion.

At the same time he built up a formidable organisation in the constituency, and drove it with unflagging energy. In the 1955 general election the Tory majority was slashed to 5,226, and four years later he captured the seat by 362 votes. Thorpe would hold North Devon for 20 years, narrowly at first, but in February 1974 with a thumping 11,082 majority. Yet he was never tempted to appeal to wavering Tory voters by trimming his Liberal views on issues such as South Africa or capital punishment.

In the House of Commons he made an immediate impression. A sketchwriter remarked of his maiden speech that 'it seemed as though Mr Thorpe had been addressing the House for the past 10 years, and got rather tired of the exercise'. But the young MP knew how to draw blood, as with his jibe after Harold Macmillan sacked several of his Cabinet in 1962: 'Greater love hath no man than this, that he lay down his friends for his own life.'

Thorpe appeared somewhat to the Left of the party, a mouthpiece for impeccable Liberal sentiments, especially on African affairs. He received the distinction of being banned from Franco's Spain.

In 1966 he advocated that Britain should cut off the oil supplies to Ian Smith's Rhodesian regime by bombing that country's railway system. The Liberal conference enthusiastically applauded the idea, but Harold Wilson inflicted permanent damage by coining the phrase 'Bomber Thorpe'.

Meanwhile, though, the young MP had been working energetically to fill the organisational void left by Jo Grimond's leadership.

Thorpe's charm made him especially effective as a fund-raiser, and in 1965 he captured the party treasuryship.

When Grimond retired in 1967, the 12 Liberal MPs elected Thorpe in his place. The new leader immediately gave a foretaste of his style by holding a rally in the Albert Hall, at which he promised 'a great crusade that will set Britain alight for the vision of a Liberal society' – a performance relayed by closed circuit television to three other city centres.

Nevertheless, in his first years at the helm the showman for once misjudged his act. 'He felt he had to move away from the image of the sharp and witty debater to being grave,' David Steel remembered. 'It was disastrous.'

Yet Thorpe did not altogether abandon frivolity. Colleagues found, to their frustration and fury, that important policy discussions had to wait upon the leader's gossipy anecdotes about the prime minister or royalty. Nor did Thorpe's continuing addiction to outmoded dress and eccentric headgear – notably the brown bowler hat he wore when electioneering – do anything to allay the growing suspicion that he was all style and precious little substance.

His critics acknowledged that he loved the *game* of politics – indeed he took a fiendish delight in its Machiavellian plots and manoeuvres – but they wondered if he knew why he was playing it.

Thorpe's Liberalism was essentially romantic and emotional. He reacted strongly against bone-headed Establishment snobbery, arrogant management or racial injustice, but showed scant interest in formulating any coherent political philosphy.

On the other hand there was no doubting Thorpe's quick mind or his keen antennae. He was to the fore in predicting the 1967 devaluation crisis and in identifying the mounting crisis in Ulster; he also showed himself a consistent supporter of Britain's entry into the Common Market.

Thorpe did not suffer fools gladly. Erring subordinates were treated to the sharp rebuke or the snappish aside; and in the face of any challenge to his authority the mask of the jester quickly gave way to a fixed, distant and icy stare. He was at his most formidable under pressure, as the Young Liberals discovered when they attempted to mount a coup in 1968.

The unsatisfactory opening years of his leadership culminated in the 1970 general election. Thorpe campaigned with his accustomed zeal, sweeping about the country in helicopters and cutting an impressive figure on television, but the results were disastrous.

The Liberals polled only 2.1 million votes and retained only six seats. And then, less than a fortnight after the election, Thorpe's wife Caroline was killed in a car crash.

For a while Thorpe appeared to lose interest in politics. But in 1972 and 1973 the widespread dissatisfaction with the Heath government found expression in a remarkable series of Liberal successes in municipal and byelections.

Thorpe's style was undoubtedly a factor in attracting discontented Tory voters. But his animadversions against the 'bloody-mindedness' of British life were undermined, at the end of 1973, by his involvement in a shoddy financial disaster.

Thorpe had become a director of Gerald Caplan's London & County Securities to boost his meagre parliamentary salary; in his delight at the sudden flush of income, however, he failed to heed numerous and reiterated warnings about the company's viability.

In 1972 the Liberals, and Thorpe himself, put on a notable display of piety over Reginald Maudling's involvement with the Poulson affair. It was therefore more than a shade embarrassing when it transpired that the leader was involved in a company that was charging 280 per cent on second mortgages, and when, at the end of 1973, the collapse of London & County revealed a tangled skein of financial misdemeanour.

British voters, far from being concerned, were apparently impressed by Liberal promises to tackle the national crisis with increased public spending and state control of incomes. At the February 1974 general election Thorpe, though largely confined in his marginal North Devon constituency, reached his political apotheosis. The Liberals nearly trebled their vote to six million; the only fly in the ointment was that this total translated itself into but 14 seats.

Rumour had it that Thorpe was responsive to Heath's offer of a coalition, with the promise of a Speaker's conference to consider electoral reform. His colleagues, however, have gone on record that the decision to reject these terms was 'unanimous'.

The ensuing months exposed the flaws in the Liberal revival. The party activists were radicals; many of its newfound supporters were dissatisfied Tories. Moreover, the exquisite Thorpe seemed far removed from the community politics advocated by Trevor Jones ('Jones the Vote') and his chums.

In the October 1974 general election, the Liberal leader left his North Devon constituency to its own devices and once more whisked about the country in helicopters and hovercraft. All to no avail: the Liberal vote fell by 700,000.

Thorpe was severely disillusioned. But the most remarkable thing about his political career was not that he ultimately failed to storm the heights, but that he managed to retain the sangfroid to lead the Liberals when, all the while, a large part of his energies was concentrated on repressing a significant element of his personality.

That Thorpe, in his youth, had homosexual tendencies was admitted at his trial. Nor was it in dispute – though he always emphatically denied any physical relationship – that in 1961 he had befriended a young man named Norman Josiffe, who later changed his name to Norman Scott.

Though Mr Justice Cantley's conduct of the trial was widely criticised, no one argued about his description of Norman Scott. 'He is a fraud. He is a sponger. He is a whiner. He is a parasite.' Scott claimed to have had an affair with Thorpe between 1961 and 1964, and there can be no question whatever that, as their meetings dwindled and finally ceased, he conceived a grievance that nothing but the ruin of Thorpe could assuage. (It should be remembered that homosexual acts between consenting adults were not legalised until 1967.)

In pursuit of his vendetta Scott seized every possible occasion, public and private, to advertise his sexual connection with Thorpe. As early as December 1962 he blurted out the story to the Chelsea police, and gave them two letters he had received from the MP, one of which contained the phrase – 'Bunnies can (and will) go to France' – that would become notorious when, 14 years later, it finally reached the public domain.

During that time Scott bore the menace of a time-bomb ticking away in the shadows of Thorpe's career. The fuse was unpredictable, but intermittent splutters constantly portended some vast explosion.

Thus in 1965 Scott took it upon himself to write to Thorpe's mother setting out the details of his homosexual relations with her son. This missive prompted Thorpe to make the cardinal error of confiding in Peter Bessell, a fellow Liberal MP.

One of the most striking features of the affair was that Thorpe, for all his public glamour, seemed to have no upright friend to whom he was prepared to turn for counsel. Bessell was a Methodist lay preacher; he was also, as he himself would all too willingly confirm under crossexamination, amoral, hypocritical and untruthful.

Bessell tried to contain the danger to Thorpe by going to see Scott, by purloining compromising letters, and subsequently by paying Scott small weekly sums which Thorpe refunded. He also sought, and appeared to receive, assurances from the home secretary, Sir Frank Soskice, that the police were not interested in pursuing Scott's allegations.

But Thorpe's anxiety could not be assuaged as long as the possibility remained that Scott would one day succeed in finding a newspaper to print his story. And after the Liberal leader had married Caroline Allpass in 1968, he had even more to lose – though the best man, David Holmes, wrote that Caroline Thorpe 'knew about Scott' before they were married.

In May 1969 Scott himself married; and his son was born that November. The marriage soon broke up, but not before the experience of connubial penury in a Dorset cottage had lent a hysterical edge to Scott's importuning of Bessell. Worse, there was the threat – never, in fact, realised – that Scott would use the divorce proceedings as an opportunity to blurt out his accusations about Thorpe under the protection of court privilege.

Another crisis developed in 1971. Scott, now living in North Wales, became the lover of a widow, Mrs Gwen Parry-Jones, who, treated to the usual accounts of Thorpe's iniquities, duly reported them to another Liberal MP, Emlyn Hooson. A Liberal Party inquiry into the affair ensued.

Thorpe fought like a tiger, denying the allegations point blank and enlisting the help of the home secretary, Reginald Maudling, to confirm a somewhat misleading summary of police dealings with Scott. It was Thorpe's word against that of his tormentor, and the Liberals chose to believe their leader.

Next year, 1972, Mrs Parry-Jones died, and at the inquest on her death Scott at last had the opportunity to tell his story in court. But no editor cared to print his wild ravings; nor did a South African journalist, Gordon Winter, find any takers when he gathered material from Scott.

It might have seemed that Scott had done his worst, and been repelled. In 1973 Thorpe announced his engagement to Marion, Countess of Harewood, previously married to the Queen's cousin.

About the same time Scott moved to Thorpe's North Devon constituency, where he proceeded to inflict the history of his relations with the local MP upon bemused rustics in pubs. He also told his tale to the Tory candidate, who decided not to touch it.

Just before the first general election of 1974, David Holmes succeeded in purchasing some letters from Scott for £2,500. Nevertheless, Scott the persecutor now appeared in the role of victim.

In February 1975 he was beaten up by two men in Barnstaple market. And in October, when an AA patrolman discovered him weeping beside the corpse of his great dane, Rinka, he claimed that only a jammed pistol had prevented the assailant from shooting him as well as the dog.

In January 1976 Scott, charged with defrauding the DHSS, declared under the privilege of court that he was being 'hounded by people' because of his affair with Jeremy Thorpe. This time, at last, the press did take notice. Thereafter rumour blew so loud that by March Thorpe felt compelled to defend himself in *The Sunday Times*, specifically denying both that he had hired a gunman to kill Scott, and that he had had any knowledge of Holmes's purchase of the letters in 1974.

Despite support from the prime minister, Harold Wilson, who appeared to believe that the accusations had been fabricated by the South African secret service, Thorpe was unable to hold the line. After the 'Bunnies' letter was published in *The Sunday Times* in May 1976, he resigned the Liberal leadership.

There could scarcely have been any criminal charges against him, however, if Bessell, who had long been exiled in California, had not decided to turn Queen's evidence. He believed, with good reason, that Thorpe would not hesitate to throw him to the wolves in order to save his own skin.

Bessell alleged that in 1968 and 1969 Thorpe had incited Holmes and himself to murder Scott, helpfully suggesting that the body might be chucked down a Cornish mine shaft, or cemented into a motorway bridge. 'It's no worse than killing a sick dog,' Thorpe is supposed to have remarked, before recommending research into slow-acting poisons.

The second charge associated Thorpe with Holmes and two others on a charge of conspiracy to murder in the years 1974 and 1975; this also depended partly on Bessell's evidence, though in this case the diversion of Liberal funds through Holmes's hands to the hitman, Andrew Newton, was also germane.

Thorpe behaved with marked courage in the face of the cataclysm, observing with his accustomed brio that a man who had the prime minister, Lord Goodman and MI5 on his side could hardly lose.

Even after his committal to trial at the Old Bailey Thorpe insisted on contesting North Devon at the 1979 election, where his opponents included Auberon Waugh, standing for the Dog Lovers' Party. Though Thorpe lost the seat (he remarked laconically to a television interviewer that Scott's allegations had 'hardly helped' his campaign), his vote fell by less than 5,000 compared with October 1974.

At the Old Bailey the charges failed after the defence, with the help of Mr Justice Cantley, had annihilated Bessell's character. Thorpe opted not to give evidence in his own defence, thus avoiding cross-examination.

Even so, his reputation was badly damaged by the exhibition of the financial sleight of hand which he had shown in directing funds given to the Liberal Party by the millionaire 'Union Jack' Hayward towards David Holmes. He was also revealed as a blustering bully in his attempt to dissuade his friend Nadir Dinshaw, the Pakistani financier, from telling the truth.

Dinshaw, acting on Thorpe's command, had innocently passed on money to Holmes. Before the trial Thorpe told him that if he reported the fact, 'It will be curtains for me, and you will be asked to move on.'

In short, the trial bore out the impression created by Thorpe's political career, that he was essentially a fixer and an operator. Far from being a tragic hero – a noble nature ruined by a single mole of nature – he appeared, whether innocent or guilty, amply provisioned with common human flaws, cast by his gifts and ambition into most uncommon relief.

Yet this man, who spent so many years trying to avoid imputations of homosexuality, won devoted loyalty from both his wives. 'I saw an emotional cripple take up his bed and walk,' someone remarked of his first marriage.

For a while after the trial Thorpe seemed to nurse the dream of rebuilding his career. In 1981 he applied unsuccessfully for the job of race relations adviser to the BBC, and the next year he was actually appointed director of Amnesty, only to resign the post after complaints from within the organisation.

Thorpe remained chairman of the political committee of
the United Nations Association until 1985, but in the world
of the *haut monde* that he loved to adorn, there would be no
redemption. By the middle of the 1980s, moreover, he was
afflicted with Parkinson's disease.

The North Devon Liberals, however, remained faithful to the
last, electing him as their president in 1987.

Jeremy Thorpe's second wife died in March of this year; he is
survived by his son, Rupert, from his first marriage.

Jeremy Thorpe, born April 29 1929, died December 4 2014

Gerry Wells

Collector of vintage radios and TVs whose home became a museum of the history of broadcasting

GERRY WELLS, who has died aged 85, was a self-confessed obsessive whose life was dominated by his fascination with radio apparatus.

By the time of his death he had amassed a collection of more than 1,300 radio and television sets and associated

Wells: he was a teenage rebel who fell foul of the law

equipment, covering the entire pre-transistor history of broadcasting. This had become the British Vintage Wireless and Television Museum, and today it occupies his lifelong home, a substantial Edwardian house in Dulwich, south-east London.

The collection contains many working examples, most of them found and brought back to life by Wells himself. Visitors can have the unique and somewhat unsettling experience of watching live television programmes in the old 405-line, black-and-white format, abandoned in 1984. Wells rescued the converter from the nearby Crystal Palace transmitter. He was a bit short of space at the time, so he set it up in his bedroom.

Gerald Lloyd Wells was born in the same Dulwich house on September 18 1929, the son of an insurance clerk. His future obsession with things electrical made itself known early when, aged three, he carefully inserted a piece of tinfoil into a power socket and blew every fuse in the house. Thereafter, electricity, radio especially, became his overwhelming interest.

As an unconventional child, the young Gerry was alternately ostracised and bullied at school. This, combined with difficulties at home, led him to play truant at the age of 11. He occupied his illicit free time in exploring bombed houses, scavenging for electrical switches, fuse boxes and other bits and pieces. From this he graduated to stealing radios from neighbouring flats. These he dismantled and hid in the attic; but he was found out and sent to a remand home.

This pattern of behaviour was repeated several times until, at 15, he was sent to an Approved School in Lancashire. There his skills found a legitimate outlet, and he was soon happily employed on electrical tasks, including renovating the local cinema's projector. It was correctly judged that his life of crime was over and he was released on licence.

With television starting up again after the war, and everything in short supply, he found his skills in great demand. It was a good time to set up in the repair business. The Coronation made 1953 a particularly busy and profitable year. He even designed and manufactured his own television sets.

With increasing affluence, the demand for small-scale repair work fell away, and in the early 1960s Wells turned to general electrical contracting. Never an astute businessman, he was an even worse employer, and his business struggled. That, plus a back injury, finally brought it to an end in 1974.

This was when (encouraged by friends who told him 'If Lord Montagu could do it with cars, you can do it with radios') he determined to turn his home into a wireless museum. In a very short time it had taken over every room in the house, including the attic, and spread to a sizeable wooden structure that he built in the garden. The collection continued to grow until it became necessary to purchase a strip of garden from the house next door, for a further building.

The establishment, now a registered charity, is closed at present, while his devoted team of helpers reorganise it – not least to get some of the weight off the upper floor before it gives way. But it will reopen to visitors, always by prior arrangement.

No doubt its annual summer garden party will take place again this year, at which people will crowd into a darkened room to watch BBC television 'Interludes' from the early 1950s in glorious black and white.

Gerry Wells is survived by a daughter.

Gerry Wells, born September 18 1929, died December 22 2014

The Dowager Marchioness of Reading

Aristocrat who raced stock cars and praised the fighting spirit of the English football hooligan

THE DOWAGER MARCHIONESS OF READING, who has died aged 96, was a society beauty of the 1930s and 1940s and a woman of independent spirit.

She was one of the first British women to get a pilot's licence, competed on the prewar stock car racing circuit, and became a rally driver in the 1950s. In later life she became a campaigner for animal rights and an outspoken English nationalist.

Margot Reading in 1945: she held views 'diametrically opposed to most sane people'

As Harold Brooks-Baker, the former publishing director of *Burke's Peerage*, once noted, Margot Reading had views 'diametrically opposed to most sane people'. At no time was this more clear than in 1998 when, after the maverick Tory politician Alan Clark paid tribute to the 'martial spirit' of English football supporters who had gone on the rampage in Marseille, she wrote a letter to *The Spectator* in which she observed: 'We are a nation of yobs. Now we don't have a war, what's wrong with a good punch-up?'

In a later interview she elaborated on her views. 'I love England so much and I just feel that the so-called hooligans are just sort of over-enthusiastic. How is it that we conquered the world and that our armies went over the top? It is because we are a nation of fighters ... What an English tough guy does is to fight with his fists, which is a good clean fight … With so many milksops, and Left-wing liberals and wetties around, I just rejoice in the fact that there are people who keep up our historic spirit.'

Her comments came in for severe criticism, prompting her eldest son, the Marquess of Reading, to beg her not to take any more telephone calls. 'I am very fond of my mum, but I do not always agree with her,' he explained.

One of three sisters, she was born Margot Irene Duke on January 11 1919. Her father, Percy Duke, was said to have been the last man to wear a wing collar on the floor of the Stock Exchange and, for reasons which remain obscure, divided the world into people he called 'George,' and those he called 'McGregor'. Margot's mother, Violet Mappin, would have inherited much of the fortune of the silversmiths and jewellers Mappin & Webb had she not married Percy only six weeks after the death of her first husband.

Educated at Benenden, Margot sat for leading photographers such as Angus McBean, who declared her one of the most beautiful women he had ever seen. She was, for a time, the face of Pond's beauty cream.

In 1940 she married Michael, Viscount Erleigh, MC, the eldest son of the 2nd Marquess of Reading who would succeed his father in 1960. Although she enjoyed a very happy 40 years of marriage, she never conformed to anyone's expectations.

She loved speed and, as well as becoming one of the first British women to get a pilot's licence before the war, she competed in the 1952 Round Britain car rally as co-driver with Sheila van Damm. Guests at the coming-out party for her daughter in the 1960s would recall how she took charge of a fairground carousel hired for the event and boosted it to full power, terrifying those on board. She was also a fearless horsewoman and hunted with the Mid Surrey Drag Hounds.

A woman of trenchant opinions, she once wrote an (unpublished) letter to *The Daily Telegraph* in which she proclaimed that 'the only answer to paedophiles is to cut their balls off'. In the 1960s she briefly entertained hopes of standing for the Conservatives in a general election, until her husband dissuaded her, fearing what she might say.

When it was suggested to her that she might be descended from an illegitimate son of William I, Margot Reading began to research her family, which she traced back to the 12th century, and she managed to persuade the College of Arms to accept her connection with the Conqueror. The discovery that a forebear called Anne Duke had played a small part in the 'Sealed Knot' conspiracy to return Charles II to the throne (while being in love with Oliver Cromwell's secretary John Thurloe) led to her co-writing a historical novel entitled *Anne of the Sealed Knot* (1972, with R.J. Minney).

In the mid-1990s she persuaded *The Spectator* to publish the letters of her half-brother, Sir Charles Mappin, who sailed round Tahiti in the late 1930s and went through much of the Mappin & Webb fortune before enlisting in the RAF as a rear gunner on a Wellington bomber and dying on his third mission. A lover of practical jokes, during the 1930s Sir Charles had announced plans for an 'Old Berkeley Square Cat Hunt', in which the stray felines of Mayfair would be rounded up with the aid of greyhounds. The police and RSPCA were among a number of bodies who fell for the prank.

In the last 20 years of her life, Margot Reading's great passion was animal welfare and she bombarded everyone she could think of with letters demanding they do more to protect all forms of animal life. In particular she sought better treatment for 'moonbears', which are often kept in appalling conditions in China, where their bile is extracted for use in Chinese medicine.

Her husband died in 1980, and she is survived by their daughter and three sons.

The Dowager Marchioness of Reading, born January 11 1919, died April 19 2015

Anne Naysmith

Former concert pianist who worked with Sir Adrian Boult and ended her life living rough in London

Anne Naysmith in front of her Mercedes estate: late in life she expressed the view that being a professional pianist had killed her love of music

ANNE NAYSMITH, who has died aged about 77, enjoyed a promising career as a pianist in the 1960s but latterly achieved notoriety as 'the car lady of Chiswick', a dishevelled and familiar sight to commuters in west London; she lived first in her dilapidated old blue Ford Consul and then in bushes by an Underground station.

Her concert career took her to the Wigmore Hall in 1967, where a critic noted that in her performance of Rachmaninov's Preludes Op 23 she 'blossomed most fully as an artist and drew some of the warmest and richest sonorities from her piano'. There were appearances at Leighton House in Holland Park,

St Martin-in-the-Fields, St James's Piccadilly, and venues in the Home Counties. She is said to have performed under the conductor Sir Adrian Boult.

However, after being evicted at the age of 39 from her home in Prebend Gardens, a pretty street of Victorian villas in Chiswick, Annie, as she was known locally, spent 26 years sleeping in her car. When that was towed away, she declined the offer of social housing, preferring a makeshift shelter by Stamford Brook Underground station, tending her plants and shrubs. That too was removed in August 2012 by Transport for London contractors, leaving her distraught.

Some commentators drew parallels with Miss Shepherd, the musician who lived in a van on the driveway of Alan Bennett's home in Camden and was immortalised in his play *The Lady in the Van* (1999). Others saw a link to Diogenes the Cynic, the Greek philosopher who showed his contempt for the material world by sleeping in a large ceramic jar or barrel.

She was born Anne Smith at Southend-on-Sea in 1937, adding the 'Nay' in later life. Her father, an Army officer of whom she had no memory, failed to return home from leave one day. In due course her Russian mother, Marie, who desperately wanted a high-profile musical career for her daughter, moved them to Hounslow, west London. They became estranged and Anne lived briefly with her aunt 'Tutts' in Devon.

By the age of 18 Anne had won a place at the Royal Academy of Music, studying with Harold Craxton and Liza Fuchsova. She rented a room in Chiswick, which she soon upgraded to a house, and began teaching piano at the Marist convent school in Sunninghill, Berkshire. Later she worked at Trinity College of Music, quickly saving the £800 cost of her car.

By the early 1960s Anne was making a respectable if not spectacular career in music, but within a decade her life fell apart. Her performing career never fulfilled its early promise; she withdrew from teaching for reasons that were never explained; and an intense affair with 'a handsome 6ft 5in choral singer' disintegrated.

Her eviction was, she believed, an injustice. By way of protest she began sleeping in her car – apparently her sole remaining possession of substance – insisting to anyone who came near that she should be allowed back into her former home.

Anne Naysmith's plight divided local residents, some of whom feared for the value of their homes, and in 2002 the Ford Consul was towed away. Others felt protective of their eccentric neighbour and provided her with a replacement – a Mercedes estate – but it was vandalised almost immediately.

Sometimes she would sit in on local court cases. On other days she could be found in the Barbican music library, examining scores or engaging in spirited and intelligent conversation about music and musicians; or she would chat with prommers outside the Albert Hall. On other occasions she would feed the pigeons and tend to the vegetation in her car-park home. Until recently she attended evensong at St Nicholas Church, Chiswick, her singing notable for its clarity and beauty. She was also a regular fixture at Chiswick cricket club, where she devised her own complex scoring system. Some thought that her fingers might be ghosting Rachmaninov during the bowler's run-up. Whether or not they were, she applauded between balls, called out 'good over' when appropriate, and engaged with her fellow spectators in informed discussion about the match's progress.

Her ablutions were done in public lavatories or at a doctor's surgery, and she washed her tattered clothes at a petrol station with a hose pipe, wrapping them in old newspapers to dry. She collected pigeon feathers, tying them round her feet with carrier bags to keep warm, and cooked on an open fire, giving her homemade tomato chutney to regular passers-by.

After her third eviction in 2012 Anne Naysmith became something of a minor celebrity, featuring in profiles on blog sites, in newspapers and on BBC television. Speaking to *The Daily Telegraph*, she told how being a professional pianist had killed her love of music.

'I suppose I just wanted to practise for enjoyment instead of for a concert,' she reflected. Yet she insisted that she would have had no trouble picking it up again: 'I haven't touched a piano seriously for over 30 years. But it's like learning to swim: if I did it for two weeks I could rush out a few things quite quickly.'

From time to time there were attempts to help her off the streets, by both official agencies and well-meaning music-lovers. Most were politely declined: if she could not return to Prebend Gardens she would remain in her car. Others were rebuffed more ferociously. Mostly, as Steven Morris noted in *The Guardian*, she remained fiercely independent, proud and dignified.

Anne Naysmith, who died after being hit by a lorry in Chiswick High Road, never married.

Anne Naysmith, born 1937, died February 10 2015

John Simopoulos

Oxford philosophy don and Dean of Degrees who was also known for his obsessive interest in telephones

JOHN SIMOPOULOS, who has died aged 91, was a founding Fellow, Tutor in Philosophy and long-serving Dean of Degrees of St Catherine's College, Oxford; he was also the sort of old-school don whose manifold eccentricities live long in the student memory.

Simopoulos was a member of a remarkable generation of Oxford philosophers, including Freddie Ayer, David Pears, Iris Murdoch, Mary Warnock, Peter Strawson and Tony Quinton, who came to dominate their field

Simopoulos: his publications included a collection of obscene limericks and a paper in the *British Journal of Venereal Diseases*

in the post-war era. Unlike them, however, he published very little. Indeed, he was perhaps best known for two publications, both outside his subject: an article, *Tetracycline treatment for non-specific urethritis*, published in 1977 in the *British Journal of Venereal Diseases* (a colleague received a copy with the inscription 'Multiplex erit scientia' – 'knowledge shall be diverse'), and a privately published collection of dirty limericks.

As Simopoulos once confessed to a fellow guest at a dinner party given by his great friends, John Bayley and Iris Murdoch (who dedicated her novel, *The Bell*, to Simopoulos): 'I used to review for an important journal ... but it packed up 20 years ago.'

Simopoulos was one of four permanent academic staff at the St Catherine's Society when it was founded in 1952, and in 1960 became a founding Fellow when it was transformed into a college. A staunch college man, he promoted reading parties to counterbalance the hearty rugger ethos that St Catz had when it was still an all-male establishment. A bi-annual dinner was founded in his honour, designed to get undergraduates and academics chatting to each other across disciplinary boundaries.

Over fine food and wine, students of all subjects were commingled, with some tutors invited to give a brief, preferably funny, talk relevant to their field, but accessible to everyone.

Simopoulos, whose father had served as the Greek ambassador to the Court of St James during the Second World War, loved ceremonial. He also became celebrated as the college's Dean of Degrees, and even after his retirement in 1988 he took pride in guiding scores of students through matriculation in the Sheldonian each Michaelmas term, as well as taking responsibility for presenting graduands at 10 degree ceremonies per year.

One former undergraduate recalled that at such occasions he was 'word-perfect, or if ever less than word-perfect, would correct himself in perfect Latin'. To his charges he would always emphasise the central importance of the oath which each student is asked to swear. The current Master of the College, Professor Roger Ainsworth, was quoted in the *Oxford Mail* as saying: 'He would tell graduands: "If you walk around Oxford, half the population will be shuffling around the pavements looking depressed. This is because they did not say: 'Do fidem' [I swear] loudly enough."'

Simopoulos did not always see eye to eye with the college's founding Master, the historian Alan Bullock – as became apparent in 1993 when the college buildings, designed by the Danish architect Arne Jacobsen, were listed Grade I by Peter Brooke, the heritage secretary, and Simopoulos dismissed this decision as a 'nonsense'. Neither he nor other college Fellows had been consulted about the design, he protested: 'Alan and his pals junketed off to Denmark for weeks and came back with this miserable Dane. Jacobsen was gloomy as hell, a symphony by Sibelius brought more or less to life ... Everyone licked Alan's arse at the time. He was very impressed by Jacobsen, even let him design the ghastly cutlery in hall. When Alan showed the Fellows the new knives and forks, they "oohed" and "aahed"; I said I thought they looked like a DIY abortion kit designed by Charles Addams.'

John Simopoulos was born on June 12 1923, when his father, Charalambos Simopoulos, was serving as High Commissioner for Greece in Constantinople. Educated at Stowe, he read Greats at Magdalen College, Oxford. For a time he taught Latin at Christ Church Cathedral Choir School before being appointed Tutor in Philosophy at what was then the St Catherine's Society in 1953.

He spoke fluent Italian (and Latin) and, in the early 1950s, also worked as a special commissioner for Oxfam, reporting on the plight of Hungarian refugees in refugee camps in Italy.

In the little he did write, Simopoulos's love for linguistic precision was always evident – even in his collection of limericks. One of his favourites ran: 'There once was a fellow called Rex, / Who'd a diminutive organ of sex. / When had up for exposure, / He replied with composure, / De minimis non curat lex ["the law does not concern itself with trifles"].'

His attention to terminological and grammatical detail was unremitting. A colleague recalled his riposte to an English tutor who accused him of being a pedant: 'At least I use the language with sufficient precision for you to say that of me, which I doubt is true in your case.'

Despite his friendship with Bayley and Iris Murdoch (whom he introduced to the Tintin books) Simopoulos loved good food (and wine). The Bayleys were not known for their fine cuisine, though it was observed that Simopoulos was 'his own barometer' in such matters, 'good' denoting what he liked and 'bad' what he did not.

This applied to other areas of life too. Thus, he was heard to remark of an acquaintance of whose chosen profession he disapproved: 'In a profession which has no standards, he somehow contrives to fall below them.'

One of Simopoulos's quirks was a fascination with telephone technology. He would spend his long vacations working in the Rome telephone exchange and, as one colleague has recalled, at a time when the Post Office ran the British telephone system and the unions ran the Post Office, Simopoulos could somehow rig up a phone in a colleague's room without having to negotiate the months-long Post Office waiting list. How he did so remained a mystery, but he liked it that way.

In retirement Simopoulos, who had a flat in London as well as one in college, indulged his lifelong fascination with the technology and became a telephone consultant in London.

He never married.

John Simopoulos, born June 12 1923, died March 4 2015

Viv Nicholson

Factory worker from Yorkshire whose life unravelled after her husband won the pools

Viv Nicholson: she dyed her hair pink-champagne blonde and spent £1,400 a week

VIV NICHOLSON, who has died aged 79, was the factory packer from Yorkshire whose husband won a record pools jackpot of £152,319 in 1961; she disastrously fulfilled her much-vaunted promise to 'spend, spend, spend', and blew the lot on a life of luxury and excess that lasted less than five years.

She and her husband won the money when she was 25. But by the time she was 30, Vivian Nicholson (universally known as Viv Nich) had not only spent it all, but had also buried her husband, Keith, and returned to her humble roots, reflecting ruefully on her fate as one of the first media celebrities of the pre-Beatles 1960s.

Portrayed in the papers as a hellcat – with the outrageous personality to match her money and her looks – Viv Nicholson laboured under the image of a working-class blonde who had led a champagne-fuelled life of depravity and whose fall, when it came, was no less than she deserved.

Certainly she had struggled with the culture shock of winning such a stupendous amount of money – the equivalent of more than £5 million today – and felt alienated from people of her own sort who, in turn, could no longer relate to her.

It was scarcely surprising. Two months after her win, she estimated that she was spending money at the rate of £1,400 a week. After the £4,000 luxury bungalow came the cars, a silver Chevrolet and a pink Cadillac, in which (once she had learnt to drive) she would roar up the gravel drive and over the manicured lawns of her children's private school, having dyed her hair pink-champagne blonde, then green, then yellow, then blue. With the cars came the clothes, furs, frocks, shoes – she once bought 14 pairs at one go – jewellery, watches and exotic holidays.

But her chief excess was drink. After the open house at their local pub near Leeds, the Miners' Arms, to celebrate their win, there were lavish parties at the new home they had named the Ponderosa, with its own corner cocktail bar literally awash with alcohol, and so much champagne that Viv claimed to bathe in it. They filled their days back at the pub, with daily sessions starting at lunchtime and often not ending before four the next morning.

But four years after hitting the jackpot, Keith Nicholson was killed at the wheel of his new Jaguar, leaving an estate of just £42,000. At first Viv, who wore her funeral suit for three months, was denied access to his money.

By the time a dispute over his will had eventually been settled in her favour, she had been forced to work in a strip club to cover her children's school fees. As she divorced or mourned a further three husbands in rapid succession, she lost heavily on bad investments, what little money was left simply haemorrhaged away, and she sank into debt.

Her chronic drink problem and unquenchable urge to spend eventually led her back to where she had started, the fancy house and cars sold, the last of the money scraped together to buy a tiny terrace house in the shadow of a grimy factory and where she stored her collection of 1960s haute couture in five wardrobes.

But this was not the end of her cautionary tale: her memoirs, *Spend, Spend, Spend*, published in the 1970s, earned her £60,000 and a West End musical of the same title about her life a further £100,000. This money, too, seemed to trickle through her fingers; she lost £12,000 in a failed boutique venture because – out of guilt – she gave the clothes away.

Even in her impoverished retirement, Viv Nicholson retained a penchant for 'spiffing' clothes and £70 bottles of perfume. She wound up penniless, on a widow's pension of £87 a week.

She was born Vivian Asprey on April 3 1936 at Castleford, a working-class satellite of Leeds. The eldest child of an epileptic miner who drank often and worked seldom, Viv won a scholarship to art school when she was 13, but was forbidden to go by her father, who sent her instead to scavenge for coal at the local pithead.

Because her mother was asthmatic, she found herself having to look after her six siblings, and although considered bright at school, Viv was forced to leave at 14 to take a job at a local liquorice factory, packing allsorts and Pontefract cakes. By 16 she was married and pregnant, but became infatuated with her neighbour, a trainee miner called Keith Nicholson, whom she married as soon as her divorce came through.

In 1961, now with four children, Viv and Keith Nicholson were between them earning £9 a week. On September 30, a Saturday night, Keith was checking his pools coupon against the football results on television when he realised he had eight score draws. Viv ran to the nearby post office to send a telegram claim to Littlewoods. For a line costing a farthing, part of Keith's stake of a borrowed five shillings [25p], they had scooped a £152,000 jackpot.

In London, emerging from their train at King's Cross, the Nicholsons were asked by reporters what their plans were. Viv's boast – that she planned to 'spend, spend, spend' – made headlines around the world and seemed to chime with the spirit of the consumer age that had coincided with the dawn of the 1960s.

Within days Viv and her family had moved out of their council house and into a detached chalet-style bungalow in the middle-class suburb of Garforth. But while her husband seemed content with his new wealth, using the freedom it bought to become a horseracing expert and a crack shot with sporting guns, Viv often moped alone at home with little to do but watch television and read the begging letters.

'All I want,' she sighed, 'is for someone to walk in the door and smile at me and really mean it – and say I haven't changed.' After her husband's death, Viv Nicholson lived in the thick of chaos.

Finding the money had run out, she drank to excess and took at least one drug overdose. Two suicide attempts took her to the edge of a nervous breakdown. But in 1979 she became a Jehovah's Witness, renounced drink, and became an energetic proselytizer, distributing *The Watchtower* door to door round the streets of Castleford.

She was enormously proud of her children, whose expensive education had been protected by a £20,000 trust fund set up immediately after the pools win.

Vivian Nicholson was married five times. Having divorced her first husband, Matthew Johnson, she married Keith Nicholson, who was killed in 1965; her third husband, Brian Wright, also died in a car crash. Her fourth, Graham Ellison, divorced her within weeks of their marriage, and her fifth, Gary Shaw, died of a drug overdose.

Her children survive her.

Viv Nicholson, born April 3 1936, died April 11 2015

Sir Raymond Carr

Convivial Warden of St Antony's College, Oxford, who pioneered a new approach to Spanish history and became a devotee of hunting

SIR RAYMOND CARR, who has died aged 96, was not only the best-known English historian of Spain of his time but also for decades a central figure at Oxford University – a don at two colleges before he became head of a third.

Carr was also a London figure, sociable and convivial, and a country figure. In middle age, he took up fox hunting and became a devotee of the chase, to the surprise of some of his friends. He wrote among his other works *English Fox Hunting* (1976) – of which Enoch Powell said, 'I always hoped that such a book would be written' – and later published *Fox Hunting* (1982) with his wife Sara.

These were peripheral to the main body of his work. Carr did not publish his first book until 1966, when he was in his forties, but it was a masterpiece which established his national and international reputation. *Spain 1808–1939* was part of the Oxford History of Modern Europe series and is written on a vast scale, reflecting throughout its author's equally vast knowledge of his subject, perhaps unequalled among his contemporaries.

Carr attempted to weave together social and political history, and to a remarkable degree succeeded. Although he was never quite an elegant writer, he marshalled a vast armoury of sources – above all from the latter half of the 19th century, about which he probably knew as much as anyone alive, Spaniard or otherwise. His learning was based on deep archival research as well as wide reading.

Towards the end of the book politics take over entirely, as Spain approached the cataclysm of the Civil War.

Just as 'le Cobb' (Professor Richard) and 'il Mack Smith' (Mr Denis) enjoyed an extraordinary fame in the countries (France and Italy, respectively) which they made their subjects, so 'el Carr' became little short of a national hero in Spain.

Some years before he received his British knighthood he was appointed a Knight Grand Cross of the Order of Alfonso el Sabio. On occasion he even represented the Spanish government when a polyglot intellectual eminence was called for – at the Frankfurt Book Fair, for example.

This lionising was partly political in cause. In the years of Franco's reign, Carr visited Spain regularly to conduct his research but, as an English liberal of his generation, he was always at arm's length from the regime.

It was after the Generalissimo's death that he came into his own in Spain, hailed not only as a great scholar but also as an apostle of constitutional democracy. By the 1980s Carr was on friendly terms with King Juan Carlos as well as with many leading Spanish politicians, and was feted whenever he visited the country.

Albert Raymond Maillard Carr was born in Bath on April 11 1919, the son of a village schoolmaster and the grandson of a blacksmith. The family lived modestly, and Carr would later speak of his need to escape, insisting that the chief impulse behind his desire to 'get away from this working-class or lower middle-class thing' was the food.

He grew up in Dorset and went to Brockenhurst School, where his academic brilliance became apparent. He went on to Christ Church, Oxford, and blossomed, for his gifts were both intellectual and social. A man of great charm, accentuated by a natural clownishness, he began to make many friends, as well as forming himself as a scholar.

Deemed unfit for military service, Carr spent most of the war teaching at Wellington College, at the same time keeping a flat in London where his social life was led. Two particular friends from the 1940s were the novelist Nicholas Mosley (Lord Ravensdale) and the Labour politician Anthony Crosland.

Although Christ Church had given Carr a Gladstone Research Exhibition in 1941, he returned to Oxford almost by accident. When the war ended and there was no longer a shortage of schoolmasters, a snobbish headmaster told him that he was not 'a public-school type'.

Carr briefly took up a lectureship at University College, London, and then, in 1946, won a prize Fellowship at All Souls, where he remained until he became a tutorial Fellow of New College in 1954. Few dons of his age had such an influence on their pupils. He was, of course, an 'Oxford eccentric', who amused – and was admired and imitated by – the young, his droll and sometimes outré behaviour the source of countless anecdotes. But he was also a man of great learning who managed to infect the brighter undergraduates with his love of scholarship, and of things Spanish.

Carr hoped to become Warden of New College, and was chagrined when Sir William Hayter beat him to the post in a characteristically envenomed election. In any case, what has been called the somewhat Lenten social life of New College was no more to Carr's taste than to that of his friend A. J. Ayer, and in 1964 he left without too heavy a heart to become director of the University's new Latin American Centre and a Fellow of St Antony's College. Three years later he was appointed Professor of the History of Latin America. But although this Chair was effectively created for him, he forsook it in 1968 to become Warden of St Antony's, a post he held for nearly two decades.

St Antony's is a post-war graduate foundation, named for its patron, the mysterious Levantine merchant Antonin Besse rather than for any known canonised saint. It specialises in international studies (as well as international students), and had at one time a reputed connection with the intelligence community. Carr presided there as cheerfully as he could, while continuing with his own work. He edited a collection of *St Antony's Papers* (1969) and *The Republic and Civil War in Spain* (1971).

In 1977 he published his own *The Spanish Tragedy: The Civil War in Perspective*. He was co-author of *Spain: Dictatorship to Democracy*, and edited *The Spanish Civil War* (1986). From his own hand came *Modern Spain* (1980), a sequel to his masterpiece.

Puerto Rico: A Colonial Experiment (1984) was a serious study, but at the same time Carr barely disguised the fact that it was written for money, at the behest of the Puerto Rican authorities who wanted a scholar to help in their campaign to become another of the United States.

He was also the editor of *The Chances of Death: a diary of the Spanish Civil War* (1995); and *Spain: a history* (2000).

Until his marriage Carr led a fairly rackety personal life.

'Freddie' Ayer recalled the old days in the Gargoyle, when the list of characters would include 'Raymond Carr and Tony Crosland from Oxford, then seldom sober.' Even later he was for a long time as likely to be seen in West End nightclubs as dining at high tables.

Writing once to Ann Fleming, Evelyn Waugh mentioned 'that tipsy buffoon don who married Mary Strickland's girl. Carr? Ker? Kerr?' and, though it caught only one side of a many-faceted character, this pithy phrase rang true.

As late as his fifties Carr took off one vacation and was sighted working behind a bar in Sweden, for reasons never fully explained, although he added that country to the subjects on which he wrote scholarly articles.

Carr married, in 1950, Sara Strickland, daughter of Algernon Strickland, of Apperley Court, Gloucestershire, by his wife Lady Mary Charteris – officially the daughter of the 11th Earl of Wemyss and actually of the adventurer Wilfred Scawen Blunt.

The Carrs entertained handsomely. For years they lived in a village outside Oxford, and it was an episode after one of their celebrated parties there which inspired Nicholas Mosley's novel *Accident*, later turned into a film directed by Joseph Losey and starring Dirk Bogarde.

The parties continued when they moved to North Oxford, and generations of undergraduates have grateful memories of their hospitality, as well as of Raymond Carr's inspired teaching.

Carr was elected a Fellow of the British Academy in 1978. He was knighted in 1987, the year of his retirement from St Antony's.

He received another kind of tribute in the form of a full-length biography by the Spanish scholar María Jesús González Hernández, published in Spanish in 2011 and then in translation two years later as *Raymond Carr: the Curiosity of the Fox*. This described, in candid detail, various bibulous antics and infidelities, as well as detailing Raymond Carr's achievements as a historian.

Carr and his wife had kept a holiday home in North Devon, where they came to know many local families. There Carr struck up one more friendship, with Auberon Herbert, brother-in-law of Evelyn Waugh and uncle of Auberon.

It was to another house in North Devon that the Carrs retired from Oxford.

After the death of his wife in 2004, Carr lived in London. He is survived by two sons and a daughter.

His second son was the portrait painter Matthew Carr, who died of leukaemia in 2011: Matthew's striking portrait of his father accompanied by a dog hangs in St Antony's.

Sir Raymond Carr, born April 11 1919, died April 19 2015

Richard West

Gifted author and travelling reporter whose writing covered Vietnam, Africa and Yugoslavia

West (left) in Vietnam, 1960s: he looked back on the conflict with mixed feelings

RICHARD WEST, who has died aged 84, was a reporter and essayist, a man of considerable learning, and a gifted writer who might have been better known and more successful if he had chosen.

In the 1960s he was a highly paid freelance who could write his own ticket to the ends of the earth and whose books were well praised. But both his views and his behaviour became increasingly idiosyncratic. He wrote for smaller papers which paid less well than the nationals but where he was free to write as he liked.

Richard Leaf West was born in Chelsea on July 18 1930, the son of a publisher and sometime journalist who was once the literary editor of the *Daily Mail*. The family were bohemian and peripatetic. West was educated at Marlborough, which he disliked conventionally, and at Magdalene College, Cambridge, which he disliked surprisingly. He read History. His education had been interrupted by wartime evacuation to Canada and the United States and was interrupted again by National Service which, in contrast to school or university, he greatly enjoyed.

Serving as an NCO in the Intelligence Corps he spent much of his time in Field Security in Trieste, at the end of the 1940s a tense trouble spot. Dick West's military duties largely consisted of propping up a bar and listening to people's conversations, a premonition of his life as a journalist.

After Cambridge he went to Yugoslavia to teach at Sarajevo university. He was sacked after one day – a brief encounter even by his standards – on party orders. But he stayed to study the language and to fall in love with the country. He then reckoned himself a Marxist and remained a man of the Left until the 1970s. But even at that time what appealed to him about Tito's republic was its bloody-mindedness, standing out against both the West and Soviet Russia.

After some months incongruously working for an Italian rubber company, his first newspaper job was on *The Manchester Guardian*. He was a reporter and then Yorkshire correspondent. He did not fit in to the austere high-mindedness of the old *Guardian*; his friends and his way of life were already unpredictable, and his conduct sometimes eccentric. A contemporary on *The Guardian*, Michael Frayn, was to remember West being sent to cover a sheep-dog trial – a regular feature of North Country life – and filing a report of the event as seen through the eyes of a sheep.

Before long West came to London and joined the *Daily Mirror*, where he was among other things letters editor. He was proud of having published a letter under the headline 'Why can't we have a teenage Pope?' (or at least he claimed he had). He also claimed to have placed an ad on the *Mirror*'s classified page: 'Beaters wanted for budgie shoot in West Midlands'.

The point of these stories was less their exact truth than the way they were woven into the fabric of the West legend. Then and later, several of the stories involved his convivial habits. In his Manchester days he returned late to his suburban digs to find that his key would unaccountably not fit the front-door lock. In a rage he smashed the door down, to discover that he had mistaken the house, in fact that of a notoriously pompous local councillor.

Years later he went on a bender in Saigon and woke up the next day in a ditch outside a tropical city. Only when he had walked some way into it did he discover on inquiry that the city was Singapore. How he had got there was never explained. Using a number of similar anecdotes the author 'Philip Reid' (in fact the journalists Richard Ingrams and Andrew Osmond) made West the hero of the 1973 novel *Harris in Wonderland*. Harris is an amiable, bibulous, baffled journalist who gets into hopeless scrapes when he writes an attack on an international mining company, a book which sounds remarkably similar to West's book *River of Tears* about the Rio Tinto-Zinc mining company.

In any case, he did not remain a newspaper staffer for long, preferring for the rest of his life the freedom and insecurity of freelancing. In the 1960s he covered British politics for a time, writing with Anthony Howard *The Making of the Prime Minister* about Wilson's victory in 1964. The book was only partly satisfactory. Neither author really liked the American model they used, although they described themselves as 'lazy supporters of the Labour Party and wary admirers of Harold Wilson'. West's disillusionment with the Left was just detectable even then.

He was happier as a travelling reporter, rather than a foreign correspondent in the strict sense, spending much time in Africa, in Latin America and inevitably in South-East Asia. Apart from magazines such as *The Sunday Times* he wrote usually for the weekly *New Statesman* and later *The Spectator*, where his individual and impressionistic style of reporting worked best.

West wrote numerous books. *The Gringo in Latin America* was a travelogue using as its peg the awkward relations between the blundering Americans of the United States and their southern neighbours. In the following year, 1968, he published *Sketches from Vietnam*, an acidulated commentary on that unhappy conflict.

He was always something of an anti-American, whether from the Left or, later, from the Right. He was an admirer of Graham Greene, who reciprocated, writing to *The Spectator* once in these terms: 'I must thank Mr Richard West for his understanding notice ... No critic before, that I can remember, has thus pinpointed my abhorrence of the American liberal conscience.' For both of them, Greene the old Lefty and West the neo-reactionary as he became, 'liberal' was the final term of abuse.

Along with his reporter's eye, West had a true historical sense. *Brazza of the Congo* (1972), warmly praised by Cyril Connolly and perhaps West's best book, tells the story of one of the most attractive of Europeans in Africa. That continent perennially interested West. He spent a good deal of time in 'UDI' Rhodesia, which he condemned politically, at least while it lasted, but whose raffishness he liked. He wrote *The White Tribes of Africa* (1965), later updated as *The White Tribes Revisited*.

His book *Victory in Vietnam*, published in 1974, took its title ironically from the tale *Victory* by Joseph Conrad, one of West's favourite writers. Its publication saw a most unusual legal action, not for libel but brought in the Family Division of the High Court on behalf of the child of an old friend of West's whose reckless life and death he had described in the book.

The action failed in the end, and the book may have marked a stage in West's own development. He could now see the results of the war after the Communists won in 1975 and, for all his anti-Americanism, looked back on the conflict in South-East Asia with very mixed feelings.

His feelings about his own country were mixed also. He had always been a cultural conservative, even when he was a political radical, notably untrendy in matters like dress. He was no dandy, but was seldom seen without a tie. He detested the desecration of England which began – or maybe reached a crescendo – in the 1960s, the property development which ruined London, the spoliation of the countryside, the rise of the new tabloid press, the abolition of the old counties, the disappearance of the Prayer Book.

These were the concerns which were to be associated with the 'young fogeys', whose godfather West in some ways was. His *English Journey* (1981) was an ill-tempered peregrination which became a tirade against social workers, architects, trade unions, pornographers and the people of Liverpool.

He returned to South Africa to write a revisionist account, *The Diamonds and the Necklace*, hostile to black nationalism and sympathetic to the Afrikaners; and to Latin America to write *Hurricane in Nicaragua* (both 1989), which, not surprisingly by then, as his views had developed, was critical of the Sandinistas. *Tito and the Rise and Fall of Yugoslavia* (1994) was a life of Yugoslavia's patriarch combined with an account of his country's demise. In 1997 he published a biography of Daniel Defoe.

At one time Dick West's way of life seemed too erratic for domestic happiness, but he found it with Mary Kenny, the Irish-born journalist and columnist for (among others) *The Sunday Telegraph*. They were married in 1974 and had two sons.

West was a journalist of unusual intelligence and literary skill. 'I like the way he writes,' Connolly said. 'I like what he has to say. He is a humanist who does not accept facile solutions, a judge of character.' In fact, it was always character which fascinated West. His books, like his articles, were partly about himself and partly about other people who caught his attention: the Afrikaner writer Herman Bosman, for example, or the Nicaraguan poet Rubén Darío. If he had applied himself to the grind of ordinary newspaper life he could have earned a steady salary, and if he had tried he could have doubtless have written best-selling books.

But he was driven always by a demon of perversity or contrariness, which marked him as much as Bosman or Darío: like them he was quirky, salty, offbeat and entirely individual.

Richard West is survived by his wife and by their sons, Ed and Patrick, who are also journalists.

Richard West, born July 18 1930, died April 25 2015

Ann Barr

Brilliant features editor at *Harpers & Queen* who launched Sloane Rangers on to the world

ANN BARR, who has died aged 85, was one of the most important features editors of her generation; perceptive and eccentric, intensely wise and oddly naïve, she made *Harpers & Queen* into the most excitingly in-touch magazine of its day.

As its features editor from 1970 to 1984, she not only launched 'Sloane Rangers' and other

Ann Barr with her parrot, Turkey

social stereotypes on to the world – *The Official Sloane Ranger Handbook* (1982) later sold more than a million copies – but also used it as a nursery for young talent. Valuing first-time writers far more than Fleet Street hacks, she snapped up a handwritten article by a 16-year-old Etonian called Nicholas Coleridge on 'How To Survive Teenage Parties', commissioned his contemporary Craig Brown to spend 24 hours with the restaurateur Peter Langan and then a whole week with Andy Warhol, and spotted and liberated dozens of other unknown talents.

Never afraid of off-beat ideas, she invited the young Loyd Grossman to write about the architecture in the Babar the Elephant books and even invented an imaginary contributor, James Zeitlinger, under whose name many scabrous profiles were printed, including a covert attack by Craig Brown on Harold Evans's *Times*.

Dithery and self-effacing, Ann Barr put the finishing touches to these pieces without seeking any credit for herself. Informed by another discovery, the failed stand-up comic Andrew Barrow, that her name practically fitted inside his, she replied, without missing a beat: 'Like a shrimp inside a whale!'

Perhaps her most notable protégé was the young Peter York, whom she first met at a film preview in 1972. She was soon proclaiming him as 'clever, clever, brilliant Peter' and it was the start of a working relationship – Peter later described Ann as his 'honorary aunt' – which eventually led to the identification of the Sloane Rangers: the country-loving, upper-middle-class, well-connected tribe of posh but not particularly rich or grand Henrys and Carolines (the men were noted for their mustard cords) who seemed to be everywhere 40 years ago.

Isabel Ann Barr was born on September 16 1929 into what she later claimed was quintessential Sloane Rangerdom. Her earliest years were spent in North Audley Street, Mayfair, but she always assumed that she would spend her life in the country. Her mother, Margaret, was a well-connected Canadian, and her Scottish father, Andrew, the son of the inventor of Barr's Irn Bru, a bright orange fizzy drink which outsells Coca-Cola in Scotland. The 'leading light' in Ann's early life, however, was her Scottish nanny, Mollie Baines, with whom she remained in close touch.

A pale-faced, red-haired child, widely known as Pannie, Ann Barr spent the whole of the Second World War in Canada. Her father, a captain in the Artillery, had been captured in Singapore in 1940 and along with other prisoners of war would spend some time working on the Burma railway. Meanwhile, Ann, her younger sister Deirdre and baby brother Greig had settled with their mother and nanny in Montreal, within easy reach of a small private girls' school called The Study, where Ann particularly relished biology lessons.

After the war, Ann's father worked for the Control Commission in Germany and his family soon settled in the still Sloane

Rangerish Eaton Square, from where Ann and her sister were sent to a girls' boarding school in Shropshire which she later dismissed as 'a total waste of time'.

After leaving school Ann found her first footholds in journalism working for John Anstey at *The Telegraph Magazine* and for Robert Harling at *House & Garden*, as well as helping Hugh Johnson, her cousin's husband, with his *World Atlas Of Wine*. By the late 1960s she was firmly established at *Queen* magazine where she encouraged the undiscovered Jenny Fabian, 'unrepentant child of the subculture', to write about the hippy underworld. In 1969 she offered a taste of things to come by publishing a much talked-about article headed 'Dirty Weekend at the Ritz'.

She stayed on as features editor after *Queen* was amalgamated with *Harper's Bazaar* the following year, under the relaxed editorship of Willie Landels. Their first edition of *Harpers & Queen* came out in November 1970. Almost all the articles which appeared under this title in the next two decades were composite efforts, with contributions from many quarters, closely overseen by Ann Barr herself. New ideas were sometimes met with: 'I'll just ring Mrs Average and see what she thinks' – an oblique reference to her sister Deirdre. She also pioneered the use of boxes, lists, sidebars and other layout devices now in wide use across the printed and digital media.

Each issue also contained a page called 'Barometer', mainly written by Ann and full of obscure, tightly phrased trend predictions.

A gardening entry claimed that there would be a summer of 'mass wisteria' and, early in 1976, 'Barometer' was the only media voice to announce that Harold Wilson would soon be resigning as prime minister to be replaced by Jim Callaghan.

Other memorable ventures included the printing of the whole of Tom Wolfe's new book *The Painted Word* in one issue; the 'Life Swap' issue in which various people, including Ann Barr herself, briefly exchanged their lives with other people across the world, and in August 1978 an edition written entirely by teenagers, with the 17-year-old Johnnie Boden as men's fashion editor. 'Teenage rebellion just isn't on any more,' wrote the future fashion tycoon. 'Even punks wear brogues.'

Meanwhile, the success of the original Sloane Ranger article, published in October 1975 and not even flagged on the cover, had surprised all those involved. Shortly after publication the Tory peer Lord Orr-Ewing had boarded an aeroplane to Greece and called out 'Any Sloane Rangers on board?' and the expression soon entered the vernacular. It was later reinforced by the appearance of the wildly best-selling *Official Sloane Ranger Handbook*, followed two years later by *The Official Sloane Ranger Diary*.

The successful promotion of these books on television by Peter York caused friction between the joint authors but in no way diminished the brilliance of their original idea. Nor did it stop Ann Barr later collaborating with Paul Levy on *The Official Foodie Handbook* and launching yet another word into the dictionaries.

At the height of her powers Ann Barr dyed her hair a startling version of its original colour and displayed her legs in quirkily patterned tights and velvet knickerbockers combined with high-fashion jackets and jewellery, topping off the ensemble with her trusty Barbour and what a friend described as 'those dreadful old shoes'.

She occupied a tiny top-floor flat in a smart block near Notting Hill Gate where she entertained with gusto a gang of friends which included the comedian John Wells, the poet Rosemary Tonks, the journalist Anthony Haden-Guest, Quentin Crisp, the designer Celia Birtwell and the oil heiress Olga Deterding.

Although Ann Barr never married, she had several romances. An affair with the concrete poet and typewriter-art pioneer Alan Riddell was followed by a long courtship with a young Mayfair art dealer.

For the past 30 years, however, Ann Barr threw in her lot with a parrot called Turkey, who accompanied her to parties and caused havoc when left alone at home, chewing at the first editions, laying an egg under the bath and then pecking her owner so savagely when she got home that precautionary injections were needed.

After she left *Harpers & Queen* in 1984 Ann Barr's later career was spent as features editor at *The Observer*, although she continued to contribute to her old magazine's 'Barometer' page. Eventually diagnosed with Alzheimer's, she remained active, selling Armistice Day poppies in High Street Kensington and telling a Sunday newspaper that surviving Sloane Rangers were 'a stratum of a bygone middle class, at least one rung down from David Cameron and his friends'. By 2010 she had moved into a nursing home in Pimlico along with a few mementoes and her beloved Turkey, now kept in a cage.

She is survived by her parrot, for whom a suitable new home has already been found, and by a host of devoted god-children.

Ann Barr, born September 16 1929, died May 4 2015

Brian Sewell

Colourful critic known for his fruity voice
who waged wittily vitriolic war against the
inanities of modern conceptual art

Sewell: he believed that 'nothing matters more than intellectual probity,
and on that altar the critic must sacrifice even his closest friends'

BRIAN SEWELL, who has died aged 84, first came before the
public as the loyal friend of Anthony Blunt when that traitor was
publicly exposed in 1979; his celebrity, however, began when he
was appointed art critic of the *Evening Standard* in 1984.

In that role, Sewell waged witty, unwavering and vitriolic battle
against what he regarded as the posturing inanities of modern
British conceptual art. His readers were at once amazed and
gratified to discover that this seemingly effete highbrow, whose
outrageously camp voice ('Lady Bracknell on acid') they knew
from radio and television, should reflect all their own prejudices.

Those inclined to scepticism over the artistic potential of
formaldehyde rejoiced to find that Sewell thought Damien

Hirst (whom he had initially admired) had degenerated into 'a fairground barker, whipping us to wonder at his freaks'. Those who recoiled from the scabrousness of Gilbert & George were delighted to read of 'the sheer vanity of this Tweedle-Dum and Dee'.

Sewell was no less severe on the British art establishment which supported the works he found so repellent. The Arts Council was chastised as 'an incestuous clique, politically correct in every endeavour, the instrument of the unscrupulous and self-seeking, rewarding the briefly fashionable and incompetent'.

In dealing with conceptual art, Sewell saw himself as the lone voice which dared to point out that the emperor had no clothes. 'Nothing matters more than intellectual probity,' he thundered, 'and on that altar the critic must sacrifice even his closest friends.'

These outbursts only increased Sewell's popularity with the *Evening Standard*'s readers, whom he had always taken good care to please: 'I think sincerely of the man – or woman, for that matter – strap-hanging home to Wimbledon. It is essential to tackle the topic with either an element of humour or such gusto as will hold the attention of someone at the end of their working day.'

For his pains in expressing his opinions Sewell was punched in the eye by a young painter, jostled at a 'video exhibition', and screamed at by feminists. But he stuck to his beliefs with admirable courage.

Brian Sewell was born in London on St Swithin's Day 1931, and brought up in Kensington. At school he was nicknamed 'Sewage'. His father, only latterly identified as the Old Etonian composer Peter Warlock, committed suicide before Brian was born but after putting out the cat. Brian would later share both his gloomy nature and his love of animals.

His mother brought him up in isolation. Brian visited the National Gallery every week, and grew up with an astonishing command of adult pursuits such as Greek mythology, Roman history and opera.

He was a regular worshipper at the Carmelite church in Kensington and was grateful for an upbringing which had enabled him to understand the intensity in Christian art.

On the other hand, he was also conscious, from an early age, of 'the irredeemable nature' of his homosexuality, which set up a conflict with the teaching of the Church. To complicate matters further, the arrival of a stepfather, Robert Sewell, when he was 11 meant a sudden change to Anglicanism. It also meant being sent to Haberdashers' Aske's School in Hampstead, which he loathed.

After leaving school he spent a year painting, from which he discovered that he had talent, but nothing to say. For a while he toyed with the notion of going into the Church: 'My ambition was to be Archbishop of Canterbury; certainly a bishop.'

He survived National Service, then turned down a place at Oxford in favour of the Courtauld Institute, where he experienced what he described as 'a conditioning of the soul'. This involved losing his faith in God and learning to appreciate art.

Originally Sewell had no intention of following up his first degree by taking a doctorate. Anthony Blunt, however, persuaded him to continue his studies, and took Sewell under his wing at the Royal Library at Windsor.

'The only trouble,' Sewell observed, 'was that he forgot to pay me.'

Even so, Blunt became a close friend, though never, Sewell insisted, a lover. His companionship proved valuable to Blunt during the crisis of 1964, when the traitor was under interrogation by MI5. Sewell, however, claimed that he knew nothing of this.

In 1958 he joined Christie's as a prints and drawings expert, and remained there until 1966. He seemed to have found his metier, until he resigned in a huff after failing to gain a place on the board.

Next, he became an art dealer, for which he was not well qualified temperamentally. On one occasion a potential buyer was informed that the picture he wanted to purchase was too good for him.

He moved into 19 Eldon Road, Kensington, in 1972, a road down which his pram had once been pushed. It was one of the most interesting and eye-catching houses in the area, adorned with higgledy-piggledy sculptures dating from the Coronation year.

On November 14 1979 Anthony Blunt was warned that the following day Margaret Thatcher would reveal his treachery to the Commons. On the morning of November 15 Sewell drove him from his flat off the Edgware Road to a hiding place at Professor James Joll's house in Chiswick.

He then stalled relentlessly as reporters pressed him to divulge Blunt's whereabouts: 'I shall tell you what he had for breakfast, but nothing more.' It was outrageous, he said, that the government should have named Blunt after granting him immunity from prosecution 15 years before.

Splashed all over the front pages, and photographed walking his dogs, Sewell instantly proved a natural for the media.

Tina Brown, then editor of *Tatler*, was so impressed by the performance that she employed him as art critic. Sewell was confirmed in this new calling – what he called 'the sad end to a once promising career' – when he moved to the *Evening Standard*. He wrote all his reviews on an old Adler manual typewriter.

In the mid-90s, *The Sunday Telegraph* employed Sewell as a general columnist. He was one of the first to attack Tony Blair's deliberate blokeishness; suggested an army composed entirely of homosexuals would have certain advantages in mobility; crusaded against cruelty to animals; and wrote a fine article against abortion.

In the winter of 1998, he left Eldon Road for a house in Wimbledon, which he described as an 'Edwardian monstrosity'. Here there was a lake, a coach house and a vast walled garden for his rampaging dogs.

Sewell was a great enthusiast for cars. At 22 he bought his first car, a vintage Wolseley, and in later middle age claimed to have once driven his gold-plated Mercedes at 140mph.

He was unable to account for the viciousness of his reviews. 'I am a church mouse,' he insisted. 'I am essentially a sweet, kind, giving sort of person, but ... it is as if I am possessed.'

He published three collections of his criticism, *The Reviews That Caused The Rumpus* (1994), *An Alphabet of Villains* (1995) and *Naked Emperors: Criticisms of English Contemporary Art* (2012). Another book, *South From Ephesus* (1988), gave a good account of both the archaeology and of the sex in Turkey, and *Sleeping with Dogs* (2013) described his lifelong affection for canine companions.

Only in the second of his two volumes of memoirs, *Outsider* (2009) and *Outsider II* (2012), did Sewell fully explain his role in the Blunt spy scandal, revealing that he had known of Blunt's treachery years before it became public, but remained loyal.

Sewell's work for television included a programme about the North West Frontier in India, which he did not like a bit, and an attack on Leonardo da Vinci.

He confronted the illnesses of his later years with the same steel that he had shown in resisting those who abused him as a critic.

Brian Sewell, born July 15 1931, died September 19 2015

Roy Dommett

Rocket scientist who developed Britain's Cold War
nuclear arsenal – with a sideline in morris dancing

ROY DOMMETT,
the aeronautical
engineer, who has
died aged 82, was
Britain's Chief Missile
Scientist during the
Cold War; as a release
from the pressures of
his top-secret job he
also developed a lively
interest in morris
dancing.

The author Francis
Spufford, in his book
*Backroom Boys: The
Secret Return of the
British Boffin* (2003),
quotes another
rocket scientist's

Roy Dommett and family, c.1970

account of bumping into Dommett in Bristol: 'These morris men
came dancing up the street, led by this big fat bloke in a kind
of Andy Pandy outfit who was bopping people on the head with
a pig's bladder – and I said to my wife: "Sweetheart, you won't
believe me, but that man is the brains behind Britain's nuclear
deterrent."' As a member of the guided weapons group at the
Royal Aircraft Establishment (RAE), Farnborough, Dommett was
a key figure in the development of nuclear missiles in Britain. He
was convinced that the principle of deterrence was morally right.
'We're not believers in using nuclear weapons,' he said. 'We're
actually believers in not using nuclear weapons. It is a
deterrent.'

He started out in the 1950s at a time when Britain's contribution to the Space Age was the building of rockets, an endeavour which had its origins in the final year of the war and the study of German V2 flying bombs. Among the experimental projects Dommett worked on with his colleagues at the RAE – all eventually cancelled – were the Blue Streak intermediate range ballistic missile, the Black Knight rocket and the Black Arrow carrier rocket.

Black Arrow was successfully launched from Woomera in the Australian desert, placing a Prospero satellite into a polar orbit (where it still circles the Earth), on October 28 1971. But the project had been cancelled just three months earlier, and Dommett later lamented that 'the ideas and the engineering were there, but everybody was squabbling over the pennies'.

By the 1970s he was updating Britain's US-built Polaris missile system, the naval upgrade known as Chevaline. Later still, he advised Margaret Thatcher on Trident.

At the same time, Dommett, who was Falstaffian in appearance with a gently bucolic voice, was applying his scholarly mind to a parallel obsession: the worlds of both morris and stave dancing (a style of folk dance from the south-west in which decorated poles are carried). He travelled around villages collecting notations for dances and tunes, lectured, gave workshops, wrote learned articles, and would often accompany dancers with his spirited accordion playing.

Owing to the sensitive nature of Dommett's scientific work, most morris dancers were unaware that the jovial, shambolic-looking figure tapping his feet in knee-bells, baldric and breeches was an eminent rocket scientist. Dommett himself relished the uncomplicated silliness of his hobby, and belonging to a community of fellow enthusiasts provided an antidote to the isolation of his 'day job'.

Roy Leonard Dommett was born in Southampton on June 25 1933, a stone's throw, as he liked to say, from the Supermarine works, where seaplanes and later the Spitfire were built. An uncle worked at the factory, and aircraft were a passion of Roy's from a young age. One of his earliest memories was seeing the Graf Zeppelin airship fly over Southampton in 1936. Every week he devoured *The Aeroplane Spotter* magazine. His father, a painter and decorator, was called up into the RAF in 1941.

During the Blitz Roy was evacuated to a house at Ringwood in Hampshire where five children had to share a double bed and the lavatory was at the bottom of the garden. When a local margarine factory was bombed, he later recalled, the blaze could be seen from 15 miles away.

One night he was visiting grandparents in East London when a V2 hit nearby. 'I can remember a strange sound,' he recalled. 'It starts with a slight whistle, a big bang, and then this noise of something coming all the way – going back up, because it was travelling faster than the speed of sound, you heard the distance sound last.' The V2s were in fact hopelessly inaccurate, but the experience fuelled Dommett's interest in missiles.

After Itchen Grammar School, where he studied aircraft engineering in the sixth form, he took a First in Aeronautical Engineering at Bristol University in 1954. One of the young lecturers was Joseph Black, who would go on to conduct pioneering research into swept-wing design.

Dommett had spent his summer vacations working with engineering firms and by the time he graduated there was a job waiting for him at the RAE at Farnborough.

In 1956 he married Marguerite Dawson, whom he had known at school, but it would be some years before he was able to disclose to her the real nature of his work. As far as she was concerned her husband dealt with aeroplane engines. But one day in the late 1960s, as she later explained, he came home and asked if they could have a talk. 'I'm working on something that I think is very important, but I can't talk to you about it,' he said. 'It might help the world in the future. What do you want me to do?' 'I trust you,' Marguerite replied. 'You do what you think is right and I won't ask questions.' She remained true to her word.

Dommett stayed at the RAE until 2000, while taking on a number of advisory roles. In 1982 he served as chief scientist for the government's Special Weapons Department; later he was a principal consultant on ballistic missiles for the Defence Evaluation and Research Agency at the Ministry of Defence.

In 2013 Dommett recorded a lengthy interview about his life for the British Library. He recalled how on one occasion, a visit to the Barley Mow morris dancing troupe at Dudley in the West Midlands caused him inadvertently to become entangled with a demonstration by the Campaign for Nuclear Disarmament.

Some dancers had started to perform a jig in the main square in front of a crowd when they were approached by a police officer. 'Not morris dancers as well?' he said, according to Dommett, then: 'Bugger off into the shopping mall!' When Dommett returned to his office at the RAE, he was ticked off by the security officer: 'You're on this film of a CND demonstration. What the hell were you doing there?' Dommett replied that it had come as a complete surprise to him.

Roy Dommett received the Royal Aeronautical Society Silver Medal in 1991, and in 1993 was appointed CBE.

He is survived by his wife Marguerite and their seven sons; one daughter predeceased him.

Roy Dommett, born June 25 1933, died November 2 2015

Sabrina

Blonde sex symbol from Stockport who shot to 1950s celebrity as Arthur Askey's sidekick

SABRINA, who has died aged 80, claimed to be Britain's first sex symbol, and achieved unprecedented fame in the 1950s as a glamour model with stupendous 41 in. breasts which she insured for £100,000.

While she could have claimed £2,500 for every inch of deflation, Lloyd's of London excluded claims occasioned by civil war, invasion or nationalisation, although at the height of her celebrity there were times when it seemed she might have precipitated any – or indeed all – of these eventualities.

Under her real name of Norma Sykes, Sabrina was discovered by BBC Television in the frenzied run-up to the launch of the rival ITV commercial service in 1955. The comedian Arthur Askey was looking for a gimmick for his BBC show *Before Your Very Eyes*, and claimed to have had a nightmare following a late supper of cold

Sabrina in Lurex trousers, c.1957

roast beef and pickled onions. In it, the diminutive comic saw himself confronted by the biggest bosoms ever seen on the small screen.

When Askey mentioned this, his producer, Bill Ward, spotted a potential publicity-grabbing wheeze and persuaded the BBC to launch a nationwide hunt, which resulted in photographs from thousands of hopefuls. The search ended when a modelling agent submitted a picture of his client Norma Sykes from Stockport.

Impressed by his discovery's voluptuous charms, but unenthused by her unglamorous origins, Bill Ward renamed her Sabrina, after the 1954 film of that title starring Humphrey Bogart and Audrey Hepburn, which was released in Britain as *Sabrina Fair*.

As Britain's first post-austerity media construct, the blonde and busty Sabrina was suddenly famous for being famous and was in huge demand at photo shoots, product launches and the opening of anything that required opening and which – underscored by her pouting, cantilevered presence – might get into the papers or on to the newsreels as a result.

She went on to become a nightclub entertainer and appeared in a handful of films before vanishing from the limelight as suddenly as she had stolen it.

Norma Ann Sykes was born on May 19 1936 at Stockport in Cheshire, the daughter of a mechanical engineer and a seamstress. While at Cale Green middle school, Stockport, she became a swimming champion and planned to swim the English Channel. By the age of nine she was swimming a mile a day at the local YWCA, beating girls of 15.

Her family moved via Leeds to Blackpool, where her mother opened a private hotel, but when Norma was 14 she contracted polio and spent two years in hospital. An operation on her leg almost led to amputation, and left her right ankle scarred (she favoured unfashionably long dresses thereafter).

Fearing that their patient might never walk again, doctors prescribed a series of exercises to develop her muscles, and she spent hours every day swimming in a heated pool and performing bodybuilding feats. Apparently her remarkable chest expansion was a direct result of these workouts.

From a seven stone wraith, Norma Sykes became a 41-17-36 anatomical wonder. Besides her overdeveloped pectoral muscles, she also acquired powerful arms and legs. But by the time she finally left hospital, she had lost touch with most of her friends during her long illness and, not wishing to return to school with younger classmates, moved to London in 1952.

After stints as a waitress and a housemaid, she worked as a 'glamour' model, posing at sessions during which she was photographed nude (she later tried to destroy the results, and reportedly wrecked a playing-card factory in the process). She signed up with an agent, and continued to pose (more or less clothed) for so-called cheesecake magazines.

Having landed the part as Arthur Askey's sidekick in *Before Your Very Eyes* on the BBC, she transferred to ITV when the show switched channels in 1956. Singularly, in all these programmes, she never spoke.

Endearingly unprofessional, she was deliberately chosen, according to Askey, because 'she had a lovely face and figure but could not act, sing, dance or even walk properly'. In truth Sabrina did little more than giggle at the endless jokes about her physique.

Her profile was further enhanced by references to her figure on BBC Radio's *Goon Show*, with exclamations such as 'by the measurements [or the sweaters] of Sabrina!' On one occasion in Birkenhead her embonpoint popped out when someone in the crowd mobbing her at a personal appearance accidentally stepped on the hem of her dress.

Sabrina's reputation in *Before Your Very Eyes* had catapulted her to overnight celebrity, and after a part in Askey's film *Ramsbottom Rides Again* (1956) she was billed as 'guest artiste' in the film comedy *Blue Murder At St Trinian's* (1957) with Terry-Thomas and Alastair Sim. In her non-speaking role, Sabrina was discovered sitting up in bed swotting from a book while the action swirled around her.

Away from the film cameras, invariably ensconced in her white Chevrolet bearing the index plate S41, by the summer of 1957 Sabrina found herself a hot public relations property.

Everywhere she went she was photographed, not only in public (being ejected from the Royal Enclosure at Ascot, or launching the Vauxhall Victor car) but also in private, leaving nightclubs with the singer David Whitfield and being, as the cheaper newspapers put it knowingly, 'squired' in Paris by the circus playboy Billy Smart. In 1959 she took her figure and her cabaret act to tour Australia and, a year later, decided to take on the United States where she became known as the 'British Bosom Lady'.

However, she made the grave mistake of visiting Cuba as a guest of Fidel Castro's new revolutionary government, a move that resulted in the condemnation of the unforgiving American press.

After several years of shuttling between Britain, America and Australia, in 1967 she married a wealthy young Hollywood surgeon, Dr Harold Melsheimer (who had never heard of her), abandoned showbusiness and threw herself into an opulent life of parties, furs and her own 40 ft yacht.

She socialised with Frank Sinatra and Dick Van Dyke and, as if to complete the California dream, furnished her Doberman Pinscher with its own bedroom and bathroom.

When her marriage was dissolved in 1977, Sabrina moved from the salubrious Woodland Hills area to a small, scruffy house in north Hollywood where she had latterly lived as a recluse. A lodger ran her errands and drove her to her medical appointments. Her neighbours knew who she was and called her by her stage name Sabrina.

Asked about her fame 44 years ago, she did not repine. 'It made me a sex symbol, which I'm not,' she confessed, 'And it made me a household name like Tide, which I am – a clean girl from the sticks. People seem to forget that I was at one time the junior breaststroke champion of Manchester.'

In 1958 Sabrina was awarded an honorary DLitt by the University of Leeds.

Her death almost a year ago was only made public recently. She had been ill for some time after botched back surgery (for which she successfully sued her surgeon).

Sabrina, born May 19 1936, died November 24 2016

John Jones

Oxford Professor of Poetry noted for the brilliance of his lectures and his love of Plymouth Argyle

JOHN JONES, who has died aged 91, was the Professor of Poetry at Oxford from 1978 to 1983.

He came sandwiched between two poets – John Wain and Peter Levi – but his tenure of the chair was in its way equally distinguished, and he was a considerable, even a great, orator. The grandson of the Hegelian philosopher Sir Henry Jones, he was possessed of the Celtic gift of utterance. He lectured

Jones: he lost his father when he was eight and never felt he had a home anywhere until he arrived at Merton College

without notes or script, in a posture which recalled Yeats's line about his father – 'his beautiful mischievous head thrown back'. (As a young ordinary seaman in the Royal Navy, Jones's nickname, among the Wrens, was 'Little Johnnie Head in Air'.)

The lectures were extraordinary. There was one about Handel, delivered in the very spot in the Sheldonian Theatre where Handel had received his Honorary Doctorate of Music. (Handel remained a lifelong love, and in his last illness Jones asked for his music to be played to him on his ancient cassette machine.)

Another spectacular lecture, given in the dining hall at Merton College, was on Platonic myth. Yet he did not write his lectures down, and had no Eckermann to record his brilliant conversations.

Jones told a student whom he had just admitted to read English at Merton: 'There will be three years of Socratic tension.' The young man did not know what was meant, but three years later, he knew. Jones was always clear in his mind – and so was Merton – that he should be given a lot of time to get on with his own reading and cogitations. He never had more than a handful of pupils on whom to exercise his Socratic gifts, and sometimes he would arrange for even this select band to be taught by someone else.

The locum tenens was usually the blind poet John Heath-Stubbs, who said things such as 'Dryden was the last poet to attend to the music of the spheres' – not the sort of sentence that would be heard in other parts of the English Faculty, which had already begun to wrestle with 'Theory' in the works of Derrida or Harold Bloom.

Jones was a celebrated literary figure but in fact did not become the English tutor at Merton until 1962, eight years after he had written his masterpiece on Wordsworth, *The Egotistical Sublime*, and in the same year that he published his *Aristotle and Greek Tragedy*, a book much admired by, among others, C.S. Lewis.

Henry John Franklin Jones was born on May 6 1924 in Burma, where his father was a doctor. He was eight, and a pupil at an English boarding school, when he heard that his father had died – as a result of being half-drowned in the river Irrawaddy. Thereafter, Jones never felt he had a home anywhere until he arrived at Merton.

He was educated at Blundell's and was taken up, while still a schoolboy, by those bizarre brothers Jackson Knight (who became the first professor of classics at what would become Exeter University) and the great Shakespearean scholar Wilson Knight. Jones remembered Jackson holding his shoulders and presenting him to Wilson as if he were a beautiful work of art: 'Just look at him!'

Jones got his scholarship to Merton, but joined the Navy – it was wartime – and studied Japanese for six months at SOAS before going East. His job was to intercept wireless messages, and he believed he was the first person in the world to learn that the war against Japan was over. He was in Colombo when the war ended, reading Hegel's *Phenomenology of Spirit* in the public library. He remained a fervent Hegelian, and would dismiss Bertrand Russell's satires on the Hegelians with almost tearful rage.

He returned to Merton, took a First in Law, and became the Law don in 1949. He had to wait until 1962 before Hugo Dyson (who had converted C. S. Lewis to Christianity) retired as the college's English don.

Some found Jones's arrogance insufferable, but he always had passionate admirers – such as Anne Barton, the Shakespearean scholar, and Iris Murdoch. Rachel Trickett, a much underestimated novelist, brilliantly evoked his character in a prophetic novel, *The Elders*, in which she fantasised, 12 years before Jones stood for the chair of poetry, that Wordsworth and Coleridge were standing against one another for election. It was in reality a novel about Jones, and what she saw was that he was a failed genius, who could not decide whether to be Wordsworth, with a body of work and no charm, or the cherubic Coleridge, whose genius was lost in talk.

A passionate football fan, Jones supported Plymouth Argyle and wrote about the game for *The Observer* from 1956 to 1959. When, in the late 1970s, he appeared on Melvyn Bragg's BBC books programme, *Read All About It*, rather than talk about something erudite, he chose for discussion a biography of the Everton legend Dixie Dean. He spent most of his slot describing a photograph of Dean heading the ball, remarking how 'he seemed to hang in the air like all great centre forwards'. Tutorials with like-minded undergraduates would often be spent discussing football.

In the year he won his fellowship at Merton, Jones married Jean Robinson, and the marriage produced two children to whom he was devoted – Jeremy and Janet. He was intensely domestic, rarely eating in college, and preferring to return to his house, Holywell Cottage, for lunch and dinner and to practise the cello.

115

Jean was a painter – Iris Murdoch believed that one day she would be as famous as Van Gogh. She was plagued by mental illness, at times so severe that she had to be hospitalised.

Jones minded intensely that his books were not more famous, and that he had not been rewarded by promotion in the academy. (It was a very dark day in Holywell Cottage when his great rival – and friend – John Bayley became the Warton Professor of English Literature.)

All this was a pity because the afternoon and evening of Jones's days were sad, when, in only slightly altered circumstances, they could have been happy. He could have had a circle of younger friends who appreciated his deep cleverness, and who enjoyed his anecdotes, and who basked in his clever, close reading of Dickens, Wordsworth, Shakespeare. Instead, there was bitterness, and a sense of things drying up.

Undoubtedly this was exacerbated by the decision to live in London.

Jean was a Londoner through and through, and was determined to get out of Oxford when Merton asked them to vacate Holywell Cottage. She persuaded the college to buy them their son's flat in Swiss Cottage and to allow them to live there for life.

There she could have had a happy time, painting on Primrose Hill by day and entertaining in the evenings, enjoying the company of friends such as Tony and Marcelle Quinton, Tony and Sarah Curtis, Robin Denniston, Gerard Irvine, and many others. She was a very good cook, and supper in the flat was nearly always an enjoyable occasion, starting with Jones dispensing egg-cup sized glasses of vodka, moving on to wine for guests, and for himself a tankard of beer.

Alas, these days were darkened by Jean's repeated descents into mental illness. Jones was an exemplary husband to her at these times, in circumstances which would have been intolerable to many others. When she finally sank, first into dementia, and then into death, he was desperately sad.

Difficult as their marriage had been, it had lasted 63 years, and those who loved them would think of their nightly routine, which Jones managed to keep going except in the very darkest times, of their lying beside one another in bed and reading jointly, and silently, the novels of Angela Brazil. John read more slowly than Jean and she would patiently wait for him to nod, vigorously, as a signal that she could turn the page of *Monitress Merle* – or *Jean's Golden Term*.

He is survived by his two children.

John Jones, born May 6 1924, died February 28 2016

The Earl of Haddington

Landowner and conservationist who was an
authority on crop circles and the paranormal

Haddington at Stonehenge: he also enjoyed keeping finches and ballooning

THE 13th EARL OF HADDINGTON, who has died aged 74, was
a landowner, conservationist, photographer and explorer of the
paranormal.

The Earls of Haddington are a great Scottish dynasty,
descending from the feudal baron Walter de Hamilton, also an
ancestor of the Dukes of Hamilton and Dukes of Abercorn. The
family seat of Mellerstain in Berwickshire is a lightly castellated
masterpiece by Robert Adam with one of the finest views in
Britain.

None of Haddington's noble predecessors could have had more grace and originality or been held in greater affection by those who knew him, indifferent as he was to age or any sort of classification. His father, the 12th Earl, was eulogised as Chaucer's 'verray, parfit gentil knyght'. The same applied to his only son.

As a hereditary peer Haddington sat for 13 years in the House of Lords until reform deprived him of his seat in 1999. Opponents of this measure argued that it turned a uniquely varied legislature into one of mundane conformity, as if a preciously preserved bio-diverse meadow had been replaced by a pesticide-drenched mono-crop.

Haddington exemplified the loss. Among his recreations he listed beekeeping, keeping finches and 'cerealogy', by which he meant an expert knowledge of crop circles. Yet this was only the tip of the iceberg. Among his many skills were ballooning and the construction of hovercrafts, in one of which he explored an Amazonian tributary. Both activities signalled his interest in physics and mechanics.

His healing powers, assisted by the use of rock crystal, gave him a Merlin-like presence in the House. Many swore by his treatment, which he dispensed on request, at exhausting physical cost, to peers, peeresses and staff alike. When Andrew Festing painted his official group portrait of the Lords debating the 1995 Queen's Speech, his friend Haddington jovially agreed to pose for the joke figure of 'the slumbering Earl' on the government side.

John George Baillie-Hamilton was born at Mellerstain on December 21 1941. His father, a Lord Lieutenant of Berwickshire and distinguished veteran of both World Wars, was a noted horseman and forester. His mother was the Catholic Sarah Cook, who played an important part in the formation of the Edinburgh Festival. His sister, Lady Mary Russell, was a maid of honour at the Coronation.

Haddington's marked transcendentalism first showed itself when he was two. He was terrorised by the ghost of a German pilot killed in a bomber-aircraft crash on the Mellerstain estate. His silence caused adult concern but he dared not betray its cause. At Ampleforth his japes were legend, and he broke the school record for the punishment of writing lines. Bomb-making involved one near-fatal detonation; but his release of an industrial quantity of laxatives into the school reservoir failed to achieve the desired disruption.

He survived the course thanks to Father Walter, his housemaster, a droll sympathiser with the anarchic tendencies of youth. His education was completed at the University of Tours and Trinity College, Dublin, both conducive to his adventurous spirit: he was a champion slalom skier and a ferocious opening bowler for the Oakland Raiders, Trinity's cricket team, with whom he toured Australia.

After university he hitch-hiked the world, exercising his talent for photography, which he exploited professionally in London on his return. A lasting achievement was his photographic reflection on Sir William Keswick's Henry Moores on the moor at Glenkiln, Dumfriesshire. Sir William was the first patron to place modern sculpture in the wild, and Moore always considered Glenkiln, which included figures by Epstein and Rodin, the best siting of his work. The collection has now been withdrawn due to vandals. Haddington's book of photographs, *Glenkiln* (Canongate), is its memorial. Another inspired assignment, commissioned by Sir Jocelyn Stevens, was to instil some of the magic and mystery of Stonehenge into English Heritage's guidebook.

In 1975 Haddington saved the world-famous Border Bows company, providing premises at Mellerstain for its factory. It ensured he was the most knowledgeable member of Scotland's Royal Company of Archers, the monarch's official bodyguard north of the border.

His interest in the paranormal alerted him early to the corn circle phenomenon. He was a sponsor of *The Cerealogist* magazine, initially edited by his friend John Michell, the radical-traditionalist author and antiquarian; and he could tell at a glance whether a circle was paranormally genuine or trodden by hoaxers.

Haddington succeeded his father in 1986 and death duties forced him to sell the family's East Lothian home, Tyninghame, and part of its estate. In the best tradition of such sporting naturalists as Lord Grey of Fallodon, Major the Hon Henry Douglas-Home (BBC Scotland's 'Bird Man'), and the great conservationist Sir Peter Scott, Haddington, a first-rate shot and fly fisherman, in 1997 founded the charity Save Our Songbirds (SOS) with its accompanying magazine *The Bird Table*.

SOS later merged with Songbird Survival, of which he was a director. In all these exploits he was hugely supported by his second wife, Jane Heyworth, whose father, John Heyworth, created the Cotswold Wildlife Park at Burford. Together they shouldered the increasingly heavy responsibilities of managing Mellerstain, a house open to the public, and the remainder of the Tyninghame estate, and both played a full part in Border affairs.

His son, George Edmund Baldred, succeeds him as 14th Earl. Haddington married first, in 1975, Prudence Hayles (dissolved 1977); and, secondly, in 1984, Jane Heyworth, who survives him with their son and two daughters.

The 13th Earl of Haddington, born December 21 1941, died July 5 2016

Johnny Barnes

Bermudian Seventh Day Adventist known as 'Mr
Happy' for his cheery daily greeting to commuters

Barnes would salute passers-by saying: 'I love you – God loves you!'

JOHNNY BARNES, who has died aged 93, was a familiar and
beloved figure in Bermuda, where he was known as 'Mr Happy'
for his habit of waving cheerily at commuters every morning for
30 years from his chosen place by the Crow Lane roundabout.

Each weekday without fail, into his nineties, Barnes would rise
at 2am, breakfast, and by 3.45 have stationed himself besides the
road into Hamilton, the island's capital. Whatever the weather,
for the next six hours he would salute passers-by, shouting: 'I love
you – God loves you!' and blowing a kiss with his hands.

A religious man who belonged to the Seventh Day Adventist
church, he was inspired by Christ's teachings on brotherly love.
'We human beings got to learn how to love one another,' he said.
'Then there wouldn't be any wars, there wouldn't be any killing.'

Bermuda's road layout meant that most traffic entering
Hamilton would pass him. Many a motorist testified that the sight
of the bearded and hat-wearing Barnes bestowing benediction

had lifted their mood. In 2011, the director Matt Morris was prompted to make a short film about him, *Mr Happy Man*, which has since been viewed online more than 100,000 times.

'I enjoy making people happy,' reflected Barnes. 'I like to let them know that life is sweet, that it's good to be alive.' In 1998, a statue of him was erected near the roundabout, paid for by local businessmen. There was some criticism of its having been done while Barnes was still alive, but he took the view that that way he could enjoy it too.

On the rare occasions when he failed to appear, radio stations would be deluged by callers anxious for news. In 2012 he suffered a fall while waving at his usual spot and was unable to get up until an ambulance arrived. He later said that he had just tripped on the hole worn by his standing there for three decades.

Never the less, he was provided with a bench and acknowledged that at his age it was time to take stock. 'When you get to 92, you have to slow down a little bit,' he said recently. 'When you have an old bike you can put oil on the wheels, but I can't put oil on these knees.'

He was born John James Randolf Adolphus Mills on June 23 1923 to parents originally from St Kitts. He recalled his mother telling him that he was born on a Saturday and so, according to the rhyme, would have to work hard for a living.

He traced his habit of greeting people back to having been scolded by his mother for delivering a message to an elderly woman as asked, but not having spoken to her. When he began work as an electrician on Bermuda's railway in the 1940s, he would wave at passers-by during his lunch hour. He continued this practice when he later became a bus driver.

Barnes is survived by his wife Belvina, to whom he was married in 1949. There were no children.

Johnny Barnes, born June 23 1923, died July 9 2016

Raine, Countess Spencer

Socialite, local politician and chatelaine of Althorp who was stepmother to Diana, Princess of Wales

RAINE, COUNTESS SPENCER, who has died aged 87, inherited the unquenchable energy and steely purpose of her mother, the romantic novelist Barbara Cartland; and like her mother, she seldom left anyone indifferent, whether as councillor in London, as chatelaine of Althorp, or as stepmother to Diana, Princess of Wales.

In the early 1970s she earned well merited praise when, as Lady Dartmouth, she played an important role in preventing the destructive redevelopment of Covent Garden. By contrast, as Raine Spencer she was excoriated for her part in the redecoration of the Spencer family seat at Althorp. 'Acid Raine' was the appellation favoured by her stepchildren. She was, as one acquaintance remarked, 'the sort of person whose eyes were always looking for someone more interesting in the room'.

It was another disadvantage that Raine Spencer seemed to be living in a by-gone age. This was not just a matter of her immaculately groomed bouffant hair and her crinoline dresses. Roy Strong remembered how, 25 years after the end of the Second World War, she would have a footman wearing white gloves in attendance at even the most informal lunch.

The aspirations of Barbara Cartland were never far distant. All through Raine Spencer's life, to the age of 60 and beyond, her conversation would be liberally laced with references to Mummy, and what she had learnt from her: 'One thing Mummy taught me: if you're sloppy and unreliable in the little things, no one will trust you on the big things.'

In the 1950s and 1960s she pursued her political career at full tilt, even while cautioning other women on the dangers of work. 'Women are doing a man's job without his physical stamina,' she complained. 'No time for love. No time to comfort, inspire and guide ...' And indeed she was divorced from Lord Dartmouth in 1970.

Yet the greater the disaster, the more Raine Spencer could be relied on to put a good face on things. 'I don't care what people say behind my back,' she remarked. 'What I want is for them to be nice to my face.'

To such a temperament, unguarded emotion was positively dangerous. 'If you absolutely must have a best friend,' Raine Spencer declared, 'make it your husband or your mother. But even with them there should be restrictions.'

She was born Raine McCorquodale on September 9 1929, the daughter of Alexander 'Sachie' McCorquodale, whose family had made a fortune out of printing, and of Barbara Cartland, who had then hardly embarked upon her career as a romantic novelist.

'What a lovely fat baby,' Princess Elizabeth (born in 1926) is supposed to have observed on seeing the infant Raine. From the very beginning Barbara Cartland set a killing social pace for her daughter. Not without reason did the Glasgow *Evening News* describe her as 'one of the smartest babies in the park'.

Her father, however, was soon cracking under the strain, drinking heavily and seeking amorous relief with a Mrs Helene Curtis. Barbara Cartland divorced him in 1932 and, after a spell at the Dorchester, went to live with her own formidable mother in Half Moon Street. Meanwhile in 1933 *Vogue* noted that Raine was evincing a 'pretty dignity of manners'.

Her mother married again in 1936, to Hugh McCorquodale, a cousin of her first husband. They lived in a flat in Grosvenor Square, and Raine soon had two half-brothers. 'I never made any nonsense of the fact that I prefer sons,' Barbara Cartland observed.

To protect her children from the war, Barbara Cartland decided to take them to Canada, where Raine briefly went to school at Mitis, a village overlooking the St Lawrence River. 'The other girls kicked her with their boots; I can't think why,' her mother recorded. 'Maybe it was the way that she talked.'

A few months in Canada sufficed to persuade Barbara Cartland to brave the North Atlantic at the most dangerous period in the war in order to return to Britain. Raine was sent to Owlstone Croft School, near her parents' cottage in Bedfordshire. She was often top of her class. 'Never mind about that,' her mother would say, 'you have a gravy stain on your shirt.'

And so to the Season. 'Eternally smiling' and an excellent dancer, Raine was voted Debutante of the Year in 1947. If she was not a flawless beauty, she gave an excellent impression of one. And when she met Gerald Legge, presumptive heir to the Earldom of Dartmouth, on a mountain in Switzerland, she immediately declared herself in love.

They were married in 1948 and installed in a large house in Belgravia, with a staff of five. Yet her love for her husband and children did not provide complete fulfilment. In May 1954 Mrs Gerald Legge became the youngest ever Westminster councillor, when she was elected for St George's Ward in Knightsbridge.

That November she hit the headlines with her vociferous complaints about the dirty cups and ashtrays on the tables in the departure lounge at London Airport. It was 'a disgrace to Britain'; worse, when she ordered the staff to clean up the mess they bolshily demurred.

She achieved better results in other fields, notably with a fund which she set up for helping old people. Yet the element of self-publicity was rarely absent. She began appearing on such television programmes as *This Is Your Life* and *Juke Box Jury*; and was ever eager to hold forth on sex education. It should be carried out by doctors, she urged.

Wags began to refer to her invariably absent husband as 'Left Legge'. In public, however, she presented herself as a model of matrimonial solicitude, a slave to every whim of her lord and master. She would love to stand for Parliament, she explained, but Gerald would not allow her to accept invitations in the evening or at weekends.

After her father-in-law became 8th Earl of Dartmouth in 1958, Mrs Gerald Legge appeared under new colours, as Viscountess Lewisham. A few weeks later, she was elected (with a majority of seven) to the London County Council for – suitably enough – West Lewisham.

The voters, she thought, appreciated her honesty: 'I always deliberately dressed up and wore all my jewellery and furs – after all everyone knows I have them.' In 1959, though, she provoked a disturbance when she shared her canvassing experiences with students at the London School of Economics: 'Often I found that where socialist voters lived there were dirty milk bottles on the doorstep.'

In 1961 the Lewishams moved to a still grander house, in Mayfair, and the next year Gerald Lewisham succeeded as 9th Earl of Dartmouth. Raine Dartmouth's political career briefly went into abeyance in 1965, when the London County Council gave way to the Greater London Council. At first she did not stand; evidently, though, she had overcome her husband's objections to her trying for Parliament, for in 1966 she unsuccessfully attempted to become the Conservative candidate for Richmond. Afterwards, in 1967, she was elected to the GLC as councillor for that borough.

As a member of the planning and licensing committee, she fought a lone campaign against giving a licence to the film of James Joyce's *Ulysses*. She had not, she admitted, seen it, but she had read the 'disgusting and degrading' book, and that was more than enough for her.

Lady Dartmouth seemed better suited to her position as chairman of the GLC's Historic Buildings Board, leading a successful campaign against the government's plan for the Tate Gallery, which would have involved pulling down the building's facade. She also foiled destructive proposals for the National Portrait Gallery by putting it on the list of protected buildings.

Her finest hour, however, came in 1971–72, when she was chairman of the Covent Garden development committee. Gradually she realised that there was no local support for the massively destructive scheme that had been advanced. Rather than forward it, she resigned.

'It has become increasingly rare for public figures to admit that they have changed their minds,' the Covent Garden Community Association commented, 'let alone that they may have been seriously wrong. The courage of Lady Dartmouth in making both decisions will not be soon forgotten.' The subsequent abandonment of wholesale development in Covent Garden, moreover, proved a decisive moment in the history of town planning. Thenceforward the more megalomaniac planners were on the retreat.

In November 1972 Lady Dartmouth announced that she would not be standing again for the GLC. But she was far from finished with public life. As chairman of the government working party on the Human Habitat, set up in connection with the United Nations Conference on the Environment in Stockholm in June 1972, she was responsible for the report 'How Do You Want To Live?' This in turn led to another chairmanship, of the UK Executive preparing for European Architectural Year 1975. As though that were not enough, from 1971 she was an active member of the English Tourist Board.

As late as 1972 Lady Dartmouth was still telling journalists that her husband was 'the Rock of Gibraltar and divine; so steady and strong and yet such humour'. A cousin of this paragon, however, observed that in private she was 'beastly to him'. But few read anything into Lady Dartmouth's appointment of Johnny Spencer (deserted by his wife in 1967) as chairman of the Youth

Panel for European Architectural Year. In fact, she had become infatuated with him.

Raine Dartmouth more or less moved into Althorp in 1975, after Spencer succeeded as 8th Earl, and endured as best she could the hostility of his children. In unguarded moments she was less restrained: 'I could have them all for breakfast if I wanted to.'

She was divorced from Dartmouth in 1976, and shortly afterwards married Spencer. 'I fell madly in love when I was 45,' she explained to the public prints. In September 1978, however, Spencer suffered a stroke, which he might not have survived but for his new wife's support. 'Nobody destroys me,' she boasted, 'and nobody was going to destroy Johnny so long as I could sit by his bed – some of the family tried to stop me – and hold his hand.'

She insisted on moving him from Northampton to the National Hospital for Neurology and Neurosurgery in Queen Square, Holborn, where he underwent a lengthy operation. When it seemed he was on the road to recovery he contracted a rare virus, which entailed another move, to the Brompton Hospital in South Kensington. Once more Raine came to the rescue, importing from Germany a new drug called Azlocillin, then unlicensed in Britain, and insisting that the doctors administer it.

In May 1979 Lord Spencer was able to return to Althorp, and by July 1981 he had recovered sufficiently to climb the steps of St Paul's and lead his daughter Diana down the aisle to marry the Prince of Wales. Raine found herself placed some way back from the Spencer family in the cathedral; her husband, though, never forgot what he owed her.

The disposal of treasures from Althorp had begun in order to raise more than £2 million of duty payable on the 7th Earl's estate; they continued, however, for as long as Raine Spencer lived in the house. In *Do You Care About Historic Buildings* (1970) she had written eloquently about the importance of handing on an inheritance; in the 1980s, though, she seemed intent on breaking up collections which had taken the Spencers centuries to assemble.

Extraordinarily, for Raine Spencer was never anybody's fool, the transactions were carried out in haphazard fashion. Sets of furniture were sold piecemeal. Dealers were allowed to snap up paintings at knockdown prices. Drawings, china and manuscripts were added pell-mell to the spoils. Frequently the buyers were able to double their money within months. As the current Earl Spencer, in his book *Althorp: The Story of an English House* (1999), bitterly recorded: 'Between 1976 and 1992, 20 per cent of the contents of Althorp were sold, which equates to a whole century of my family's five centuries of acquisitions disappearing.'

The Earl and Countess Spencer claimed that it was absolutely necessary to raise funds for the refurbishment of Althorp. Certainly, the house was extensively redecorated: as one London craftsman put it, everything that did not move was covered in gilt. Plasterwork was renewed, embroidery remounted, chairs re-upholstered, furniture and paintings restored, carpets and curtains cleaned and replaced. Even a 17th century oak floor disappeared under wall-to-wall beige.

Critics fiercely condemned the Spencers' taste. Althorp, it was said, had become 'a bordello', 'an Arab gin palace', 'a Moroccan brothel'. Raine Spencer attributed such judgments to 'personal jealousy of me because I am so lucky to have such a wonderful husband'. And, to be fair, there were a few experts such as Roy Strong who thought that Raine 'made Althorp marvellous in many ways'.

But it would be difficult to argue that all the changes made were necessary; a degree of decaying grandeur does not go amiss in a country house. In any case, the Spencers spent a good deal of their loot outside Althorp, acquiring a large new residence in Mayfair, and three houses in Bognor. They even bought a Rolls-Royce.

Raine Spencer worked hard to raise money at Althorp, renting the house out for events, and holding musical soirées. She learnt Japanese in an effort to attract business. Even so, Althorp never attracted more than 35,000 visitors a year. It did not help that she banned wheelchairs, and failed to conceal her disdain for her customers. 'Ah, the dreaded public,' she exclaimed one day when she emerged from the private wing to see a group of tourists.

She still had sufficient energy for activity beyond Althorp, serving on the Advisory Council of the Victoria and Albert Museum from 1980 to 1982, and once more working for the British Tourist Authority. The two books she published with her husband, *The Spencers on Spas* (1984) and *Japan and the East* (1986), did not sell well.

Raine Spencer's connection with Althorp was abruptly ended by the death of her husband in March 1992. The new Earl immediately took steps to eradicate her influence. It was reported, moreover, that when her maid packed her clothes into suitcases bearing the Spencer emblem, the Princess of Wales ordered that they should be removed and put into black bin liners instead.

But Raine Spencer was never one to repine. She had been left very well off, and in May 1993 announced her engagement to a French count, Jean-François de Chambrun.

The 63-year-old bride informed the press that she was madly in love, and even hinted at lubricity. 'Well, at our advanced age,' she coyly acknowledged, 'no one would think we'd only just held hands.' Yet even before the wedding there were worrying signs. The Château de Garibondy above Cannes, where the count lived, far from being an ancestral possession, had been acquired from the count's first wife, an American heiress, as part of a divorce settlement. Now, it transpired, it was let out for the making of pornographic films. The bailiffs were hovering.

Nevertheless, in July 1993, Raine Spencer went through with the wedding. 'We can only pray for them,' Barbara Cartland observed. Within two months the new Contesse de Chambrun was obliged to deny rumours that she was separating from her husband; and within three years the rumours were denied no longer. The parting, it transpired, had been 'very amicable'.

Afterwards Raine Spencer kept a lower profile, promoting Harrods, the London department store to whose owner,

Mohammed Fayed, she and Johnny had been close. In December 2007, however, she emerged to give a bravura appearance at the London inquest into the death of her stepdaughter, Diana, Princess of Wales, dramatically begging the coroner 'to do your utmost to solve this mystery, to tear aside anything that could be a cover-up, and sift through everything possible and, indeed, impossible in order to allow poor Diana and poor Dodi to, at last, truly rest in peace'.

The story, she clearly wanted the inquest to understand, did not end there. In often piquant testimony she described how she and stepdaughter had achieved a rapprochement. 'Diana always said I had no hidden agenda,' recalled the countess. 'So many people – because she was so popular and so famous – wanted something out of her.' She told of their shared fascination with horoscopes, and the princess's belief that the stars would eventually guide her towards true love. 'We all want the dark, handsome gentleman to walk through the door,' she observed.

In her book *The Diana Chronicles*, Tina Brown claimed that her own experience of separation and divorce had made the Princess see her old adversary in a new light. In her grief following the death of her father, she had recognised that Raine had loved him too and had invited her for a 'weepy reconciliation lunch' at Kensington Palace. 'Afterwards,' wrote Tina Brown, 'the princess and the countess were often sighted deep in a tête-à-tête at the Connaught Grill.'

To her immense credit, Raine Spencer never sought to capitalise on this rapprochement. In fact she never spoke of her relationship with her stepdaughter until she was called to give evidence at the inquest, 10 years after the Princess's death.

Raine Spencer had three sons and a daughter by her first marriage to the 9th Earl of Dartmouth, who died in 1997.

Raine, Countess Spencer, born September 9 1929, died October 21 2016

Benjamin Creme

Glaswegian artist who claimed to be in telepathic contact with a 'new world teacher' called Maitreya

BENJAMIN CREME, who has died aged 93, was a Scottish painter, esotericist and author who spent much of his life as an evangelist for the coming of a 'new world teacher', whom Creme called Maitreya.

Creme, who claimed to be in telepathic communication with one of a community of ascended Masters living in the Himalayas, travelled the world espousing his message of Maitreya's coming, gathering a large following.

He first came to international attention in 1982, when he took out a series of full-page advertisements in newspapers in Europe and America and staged a press conference in Los Angeles proclaiming the arrival of Maitreya who, according to Creme, had left his abode in the Himalayas in a 'self-created' human body and flown from Pakistan in a jumbo jet to London, where he was working as a night porter in a hospital. There, he was preparing for the 'Day of Declaration', in which he would reveal himself via global television and usher in a new age of peace and harmony.

Creme's announcement prompted an unseemly rush of news reporters to the East End of London, making enquiries about the possible whereabouts of this 'new Christ'.

To facilitate his work, Creme established a magazine, *Share International*, which published communications purportedly coming from Creme's own Master and regular bulletins about Maitreya's ongoing, if hidden, influence in world affairs.

It was due to Maitreya's influence, it was claimed, that the German chancellor Willy Brandt had set up the Brandt Commision to further negotiations on global development. Maitreya had also held secret discussions with the chairman of the BBC, Alasdair Milne, about a proposed television appearance. In 1988 *Share International* published a photograph of a bearded man dressed in a robe who had reportedly made a fleeting appearance at a prayer meeting in Nairobi, explaining that this was Maitreya, and that the Day of Revelation was nigh.

The utopian optimism of Creme's mission gained considerable purchase among enthusiasts of 'New Age' beliefs. *Share International* was published in 70 countries, and Creme travelled throughout Europe, America, South America and Japan addressing public meetings, as well as speaking frequently on radio. He also wrote 16 books on esoteric subjects.

In the parallel universe of millenarian enthusiasm, his claims seemed to be taken equally seriously by some fundamentalist Christian organisations, who regularly attacked the mild-mannered Scotsman as an apostle of the 'anti-Christ' prophesied in the Book of Revelation, and an avatar of the dreaded spectre of 'World Government'.

Benjamin Creme was born in Glasgow on December 5 1922, into what he described as an 'upper-working class' family. His Russian Jewish father was an importer and exporter of china. His mother was an Irish Catholic who for a brief time took up spiritualism, christening her new-born son by the spiritualist name of 'Light'.

Creme had early ambitions to be an artist, and left school at 16 to concentrate on painting; throughout his life he would earn a living from selling his works. His interest in metaphysics and the occult was first awakened at the age of 14 when he encountered the writings of the Belgian-French explorer and Buddhist Alexandra David-Néel, who had travelled through Tibet in the early 20th century, reaching Lhasa at a time when the city was closed to foreigners. Creme claimed that through close study of her books he was able to master the Tibetan yogic practice of 'tumo', or inner heat.

He extended his studies through the teachings of Gurdjieff, Ouspensky and the Indian swamis Yogananda and Sri Ramana Maharshi, but it was the writings of Madame Blavatsky, the Russian occultist and founder of the Theosophical Society, and the esotericist Alice Bailey, that were to prove formative. Blavatsky had maintained that she was in contact with a group of advanced spiritual adepts whom she called the Hierarchy of Masters, and talked of the coming of a new world teacher named Maitreya – the fourth historical Buddha in Tibetan Buddhist cosmology. Blavatsky's millenarian message was further elaborated by Alice Bailey, who in 1923 broke away from the Theosophical Society to found her own Arcane Society, and claimed to be in contact with her own realised Master whom she called 'The Tibetan'. Alice Bailey believed that the hierarchy of Masters inhabited the mythical city of Shamballah, which had been founded by Venusians some 18 million years ago on a site in the Gobi desert.

Thus inspired, Creme became a member of the Aetherius Society, a UFO-contactee group which had been founded by the eccentric 'Sir' George King, who had been working as a taxi driver until one day in 1954 when, while he was drying some dishes, a loud voice instructed him: 'Prepare yourself! You are to become the Voice of Interplanetary Parliament.' King claimed the voice came from an entity living on Venus named Aetherius.

Creme became the society's vice-president, but broke with them in 1958 following a disagreement with King. The following year he experienced his own epiphany, claiming to have had his first telepathic communication with one of the same Hierarchy of Masters who had been in contact with Blavatsky and Bailey. This Master, Creme maintained, instructed him to pave the way for the coming of Maitreya. Creme gathered a small group around him and began to hold public lectures to spread his message.

A highly engaging speaker, his meetings would often begin with a tape recorder, operated by a bespectacled woman in a cardigan, playing recordings of his Master 'speaking through' Creme. At an appropriate point in the proceedings he would warn his audience that he was about to enter a meditative state during which he would be 'overshadowed' by the power of Maitreya and that they should not be alarmed if they noticed anything unusual. Thus prepared, it was not uncommon for some to report having witnessed Creme suffused in a golden glow, or to have seen the face of Maitreya super-imposed on his.

Creme was a genial and cultivated man with a compendious knowledge of art, philosophy and classical music, and a love of cricket. He had a particular disdain for the tinkly banalities of 'New Age' music, which he pronounced 'newage', to rhyme with sewage. He lived modestly in a semi-detached house in Tufnell Park, receiving no money for his talks, and claiming that it was actually 'embarrassing' to have been 'chosen' as the emissary of the new Christ.

'My job,' he once said, 'has been to make the initial approach to the public, to help create a climate of hope and expectancy. If I can do that, I'll be well pleased.' Nor did he seem in any way discouraged by Maitreya's apparently obdurate reluctance to appear as promised, explaining that it would be in contravention of man's free will for him to do so without an invitation from suitably high-ranking figures from politics and the media.

These requirements appeared to have been met when in December 2008 Creme made his most emphatic declaration to date, claiming that 'a bright star' would shortly appear in the sky heralding Maitreya's appearance on a major American television programme when he would finally reveal himself.

Over the years, Creme became accustomed to ridicule and mockery, which he treated with equanimity. 'Scepticism is fine,' he once said. 'But I don't like cynicism. I say, keep an open mind.'

His first wife, Peggy, died in 1965. He is survived by his second wife, Phyllis, whom he married in 1968, by their son and daughter, and by a son of his first marriage.

Benjamin Creme, born December 5 1922, died October 24 2016

Stanley Reynolds

Convivial, bibulous editor of *Punch* who once
predicted the Beatles would be a '12-month wonder'

STANLEY REYNOLDS,
the journalist and
novelist who has died
aged 82, was one of
old Fleet Street's most
convivial figures, and,
with his friend the
cartoonist Michael
Heath, one of the
last editors of the
venerable weekly
Punch.

'Stan' was a
notable dandy and
wit. An American from Massachusetts – he called himself 'a
swamp Yankee' – he affected the elaborate outfits of an old-
fashioned English gentleman: a Savile Row suit with a silk
handkerchief in the breast pocket and a watch chain looped
across the waistcoat; handmade shoes; a Jermyn Street shirt with
a detachable collar; a Locks hat; a monogrammed umbrella from
Swaine Adeney Brigg; and spectacles with frames he said were
made of teak.

His wit, delivered in a rapid growling drawl, was combative,
perverse and provocative, and although he was essentially kind
it could also sometimes be cruel. While he reduced some to tears
of laughter, others – the drama critic Sheridan Morley was one –
wept tears of pain; and nowadays his sexism and racism would
result in his arrest.

The cruelty was largely attributable to alcohol, and although
he practised drinking assiduously he was never much good at it.
At the weekly lunch at the historic Punch Table (which is now in

the archives of the British Library), he would scintillate over the hock, and set the table on a roar over the claret, but when the port appeared the cry would go up: 'Not the port, Stanley!'

Drink damaged his liver, and on medical advice he would swear off it for prolonged intervals, which made him easier company. But he would study the palms of his hands, which his liver had turned cricket-ball red, and when a patch of white appeared he would embark on the binges he called 'periodicals', until it was swallowed up again by the red. In 1993 he gave up entirely, and never seemed to miss it.

Stanley Ambrose Harrington Reynolds was born in Holyoke, Massachusetts, on November 27 1934. His father was a businessman of Irish extraction; his mother was French and, as he recalled, 'a bit daffy', so in his infancy he was cared for mainly by her mother. He spoke French as a child, but not as an adult. He suffered from psoriasis and had spells in hospital, which left him with an enduring anxiety about his appearance, and the sense that he was an outsider.

At Williston, a private school in nearby Easthampton, he abandoned his family's Roman Catholic faith and became a fierce atheist, objecting to public prayers as unconstitutional. He also became a fervent admirer of FDR, and a lifelong Democrat, so much so that he became estranged from his older sister, a Republican.

On leaving school he joined the US Army and served for two years with the 1st Infantry Division, rising to the rank of sergeant. An accomplished marksman, in later life he would speak authoritatively of such sharpshooting arcana as 'Kentucky windage' and 'Arkansas elevation'. On one occasion he confused the grid references on a map and marched his platoon over a bridge and into Canada, which was reported in the local press. 'Did you know,' he liked to ask fellow drinkers in Fleet Street, 'that I once invaded Canada?'

After night school at Boston University he found employment on the *Holyoke Transcript-Telegram*. 'I used to churn out Society Jottings,' he recalled unconvincingly, 'like "Big Nose

138

Sam Saraceno is on the town with a pack of his Wop pals. *The Transcript* takes the opportunity of letting Sam know he is a low-down dirty stinking rat."' (He was a Damon Runyon fan.)

Having fallen in love with a visiting Englishwoman – Gillian Morton, who would later become this newspaper's radio critic – he followed her home to Liverpool, married her, and then took her back to America, where in 1958 he became a reporter on the *Providence Journal* in Rhode Island.

Two years later they returned to Britain, where he worked first for the *Manchester Evening News* and then for the *Liverpool Daily Post*, covering crime and sport, and also foreign stories such as JFK's election, and conditions in Cuba under Castro. After a stint as a 're-write man' for Reuters in London he joined *The Manchester Guardian*, a long-standing ambition inspired by Alistair Cooke's reports for that paper from America.

Reynolds wrote about anything that came his way. He reviewed a Beatles concert in the Cavern, and in 1963 declared that they were 'about to fade away from the charts, to the Helen Shapiro hinterland of the 12-month wonders ... it was a good exciting sound while it lasted'. (He preferred the Rolling Stones.) Perhaps because his address was Menlove Lane, he was asked to investigate Liverpudlian attitudes to homosexuality, so he pinned on a 'Glad to Be Gay' badge and went on a pub crawl in the docks, ending up in a fight.

He also wrote brilliantly about cricket, an unlikely passion of his – 'a former baseball third baseman, I became a demon fast-bowler'. And twice a week he wrote the long-running, 'supposedly humorous' column that would eventually lead him to *Punch*.

He also tried his hand at literature. Besotted by Jack Kerouac – to the extent that for a time he dressed as a Beatnik – he wrote a play about him, *Desolation Angel*, which was staged in Liverpool and London. He was delighted when Pete Postlethwaite, playing Kerouac, paused mid-performance to ask the audience: 'Can you believe some guy actually sat down and wrote this shit?'

He also claimed to have rewritten a novel 21 times, which was never published. Then he spent a fortnight writing *Better Dead*

Than Red, a satire on the American Right, which was published in Britain and America in 1966, translated into German and Italian, and earned him the equivalent of two years of his *Guardian* salary.

In 1972 he left *The Guardian* and became television critic of *The Times*, while writing book reviews for *The New Statesman* and a weekly article for *Punch*, where in 1980 he succeeded Miles Kington as literary editor.

Despite the chaos, noise and occasional violence that prevailed in the cramped office he shared with Michael Heath, he proved an excellent editor – attentive, meticulous, always keen to bring out the best in his contributors. But *Punch* was on the skids, out of touch, eclipsed by *Private Eye*, with falling circulation and inept management. In 1988, as a last throw of the dice, and to general amazement, including theirs, he and Heath were appointed joint editors. Neither of them could remember much of their brief reign, though Reynolds did recall dancing on the Table: 'It was OK because I was the editor.'

After the death of *Punch* he moved with his partner by this time, the writer Jane McLoughlin, from Islington to the country, first to Oxfordshire and then to Somerset. He was an enthusiastic adopter of roles, in which he exaggerated aspects of his own personality. So just as he felt obliged to drink and swear a lot as a journalist, in the country he became keenly interested in such things as flowers and pigs.

For a while he kept up his journalism, with columns in *The Oldie* and the short-lived *European*, and obituary writing for *The Daily Telegraph* and *The Guardian*, but he soon settled down to write books.

'At a great age,' he announced on the blog set up for him by one of his sons, 'sitting in a corner of my bedroom in my 17th century West Country cottage, in a tweed jacket and club tie, and with a fountain pen' – he never mastered the electric typewriter, let alone the computer – 'I have been writing what pleases me.'

What pleased him was old-fashioned whodunits or 'murder mysteries', set in the quaint New England township of North Holford (based on the Holyoke of his childhood), and featuring

Detective 'Boomer' Daniels, who sounded rather like his author. He wrote six of them, beginning with *Death Dyed Blonde*, but despite the gushing endorsement of Jilly Cooper they did not sell well. *Murder in Arcady*, the fourth in the series, sold one copy.

He was happy enough, though, scribbling away and mowing his lawn, even after he was somewhat incapacitated by a heart attack. But over the past few years he became progressively iller, and could no longer walk, which was a misery and a torment.

It is said by those closest to him that his life was prolonged by the recent election in America, and ended by its outcome.

He was twice married: in 1958 to Gillian Morton, by whom he had three sons (marriage dissolved); and in 2004 to Jane McLoughlin.

Stanley Reynolds, born November 27 1934, died November 28 2016

The Right Reverend Eamon Casey

Ebullient Irish bishop and campaigner who left the country after it emerged that he had fathered a son

THE RIGHT REVEREND EAMON CASEY, who has died aged 89, was the Roman Catholic Bishop of Galway who resigned following the revelation in 1992 that he had fathered a son 17 years earlier, and that he had paid the boy's mother, an American divorcee, some (Irish) £75,000 from diocesan funds after negotiations with her lawyers.

Bishop Casey, second from right: he had a taste for fast cars, which he frequently crashed

An ebullient and gregarious figure, Casey was the most popular, the most socially involved, and the most dynamic campaigner against poverty and injustice of his generation of Irish bishops. He was also a noted *bon vivant*, with a taste for fine claret and fast cars, which he frequently crashed. But he maintained that 'any clergyman with more than four figures in the bank has lost the faith'.

Eamon Casey was born on April 24 1927 at Firies, near Tralee, Co Kerry, one of 10 children of a creamery manager. Raised in Co Limerick, he was educated at St Munchin's College there and studied for the priesthood at St Patrick's College, Maynooth.

He was ordained in 1951 and became a curate in Limerick, where he said his social conscience was shaped by the misery he saw in working class housing estates. In 1960 he moved to

Slough to work among Irish immigrants. Impressed by Casey's efforts among the homeless, Cardinal Heenan of Westminster asked him to turn his Catholic Housing Aid Society into a national organisation in 1963.

In 1966 Casey also helped to found Shelter, in a spectacularly effective campaign to press government for action on homelessness. In 1968 he became chairman of Shelter, demonstrating great managerial and fund-raising acumen, and was helped by his television appearance in *Cathy Come Home*, a powerful drama-documentary. Casey's chubby, grinning face and engaging manner endeared him to charity workers and prospective donors alike.

In 1969 he was recalled to Ireland to become Bishop of Kerry. At 42 he was the youngest member of the Irish hierarchy. The novelist Kate O'Brien asked: 'Why is this young man of action, this Samaritan who wears his heart on his sleeve, being trapped into a mitre away from his great vocation?' Cardinal Heenan, in a sermon, said the appointment of Casey, a friend and father of the poor, was a sign of the changing Church.

But Casey's mitre did not trap his effervescence and he launched a series of high-profile local campaigns. He ended the archaic ban on Saturday night dances in Kerry church halls, pressed for the maintenance of the compulsory Shannon airport stopover for transatlantic traffic, which provided local jobs, blessed an unauthorised bridge to Valentia Island, and kept up a barrage of abuse of the government for failing to fund poverty programmes.

If he was criticised for any of his activities it was for his style, not his sincerity. When Cardinal Conway set up the Irish development agency Trócaire in 1973, Casey was appointed chairman. Trócaire, 20 per cent of whose budget was devoted to education and propaganda, supported liberation theology, and in El Salvador and Nicaragua backed bishops Romero and Ortega, incurring the anger of the Pentagon.

When, in 1983, the US government accused the agency of being anti-American, Casey organised a boycott by the Irish Catholic bishops of President Reagan's visit to his ancestral home in

Tipperary. Trocaire also embarrassed the Irish republic's power generation company ESB, by claiming that it had driven people from their homes in the Philippines during construction of a hydro-electric project under contract to the Marcos regime.

In 1974 Casey chaired a Dublin meeting of Cherish, a support organisation for unmarried mothers. Commending the women, he bitterly castigated fathers who failed to recognise their responsibility to their children. Unknown to his audience, his own unacknowledged son had just been born, the issue of a clandestine affair with Annie Murphy, a 26-year-old American divorcee.

Miss Murphy, a distant relative of the Bishop, had been sent to Ireland in the spring of 1973 to help her recover from a disastrous marriage and a miscarriage. In her book, *Forbidden Fruit*, co-authored with the former Jesuit Peter de Rosa in 1993, she offered a lurid account of her relationship with the bishop, who, she said, had tried to browbeat her into having the child adopted to conceal the affair. She also suggested that he might have had other affairs. Describing his boudoir technique, she remarked: 'He was a goddam bishop. Where had he learnt all this?'

In 1976 Bishop Casey was transferred to the more urban diocese of Galway, a move prompted by local agitation for a more liberal prelate to replace the arch conservative, Bishop Michael Browne. But although Casey happily wore the liberal tag bestowed by observers of his social conscience, his theology was conservative.

He kept a low profile in the public controversies over socio-sexual issues in the 1970s and 1980s but negotiated a secret accommodation with the medical staff at Galway's Galvia Hospital, who agreed to ban sterilisation and in vitro fertilisation, both of which were against Catholic teaching, as well as amniocentesis, which was regarded as a prelude to abortion.

In 1986, after he was arrested and banned for drink-driving in London, he made a tearful public confession to the people of his diocese. In an editorial, *The Irish Times* praised the honesty

144

and humility of this extrovert, warm-hearted and impulsive man whom car salesmen sought out – Bishop Casey, whose regular collisions ensured a brisk turnover in new models.

Having a preference for Italian cars, the bishop wrote off several Lancias, but also crashed a Mercedes. He was an occasional entrant in saloon car races at the Mondello Park circuit in Co Kildare.

In 1991 persistent rumours began to circulate about his affair with Annie Murphy, whose son Peter, now aged 17, was pressing for public acknowledgement by his father. Although several Irish newspapers were approached with the story, none dared publish a line. But the public whispering reached a pitch in May 1992 and the bishop resigned while on a visit to Rome.

In a statement, he said merely that he had left for personal reasons and would devote the rest of his active life to work on the missions. He disappeared from view for almost a year but was tracked down to a convent in Mexico by the author Gordon Thomas, who photographed the now bearded bishop and described his secluded but comfortable lifestyle.

Much embarrassment was caused to the Church authorities by the revelation that Casey had appropriated diocesan funds to give to Miss Murphy; later, it was announced that the losses had been made good by an unnamed well-wisher. Bishop Casey continued his exile in Central America, but returned to Ireland for brief visits to funerals and family occasions.

Having worked on the missions in rural Ecuador, Casey later found himself a retirement job in Britain in the tiny parish of Staplefield near Haywards Heath, Sussex.

Here he devoted himself to visiting the sick in the local hospital, where his ministry was greatly valued. Known as Fr Eamon, he was much loved by local people for his warm-hearted approach. The bishop having done penance for his sins, the people of God had clearly forgiven him for his transgressions.

In 2006, Casey, now almost 80, returned to Ireland, settling in the small east Galway village of Shanaglish. About a year after that he recorded several hours of interviews with an

Irish folklorist called Maurice O'Keeffe. He did not discuss the circumstances of the scandal, but revealed that when he knew that his secret relationship was about to be exposed he went to the Vatican to hand in his resignation and 'acknowledge [his] wrongdoing'.

The Pope's representative, however, 'wouldn't accept it', Casey claimed. 'He said the Holy Father doesn't want to accept it.' He also recalled a stay in a North American monastery in which he had twice set off the alarm by smoking (contrary to the rules) in his room late at night.

In 2011 Eamon Casey was admitted to a nursing home in Co Clare suffering from Alzheimer's disease.

The Rt Rev Eamon Casey, born April 24 1927, died March 13 2017

Michael 'Dandy Kim' Caborn-Waterfield

Adventurer who dated Diana Dors, spent time in a French jail and founded a famous sex shop

MICHAEL 'DANDY KIM' CABORN-WATERFIELD, who has died aged 86, was a colourful character in post-war London, a gentleman adventurer who had a relationship with Diana Dors, smuggled guns into Cuba, served time in a French jail and set up the first Ann Summers sex shop.

In his memoir *Fast and Louche: Confessions of a sinner* (2002), Jeremy Scott described Waterfield as 'an amusing, good-looking man', who 'seemed to take nothing entirely seriously, including himself. But he shared with Lord Byron a reputation of being dangerous to know.'

Whether or not the reputation was justified in Lord Byron's case, it certainly was in Waterfield's.

Michael George Kimberley Caborn-Waterfield was born on New Year's Day 1930, the son of Vivian Conrad George Colnaghi

Caborn-Waterfield, a pilot in the Fleet Air Arm who died in 1944. Kim was educated at Cranleigh, from which he ran away aged 16 to a racing stables where he briefly pursued an ambition to become a jockey.

When that did not work out, he became an actor and a trader in black-market nylons. Reputed to have several West End stage-doormen on his payroll, by the late 1940s he had three cars and a flat in St John's Wood.

On New Year's Eve 1948 he was holding court in the Cross Keys pub in Chelsea when he set eyes on the 17-year-old Rank starlet Diana Dors. 'I glanced away from my friends to see a boy with the most disturbing eyes that seemed to pierce right through me,' she recalled in her 1981 autobiography. 'His dark good looks were almost beautiful ... I half-smiled in his direction, but abruptly he turned away as if he hadn't seen me.' As he had expected, his lack of interest intrigued her and they became lovers.

The relationship ended after two years, though they remained good friends, and she went on to marry Dennis Hamilton, a door-to-door salesman with whom Waterfield would become involved in a fracas at the Embassy Club in 1955, resulting in a conviction for 'insulting behaviour'.

In the meantime Waterfield had become the leader of a smart Chelsea set, throwing parties attended by the likes of Lord Lucan, his good looks and natty dress sense (a friend recalled his collection of 25 handmade suits) earning him the nickname 'Dandy Kim'.

A succession of women fell under his spell. In his memoir *Serendipity ... a Life* (2012), Peter Watson-Wood recalled how after seducing one such unfortunate – the daughter of an American millionaire – Waterfield had swept her off to Gretna Green for a quick marriage: 'The American tycoon had to part with very considerable money in order to rescue his beloved daughter from this unsuitable union. Kim did the decent thing and, with the bank seriously topped up, he told the girl it wouldn't work out after all and she should go back to daddy.'

He also went out with the actress Samantha Eggar, though he claimed to have resisted the charms of the ex-wife of Randolph Churchill (née Pamela Digby, later Pamela Harriman, the US ambassador to Paris), whom he described as 'a true redhead ... aflame, mop, collar and muffs'.

In the mid-1950s he took up with Barbara Warner, daughter of the Hollywood mogul Jack, and in 1956 was found guilty *in absentia* by a French court of the theft of £23,000 (in francs) from Warner's home on the French Riviera and sentenced to four years in jail. During the trial Waterfield was described as 'seductive, witty, courteous, unscrupulous and the possessor of a criminal record'.

During a case which threw up a number of mysteries that remain unresolved, Barbara Warner claimed that Waterfield had forced her to reveal the whereabouts of Warner's safe by threatening that 'if I didn't help him to find it, he would tell my father about things that happened the previous year'. In 1960, after running guns for the Cuban dictator Batista, opening a water-skiing school in Tangiers (from where he claimed to have been spirited back to Britain by the Kray twins after the French authorities tracked him down), Waterfield was eventually extradited to France, but only served 12 months of his sentence.

According to Douglas Thompson in *The Hustlers* (2007), Jack Warner's lawyer had been informed about 'sensitive' documents that Waterfield had stolen along with the cash. So 'potentially explosive' were these papers that pressure had been applied 'at the highest level', and as a result Waterfield was freed and the order for him to repay the stolen money was rescinded.

After his release Waterfield bought a manor on the Dorset-Wiltshire border and became a keen rider to hounds with the South and West Wilts Hunt. Back in London he returned to the Chelsea social scene, cruising the King's Road in his Bentley and hosting parties frequented by, among others, Stephen Ward, the society osteopath, who turned up with Mandy Rice-Davies and Christine Keeler. In 2001 Waterfield would sell a collection of portraits by Ward, who had committed suicide in 1963, including studies of Keeler and a naked Rice-Davies and a pornographic sketch, which he claimed to have bought to protect a friend.

By the late 1960s Waterfield was ready for a new venture. By his own account was given an idea by the society lawyer Lord Goodman, who had been impressed by a sex manual Waterfield had published under the nom de plume Terence Hendrickson and 'wondered if I could do the same with goods aimed at the woman's market'. In 1970 he opened the first Ann Summers sex shop near Marble Arch, naming the enterprise after a former girlfriend who was working as manager of his Dorset estate. He felt that his own name and notoriety might be bad for business.

The ex-girlfriend (Annice Summers) agreed to help with the new venture and for 12 months Ann Summers and 'her' shops – a riot of multicoloured plastic 'massagers', exotic lotions and inflatable partners (puncture repair kit extra) – were a sensation. In the face of horrified opposition from church groups and councils, the 'convent-educated' Ann became famous as the standard-bearer for the sexual revolution. In 1971 the *London Evening Standard* named her Woman of the Year.

But later the same year she resigned, saying that she had become concerned about some of the products sold under her name, as well as the fact that the financial rewards Waterfield had promised had not materialised. She went on to spill the beans – revealing that she had simply been a front person for the enterprise while Waterfield had been the brains. 'It was disastrous for the business,' Waterfield said. 'Until then it was perceived as being naughty-but-nice. Her revelation condemned the Ann Summers shops to seediness.' A postal strike did not help, either.

The name was resurrected later that year by the Gold brothers, soft porn and property tycoons who turned it into a high-street chain. Waterfield went on to fall out with the Golds and in 2013 lodged a High Court claim for more than £500,000 in damages, alleging that he had been defamed in *Please Let it Stop*, the 2008 autobiography of Jacqueline Gold, the chief executive of

Ann Summers, who, he claimed, had suggested that he had had an 'adulterous relationship' with Princess Margaret and was in the habit of illegally landing his helicopter in Hyde Park.

In 1972 he married Penny Brahms, a model and actress who had co-starred with Joanna Lumley in the 1971 sex comedy *Games That Lovers Play*, and with whom he had a daughter, although the marriage did not last. In 1976 he proposed a Miss Topless World beauty pageant, which did not, in the end, come off.

A friend recalled that Waterfield, a 'restless spirit', had a somewhat cavalier attitude to banks and when he was short of funds had a habit of 'evaporating' into thin air. For a time he lived in Australia. In 2000 the *Daily Mail* reported that he had 'eschewed his natural milieu of a flat in Chelsea's Kings Road to pursue the life of a "tax exile" near Dublin'.

'At first,' the paper reported, 'he denied he was Dandy Kim. But very few 70-year-olds sport shoulder-length white hair, tight jeans, denim shirt, suede boots and cut-glass accents.' Later he moved back to London.

His daughter survives him.

Michael 'Dandy Kim' Caborn-Waterfield, born January 1 1930, died May 4 2016

Sarah Holman

Highland countrywoman and 'compulsive fund-raiser' who upheld all that was best about stalking

SARAH HOLMAN, who has died aged 65, stood out among a dwindling number of Highland landowners who hold the view that owning an estate carries with it a duty and responsibility to the land and the local community.

She took an active part in the life of the villages of Ilmington in Warwickshire and at Acharacle, Argyll, where she delighted local residents with her eccentricities, and a family trust made land available for a new primary school, a commemorative woodland walk and an extension to the graveyard.

Her own great love was

Sarah Holman: a woman of forthright views, described by a friend as '95 per cent wonderful and 5 per cent maddening'

stalking on the family's Shielbridge estate in Argyll, on the west coast of the Scottish Highlands. There was nothing she liked better after a morning swim in the icy Atlantic waters, which she did every day summer or winter, than setting out for the high tops, often not returning until late evening.

Where deer were concerned she was a traditionalist and upheld all that was best and grand about stalking. Not for her a short walk, an easy beast in the early morning mist or loosing off a few rounds from an all-terrain vehicle. She was an

152

accomplished stalker and got involved in all aspects of the day, including the gralloching, which she once performed wearing a pair of Marigolds.

The eldest of four daughters of Christopher Boot Holman and his wife Winifred, née Ponsonby, Sarah Charlotte Holman was born in London on July 9 1951. A paternal great grandfather was Jesse Boot, the first Lord Trent and founder of Boots the Chemists. In 1930 he had purchased the 50,000-acre Ardnamurchan Estate (of which Shielbridge formed a part), the most westerly property on mainland Britain, from the father of the art historian Kenneth Clark. The estate comprised a 70-stag deer forest and the south bank of the river Shiel, famous for its early run of sea trout and heavy salmon. Also included was the massive red-sandstone Glenborrodale Castle and Shielbridge House.

Sarah developed diabetes when she was five, but never made a fuss, always telling her family that she was as fit as a fiddle, had her diabetes under control and that her doctor recommended a bottle of red wine a day. This was a prescription she adhered to until this year when she announced that she was giving up wine for Lent, though when asked how she would manage she replied: 'I'm drinking whisky instead.'

When she was 10 her parents bought Foxcote House, a magnificent 18th century manor near Shipston-on-Stour in Warwickshire, which, until the death of Robert Canning in 1848, had been the seat of the Canning family since the reign of Henry VI. There she was taught to ride and she hunted with the Warwickshire all her life. Sarah was educated at Lawnside in Malvern, the Sorbonne in Paris and the Royal Agricultural College, Cirencester.

Despairing of her getting married, when she was 35 her father asked her to take over the running of the Shielbridge estate, by now reduced to 10,000 acres. Moving to the Old Manse at Acharacle, she provided generous entertainment for a shifting cast of guests, the quality of her wines making up in some measure for such dubious delicacies as mushroom and mackerel paté. The sporting artist Ian MacGillivray was a frequent guest; some of his best deer paintings were done on the estate with the Inner Hebrides as a backdrop.

Sarah Holman served as chairman of the Ardnamurchan Deer Management Group and on the executive committee of the Association of Deer Management Groups. Always concerned for animal welfare, she disliked the commercial aspects of stalking and nothing annoyed her more than being told by Scottish Natural Heritage that more deer needed to be culled to make way for yet more trees – although numbers were already at an all-time low.

Sarah Holman served as a Deputy Lieutenant and High Sheriff of Warwickshire as her father and various ancestors had before her. She was always organising events to raise money for her many charities. When her bank manager asked her what her job was she replied: 'compulsive fund-raiser'. For the last 20 years of her life she ran the Cheltenham Countryside Race Day, for the Countryside Alliance, raising more than £2 million and bringing attendance numbers up from 6,000 to 20,000. When the committee tried to retire her, giving her a farewell lunch, she refused to take the hint and raised a record amount the next year.

Sarah Holman had no airs and graces and at a smart charity lunch in Gloucestershire last year she invited her carpenter, her gardener, her plumber, her rat catcher and Barry her local taxi driver, and had the most fun of all the tables there.

A woman of forthright views, described by a friend as '95 per cent wonderful and 5 per cent maddening', Sarah Holman lost her keys, wallet and telephone on a regular basis and was oblivious to any rules that did not suit her. On one occasion, rushing back to Foxcote at high speed late at night, she was pulled over by the police. She explained that she had been playing the part of a tart in the village play and when she saw the lights of a car behind apparently giving chase, she was terrified that she was being pursued by two men in the audience who had been eyeing her up. The policemen were so impressed by her defence that they sent her on her way.

On another occasion, arriving at the airport check-in desk and finding herself barred from her holiday flight since she had an out-of-date passport, she demanded to speak to the pilot.

Sarah Holman was unmarried, explaining that she had had two lovely proposals when she was younger, but had turned them down, as 'things were great as they were'. She was adored by her sisters, nephews, nieces and godchildren and welcomed them to the Old Manse each year. She is survived by Corrie, her beloved Norwich terrier.

Sarah Holman, born July 9 1951, died June 7 2017

Sir David Tang

High-living entrepreneur who cheerily marketed a version of Chinese style to western consumers

Tang: 'one of those rare people who cheers the world up'

SIR DAVID TANG, who has died of cancer aged 63, was a larger-than-life Hong Kong-born entrepreneur, style guru and bon viveur who embodied both the potentialities and the cultural contrasts of the interface between China and the west.

Tang's business brainwave was to sell upmarket western consumers a conception of 'modern Chinoiserie' that made the emergent eastern superpower more accessible by poking gentle fun at it. In 1991, at a time of deep foreboding in Hong Kong over the looming handover of power to Beijing, he opened the China Club in the penthouse of the monumental former Bank of China building – from the balcony of which Maoist cadres had

156

once incited the populace by megaphone to turn violently against British colonialist 'devils'.

The club's décor mixed Cultural Revolution memorabilia with Qing Dynasty teahouse furnishings and the boldest of Chinese contemporary art. Staff in white Mao suits with red military flashes served cocktails to taipans and visiting celebrities in the Long March Bar – and, with the addition of China Clubs in Beijing and Singapore, the operation became a focal point for the kind of power-networking at which Tang himself excelled, and of which he never tired.

Quite simply, he knew everyone – from Fidel Castro, who made him Cuba's honorary consul in Hong Kong, to the Duke of Marlborough, who invited him to Blenheim for shooting parties; from Margaret Thatcher to Tracey Emin and Kate Moss; and from the Prince of Wales to Deng Xiaoping. Tang's ambition of arranging a social encounter between the last of those pairings was thwarted only by the death of the Chinese supreme leader, whose artist daughter's work adorned the China Club.

Tang acknowledged no contradiction in being both a proud Chinese patriot and a passionate Anglophile, preferring to see himself as a 'benign mediator'. Though he claimed to own a T-shirt which said 'F--- Off, I've Got Enough Friends', he greeted new ones and old ones alike with his mischievous, discursive bonhomie: the last British governor of Hong Kong, Chris (now Lord) Patten, called him 'one of those rare people who cheers the world up'.

Meanwhile, the project of turning himself into a global brand took a second major step in 1994 with the opening of Shanghai Tang, a ready-to-wear clothing and accessories store in the Central district of Hong Kong which in due course became a chain with branches in Beijing, Macau and Shanghai. Its signature garment was a Chinese evening jacket in bright red or green velvet, and its range included Mao caps and Cultural Revolution T-shirts – all labelled 'Made by Chinese' because Tang believed 'Made in China' carried connotations of shoddiness.

The expansion of Shanghai Tang required deeper pockets even than those of its founder's handmade suits, so the Swiss-based luxury goods group Richemont was brought in as a partner. But relations soured after a fraud by a staff member was uncovered, and Tang found himself squeezed out of corporate power; he sold his remaining stake to Richemont in 2007.

The Tang persona was oblivious to any distinction between business and pleasure. A world-class cigarman and prolific consumer of fat Cohibas, he acquired the distribution rights for Cuba's national product throughout Asia and Australasia and opened a chain of opulent Cigar Divan boutiques, the first of them in Hong Kong's exclusive Mandarin Hotel. Likewise he was both a partner in Hong Kong's leading contemporary art gallery, Hanart TZ, and an avid private collector.

'The most profitable of all my investments has been my collection of paintings,' he observed of his business philosophy. 'I had no idea that was going to happen. Of course you do what you can to seize the opportunities. But you have to be in the right place at the right time, and then it just happens. You can't go out and seek it. It's like love.'

David Wing-cheung Tang was born on August 2 1954. His grandfather, Sir Shui-kin Tang (from whom his father was estranged), founded the Kowloon bus company and became one of Hong Kong's 'great and good' before the Second World War as a member of its urban council and chairman of the Tung Wah public hospital.

Brought up a Roman Catholic, David Tang was educated first at La Salle College in Hong Kong and, from the age of 13, at the Perse School in Cambridge – because, he said later, his English was not good enough to gain entry to Eton or Harrow.

By the time he had gone on to study Philosophy and Law at London University, however, his command of the language was ornate – and for the rest of his life he alternated bizarrely between Wodehousian plumminess and the harsh tonalities of his native Cantonese. Likewise in sartorial style, he was sometimes the retro Savile Row dandy but more often, in loose-fitting tunics

158

and pyjama-like trousers that disguised a spreading waistline, he might have been an actor playing the part of a Confucian gentleman-scholar.

But there was indeed an intellectual – as well as an exponent of informal diplomacy and a very shrewd dealmaker – behind the life-and-soul façade of 'Tango', as he was known to British friends in Hong Kong. He lectured in philosophy at Peking University and translated Roald Dahl's *Charlie and the Chocolate Factory* into Chinese before entering the business world in 1985 as Asian representative for the oil and mining adventurer Algy Cluff.

It took a while, he claimed, to persuade Cluff to let him do 'anything more than photocopying', but the job was an outward-bound education in entrepreneurship. Each of Tang's own commercial ventures was based on detailed research and attention to design detail, plus a characteristically Chinese attention to cash flow.

Tang was a director of several major Hong Kong companies, and an adviser to the Savoy Hotel group, the investment firm Blackstone, the Tommy Hilfiger fashion brand and the jewellers Asprey & Garrard. Among his later ventures were the China Tang restaurant in the Dorchester Hotel, and the Cipriani restaurant in Hong Kong.

Having long declared himself 'awfully backward' in technology ('I clung on to my fax machine as long as I could'), Tang finally entered the digital arena in 2011 as the founder of ICorrect. com, a website on which celebrities who feel they have been misrepresented elsewhere can put the record straight – for a subscription of $1,000 a year.

It was for his tireless work in the charitable field that Tang was appointed OBE in 1997 and was knighted in 2008 – wearing a black silk Mandarin suit for the investiture. He was founder chairman of the Hong Kong Cancer Fund, vice chairman of the European Organisation for Research and Treatment of Cancer, and founder president of the Hong Kong Down Syndrome Association. An accomplished but self-deprecating pianist, he was president of the London Bach Society, an adviser to the LSO and the English Chamber Orchestra and a governor of the Hong Kong Philharmonic. He was also a trustee of the Royal Academy, chairman of the Asia-Pacific acquisitions committee of Tate Modern, and patron of the Hong Kong Youth Arts Festival.

He maintained a town house in Belgravia – presided over by an English butler – as well as homes on Hong Kong island and at Sai Kung in the New Territories. Though he travelled constantly he found time to write weekly columns for *Apple Daily*, a Hong Kong tabloid, and the *Financial Times*, in which he offered magisterial answers to readers' questions on issues of style and manners.

One FT reader asked him to describe his own 'perfect day'. The answer included a high partridge drive in Northumberland; lunch at the rooftop restaurant of the Danieli in Venice, followed by 'a Punch Double Corona at the Cuban National Ballet school in Havana while watching an exercise class and drinking a double espresso'; sunset on Malibu beach; a performance of Brahms piano pieces Op 118; 'and so to bed'.

He published two anthologies of his journalism, *An Apple a Week* (2006) and *A Chink in the Armour* (2010). He was adept at card tricks, and enjoyed casino gambling.

David Tang married first, in 1983, Susanna Cheung Suk-yee, an Australian-Chinese film actress; they had a son and a daughter. The marriage was dissolved in 1994 and he married secondly, in 2003, his long-time girlfriend Lucy Wastnage, whom he met when she was personal assistant to the publisher Naim Attallah.

Sir David Tang, born August 2 1954, died August 29 2017

Gavin Stamp

Historian and conservationist who waged a lifelong campaign against architectural vandalism

GAVIN STAMP, the architectural historian, who has died aged 69, was 'Piloti' who wrote the 'Nooks and Corners' column in *Private Eye* magazine; a television presenter of great charm and humour; a conservationist who personally saved one of the finest Arts and Crafts buildings in London; a photographer, draughtsman and writer of prodigious talent.

In 1966, the poet Christopher Logue wrote a satirical poem about the general election being held that year, the second in 17 months: 'I shall vote Labour, because deep in my heart, I am a conservative.' Logue could not possibly have known it, but he was describing the character of Stamp, who would one day marry Logue's widow, Rosemary Hill.

In his youth a man of the Right, Stamp became, by the end of his life, an impassioned defender of the European Union, and a socialist – homesick, as he openly admitted, for the England of his childhood, of free orange juice and nationalised steam railways. He rather despised the inability of many contemporaries to change their minds.

His most celebrated piece of journalism, in the *Spectator* in 1985, was a defence of the telephone boxes designed by Sir Giles Gilbert Scott, later worked into a fine illustrated book. 'No vandalism meted out to a kiosk by an individual has equalled that practised systematically by British Telecom,' he wrote. The article inspired a campaign by the *Spectator* which led to about 2,500 of the boxes being listed.

Gavin Mark Stamp was born on the Ides of March 1948 in Bromley. He shared with his younger brother Gerard, the architectural watercolourist, an early passion for buildings. At Dulwich College, when Stamp was a boy there, there was a plan to put plate glass into some Victorian cloisters. It was his first shocked encounter with architectural vandalism, against which he would campaign with fervour for the rest of his life.

Gonville and Caius College, Cambridge, where the arch-conservative John Casey was a Fellow, had a profound effect on Stamp. The prevailing ethos in English universities at that time was Leftist and anti-historical. Casey's disciples rebelled against this by wearing suits and watch-chains and polished leather shoes. Stamp was always thus attired until his forties. (In the 1980s he was labelled, with others, a 'Young Fogey').

For three years he studied Architecture under Dr David Watkin, who influenced a whole generation to rethink their ideas about modernism, and who pined for the neoclassical values which underpin the great European tradition. Stamp later distanced himself from the ethos of Peterhouse Right, finding their misogyny and anti-Semitism so repellent as to call into question their aesthetic judgments.

But he retained an intense and very Cambridge intellectual seriousness. When he left the university he moved to London and gravitated to the Architectural Press in Queen Anne's Gate. The Bride of Denmark, the Victorian pub in the basement there, was where he formed many of his lasting friendships, including that of his hero John Betjeman.

Stamp became close friends with both the Betjemans. With Sir John, he would enjoy long lunches at the Ritz, and jokes about the 1890s, while imbibing the poet's passion for architectural conservation.

Betjeman had started the 'Nooks and Corners' column in *Private Eye*, devoted to exposing the vandalism of plansters, bishops and others who were intent on wrecking England. After Betjeman ran out of steam, he recommended that Stamp should take over the column. He wrote it every fortnight for the rest of his life, lambasting fraud and vandalism with even-handed anger. Penelope Betjeman also woke in Stamp his fascination with India, where she had been born and on whose architecture she was a distinguished expert.

At this time he also worked at the RIBA Drawings Collection with John Harris. Stamp was responsible for a memorable exhibition there of War Memorials from the First World War. He designed and drew the catalogue and found many things of overlooked value and beauty.

His own architectural drawings were exquisite. His drawings of Holy Trinity, Sloane Street, the 'cathedral of Arts and Crafts' in Belgravia, illustrated his impassioned pamphlet written to support Betjeman's successful campaign to save that great building from demolition.

The architect Roderick Gradidge was another friend made at this time. Born in India, like Penelope Betjeman, Gradidge educated Stamp in the ways of English architects in the sub-continent – above all Lutyens, but many others less well-known. Gradidge, his long hair plaited in a pigtail, his tree-trunk legs visible beneath a kilt, was a distinctive figure with the barking voice of an Indian Army colonel. He was an advanced Anglo-Catholic, and Stamp, who had loved church architecture since he was a boy, began to be a churchgoer.

Somewhat to the horror of Gradidge and other bachelor friends, Stamp married Alexandra Artley, a clever English graduate from the University of Leeds, who worked as a secretary at the Architectural Press and would eventually establish a name for herself as a witty columnist in glossy magazines. The bachelors never appreciated the fact that Stamp was always deeply attracted to clever women. The Stamps had two daughters, Agnes, named after the lost church of St Agnes Kennington, and Cecilia.

Since neither Stamp nor his wife did anything which a building society would have regarded as useful, they were unable to get a mortgage, but Barclays Bank Redcar (Artley's local bank) lent them £50,000 to buy an elegant little house near King's Cross Station – 1, St Chad Street. It became a mecca for all their friends, and they held more or less open house. Gavin would stand by the old-fashioned hissing gas fire (bought from architectural salvage) dispensing whisky, while Alex, puffing cigarettes at the other corner of the room (a habit of which Stamp hotly disapproved) would keep their friends howling with laughter.

One of the children, surveying the everlastingly unfinished process of 'restoration' in which their house existed – the bags of cement, the neatly hung architectural prints on the scraped, but undecorated walls – once asked, 'Why don't we live in a house like other people's houses?' Alex immortalised their domestic chaos in her columns, eventually turned into a book, called *Hoorah for the Filth Packets*.

Stamp always said he would never take a job and never leave London. He continued to write the Piloti column, to turn out a series of well-received books, and to join the likes of Colin Amery and Dan Cruickshank, Lucy Lambton and the Betjemans in trying to prevent the wreckage of Britain.

But the Stamps were poor and it was flattering to be asked to become the Professor of Architectural History at the Mackintosh School of Art in 1990. They sold the St Chad Street house before the property boom really took off – and always regretted doing so. In Glasgow, they bought the house built by the neoclassical architect Greek Thomson, and started the Greek Thomson

164

Society. (Stamp loved societies, was a keen member of the Victorian Society and was the founder member of the 1930s Society, which morphed into the Twentieth Century Society).

He was much loved in Glasgow. His lectures were dazzling slideshows, with more than 200 images per lecture, as he shared his encyclopaedic knowledge and infectious enthusiasm. But it was a taxing time domestically. His marriage unravelled, and when he returned to live in London, it was alone.

He told Glasgow friends that he was homesick for the sight of the backs of London stockbrick houses, seen from the train. He went to live in what was in effect a bedsit in Forest Hill.

Although he had produced many fine books, including those which reflected his passion for photography, Stamp never wrote the single great architectural monograph that might have been expected. In some ways his most beautiful book is *The Memorial to the Missing of the Somme*. It reflects his passion for Lutyens, and his obsession with the First World War. It is also a demonstration of his brilliance as a writer, with what he called 'a sense of the eternally tragic'.

In the last phase of his life, Stamp, the hater of cigarettes, fell in love with another smoker, Rosemary Hill, biographer of Augustus Welby Pugin. They married. It was a meeting of minds, as well as a love match.

Gavin Stamp, born March 15 1948, died December 30 2017

Mark E. Smith

Lead singer of Mancunian band The Fall whose
abrasive exterior concealed a deep poetic sensibility

Smith in later life: 'If it's me and your granny on bongos, it is still The Fall'

MARK E. SMITH, who has died after a long illness aged 60, was
the incorrigibly truculent lead singer with The Fall.

Smith's group was formed in north Manchester in 1976.
Over the following four decades, during which period their
contemporaries became gradually subdued, diversified their style
or simply retired, The Fall remained tenaciously committed to the
abrasive spirit of the punk movement. Mark Smith did not mellow
with age.

His character was an unusual combination of deep poetic
sensibility and belligerence. His encounters with the press tended
to be eventful and, despite his slight build, he often struggled
to refrain from violence. 'Mark E. Smith will be remembered as
a man who believed that the pen is mightier than the sword,'

Robert Chalmers wrote in *The Independent on Sunday* in 2011, 'but who did not always have a pen to hand.'

Among the things for which Smith expressed a particular loathing were: London; doctors; Jane Austen; Beaujolais; psychologists; Manchester United; *The Guardian*; David Bowie; the NYPD; 'soft lads who blab'; John Lennon; nouvelle cuisine; Australia; Princess Diana; the smoking ban in pubs; Bob Geldof ('a dickhead'); the football pundits Alan Hansen and Alan Shearer ('they look like retired policemen: I bet they go shopping together'); Brighton ('s--t pubs, s--t music, s--t beaches'); the works of J. R. R. Tolkien; David Cameron; 'beer-minded proles'; Kojak ('a t--t'), and the town of Stockport.

To refer to The Fall as a group is somewhat misleading, in that the band's personnel functioned as a vehicle for Smith's perverse but inspired songwriting. 'If it's me and your granny on bongos,' Smith once said, 'it is still The Fall.'

As a singer he favoured a distinctive declamatory style which was more notable for its volume and tone of sardonic menace that for its adherence to the chromatic scale. The music was diverse, sometimes poppy but typically uncompromising, and underpinned (from 1979 to 1998) by the propulsive bass guitar of Stephen Hanley, who played, one critic remarked, 'with the remorseless concentration of a communist factory operative'.

The band could never have been said to function as a democracy, and Smith, who played God in a 2007 episode of Johnny Vegas's television comedy series *Ideal*, sacked so many group members that there is a book, *The Fallen*, by Dave Simpson, cataloguing the experiences of former accompanists: their total, excluding Smith, is estimated at 66. He once dismissed a sound engineer for having ordered a salad.

The most famous musician dismissed by Smith was Marc Riley (now a DJ on BBC Radio 6 Music), who, despite having been sacked on his wedding day in the wake of a punch-up, still describes Mark Smith as 'a genius'.

For all his less amenable impulses, Smith was one of the true originals of popular music, and The Fall was tirelessly championed by enthusiasts such as the broadcaster John Peel. 'With The Fall,' Peel said, 'you can never be quite sure of what you are going to get. Sometimes it might not be what you want.'

Smith was brought up at Sedgley Park, a working-class neighbourhood of Salford. His first wife, Brix Smith, was a graduate of the august Bennington College in Vermont. Born Laura Elisse Salenger – she adopted her *nom de guerre* in homage to the song *Guns of Brixton* by the Clash – she came from a privileged background in California.

In her 2016 memoir *The Rise, The Fall, and The Rise*, she gives her first impressions of coming to live in Smith's rather modest flat, equipped with neither shower nor washing machine: 'I never expected Manchester to be so grim. Its glowering Victorian red-brick buildings looked like mean structures where horrible atrocities had been committed ... The people seemed joyless. Nobody smiled ... Mark loved this city.'

Smith, a former docks worker, wrote songs with refrains such as 'Yeah Yeah, Industrial Estate' – from *Industrial Estate*, a track on the band's seminal 1978 album *Live at the Witch Trials*. Just as the comforting opulence of California summers had infused the songs of the Beach Boys with a sunny joie de vivre, so the more challenging landscape of Manchester after dark nurtured the furious defiance in Smith's songwriting – and attitude.

'Nobody,' said Tony Wilson, the founder of Factory Records who first put The Fall on television (on Granada in 1977), 'exemplifies attitude more than Mark E. Smith. He is attitude personified. The Fall was always more about attitude than music.'

Mark Edward Smith was born at Lower Broughton, Salford, on March 5 1957. The house in which he spent his infancy is in the shadow of the Cliff, then the training ground for Manchester United. The neighbourhood is dominated by that club's supporters; Smith, unsurprisingly, professed a fervent allegiance to Manchester City.

His father Jack was a plumber, like his father before him; his mother Irene worked for the post office. 'My dad's attitude,' said Smith, 'was either you follow me into the business, or you join the Army.' He had three younger sisters. Having passed his 11-plus, Smith attended Stand Grammar School, where his academic performance, especially in English, was commended as outstanding.

As a schoolboy he displayed a sensitivity that he would spend the rest of his life seeking to deny, preferring to espouse the values of his father and paternal grandfather, both no-nonsense ex-servicemen. 'Manchester has always produced men like this,' Smith said. 'Hard men with hard livers. Men with faces like unmade beds.'

He left school on his 16th birthday and worked on Salford docks, initially as a cargo-handler, then as a clerical worker. In the evenings, he attended a class in A-level English literature but never took the exam. An admirer of Aleister Crowley and H. P. Lovecraft, he named his group after the novel by Albert Camus, *La Chute*.

While in public he enjoyed sneering at the notion of art and literature, Smith would go on to produce two acclaimed albums of his own poetry. One of his most notable achievements, produced at the Edinburgh Festival in 1988, was the ballet *I Am Curious, Orange*, an ambitious collaboration with the dancer and choreographer Michael Clark. (It became the album *I Am Kurious Oranj*.)

As a teenager Smith listened to Northern soul and had a fondness for mainstream pop virtuosos such as Joni Mitchell. He began writing performance poetry and experimenting with music with his first girlfriend, a psychiatric nurse called Una Baines, and a gifted young guitarist, Martin Bramah. As a youth, Una Baines recalled, Smith was an ardent socialist and committed feminist.

If his early influences – such as the German electronic ensemble Can, Iggy Pop and the Sex Pistols – remained detectable, there was always something about Smith that suggested he was in touch with another reality. Considered by many friends and family members to be psychic, for some years he gave tarot readings. On a childhood holiday, Smith said, he 'began speaking in tongues, in Rhyl'.

The first serious incarnation of The Fall, including Smith, Una Baines and Bramah, seemed to arrive fully formed. The broadcaster Danny Baker early on recognised the unhinged ferocity of songs such as *Totally Wired* and the peculiarly compelling poetry of titles like *Hex Enduction Hour* (1982), the fourth album. Jonathan Demme used one of The Fall's best known anthems, *Hip Priest*, in his film *The Silence of the Lambs*. Another Fall track, *Touch Sensitive*, was used to advertise the Vauxhall Corsa. ('I needed the money,' Smith explained. 'We are not all Elton John.')

It was 1983 before the group appeared on national television, at John Peel's request, on Channel Four's *The Tube*. By this time the singer's liking for alcohol and amphetamines was already public knowledge.

Although Peel adored The Fall's work, he and Smith were not soulmates. 'Never in my life,' Peel said of one encounter, 'have I been in a room that so crackled with malevolence.'

Smith, though he remained a dedicated advocate of socialism, surprised many of his supporters when, in 1982, he vigorously endorsed Margaret Thatcher's decision to engage with Argentina over the Falkland Islands.

Mark E. Smith married three times. He met Brix Smith at a club in Chicago in April 1983; they were married in north Manchester that November. He left her in 1989 for Saffron Prior, the daughter of a friend, who ran The Fall's fan club; their marriage was dissolved in 1995.

He met his third wife, the Greek Elena Poulou, at a bar in Berlin in 2000. His last partner was the photographer Pamela Vander, three decades his junior, who managed the group.

He tended to recruit his wives and girlfriends as members of the band. The most significant contributor was Brix (subsequently romantically linked to the violinist Nigel Kennedy). She was The Fall's guitarist between 1983 and 1989 and would rejoin for two years in 1994. She helped to engineer the band's most commercially successful periods.

Brix Smith persuaded the scruffy-looking Smith and the rest of the band to dress with some concessions to style. For a time they achieved mainstream recognition with songs like their covers of R. Dean Taylor's *There's a Ghost in My House* and The Kinks' *Victoria*, both of which entered the Top 40, as well as *Mr Pharmacist*, first performed by the San Francisco hippy group The Other Half. In the late Eighties, for a while, they were almost fashionable.

'Always different, always the same,' John Peel said of The Fall. Smith released 32 studio albums with the group. Some, like the most recent, *New Facts Emerge* (2017), could be disappointing. Others, such as *The Light User Syndrome*, a 1996 album which includes one of his finest songs, *Cheetham Hill*, were magnificent.

Theme From Sparta FC, from the 2003 album *The Real New Fall LP*, was for some years used to introduce the football scores on BBC One's *Final Score*.

By the late 1990s he was collaborating with his girlfriend Julia Adamson, and his altercations with male band members were increasingly frequent and public. 'I have never molested a woman,' Smith observed, 'or hit anybody who didn't deserve it.'

In 2004 BBC Four made *The Wonderful and Frightening World of Mark E. Smith*, a documentary in which Alan Wise, who managed both The Fall and the German chanteuse Nico, said: 'Mark's tremendous use of drugs, notably speed, clearly shows in his face. Mark is a hard drinker and a tough man. He has great talent. He has charisma. He is not "a nice guy".'

Smith himself said: 'I am one of the three per cent who were born to take speed. It helps me sleep.'

On another occasion, he boasted: 'People are s--t scared of me. I do actually enjoy that. I do not want or require security guards. I don't think that security guards are very good for your writing.'

In 2004, after the death of John Peel, *Newsnight* interviewed Smith live. 'Who are you?' Smith snarled, having pointed out that he scarcely knew Peel, to a visibly perturbed Gavin Esler. 'Who are you anyhow? The next DJ?'

In 2017 he cancelled a string of concerts in the United States and Britain, citing lung and dental problems. Friends said that he had developed osteoporosis, a condition sometimes associated with alcoholism.

Few were surprised when on March 5 2017, Smith's 60th birthday, the BBC mistakenly announced his death. Defiant to the last, he gave his final performance in Glasgow on November 4 2017, from a wheelchair and with his right arm in a sling. 'I think it is over,' he proclaimed. 'I think it is ending.'

For many years his concerts would end with the crowd singing along to the chorus of *Hip Priest*: 'He is not appreciated.' If those admirers had to identify a single source of regret at his disappearance, it might be that his aberrant behaviour earned the troubled artist a level of public recognition that his music would never achieve, at least in his lifetime.

Mark E. Smith, born March 5 1957, died January 24 2018

Hannah Hauxwell

Farmer whose frugal and solitary life in the Dales
featured in an acclaimed documentary

Hannah Hauxwell: her farm had no electricity, running water or central heating.
'I'm always amazed that people should be interested. I've led a very simple life'

HANNAH HAUXWELL, who has died aged 91, was a Daleswoman
who in 1973 captured the hearts of the nation when her solitary
life on the remote Low Birk Hatt Farm, near the North Pennine
village of Baldersdale, then in the North Riding of Yorkshire (now
in County Durham), became the subject of an award-winning
Yorkshire Television documentary, *Too Long a Winter*.

Three years earlier she had been the subject of an article in
the *Yorkshire Post* entitled 'How to be happy on £170 a year'. By
the time Barry Cockroft turned up to make his film chronicling a
community of North Country people and their struggle to survive
in the harsh Pennine winters, her income had risen to around
£250 a year. The average salary at the time was £2,000.

Hannah Hauxwell had inherited her parents' dilapidated
80-acre farm when she was 34. There was no electricity, running

water or central heating, and she tended her small herd of cattle in layers of raggedy clothing when temperatures were below freezing. It was mainly from the sale of a few of these 'beasts' that her modest income was derived.

Though she had lived an isolated life, often going for a fortnight without seeing another human being, Hannah Hauxwell turned out to be a television 'natural'. As Sean Day-Lewis observed in a review of the documentary in *The Daily Telegraph*, she 'upstaged people and beasts and even the grand surrounding landscape' with her 'extraordinary dignity, simplicity and acceptance [which] shone without a hint of acting or editorial manipulation'.

Hannah, then 46 and unmarried, was shown hauling water from the stream, lugging logs, setting out in blizzards to tend her animals and breaking the ice on a pond to keep them watered. Pink-cheeked, white-haired, twinkly, and with a simple, old-fashioned turn of phrase, she was seen unaffectedly discussing the cow pail she used as a bath, the bread deliveries which were left at a gate three fields away, and the night the chimney above her kitchen coal fire collapsed and she ended up sleeping in the byre with her favourite cow.

Other sequences showed her obviously enjoying a rare night out at a harvest festival supper and dance, and hanging food in plastic bags from hooks in the ceiling (formerly used, she explained, 'for funerals and pig killings') to prevent it being eaten by rats.

Although Hannah Hauxwell had been hermetically sealed from the modern comforts most people take for granted, her other-worldliness struck a chord with viewers. Her almost beatific contentment with her lot, her immaculate manners and quiet strength, shaped by adversity, seemed to provide evidence that modern society, with all its getting and spending, had forgotten something essential and human.

The film made Hannah Hauxwell into something of a celebrity. She found herself travelling halfway around the world for further documentaries, with accompanying books including *Seasons of My Life* (1989) and *Daughter of the Dales* (1990).

She was guest of honour at a Women Of The Year gala at the Savoy Hotel in London (wearing the first dress she had bought since her mother's funeral), attended a Buckingham Palace garden party and appeared on *This Is Your Life*, when she seemed genuinely to have no idea who Michael Aspel was.

Yet she continued to live a frugal life and remained unspoilt by fame: 'I'm always amazed that people should be interested,' she said in 2008. 'I've led such a very simple life.'

An only child, Hannah Hauxwell was born at Baldersdale on August 1 1926 and was three when her family moved to Low Birk Hatt Farm. It was too small to be a commercial hill farm, and her father had paid too much for it at auction for it ever to be a going concern. He died when Hannah was still a girl, and her uncle moved in to help her mother Lydia try to make a go of it.

Her mother died in her sixties, followed three years later by her uncle. 'And then the loneliness came down,' she told *The Daily Telegraph* in 1996. 'You can't be in a household with people who care about you and then be the only one left without it hurting.'

When *Too Long A Winter* was aired, her life was changed. Yorkshire Television's switchboard was inundated for several days with viewers wanting to offer help. A local factory raised money to connect her farm to the National Grid and she received letters and donations from well-wishers around the world. She was given a cooker, and an electric kettle ('such a blessing,' she recalled): one winter she had gone without a hot drink, apart from warm milk from Rosa the cow, for four days.

In 1988, however, after decades of running the farm on her own, ill health and a series of bitter winters persuaded Hannah Hauxwell to sell up, prompting the Yorkshire Television team to return to film a second documentary, *A Winter Too Many* (1989). The film showed that she had a little more money, which she had invested in a few more cows, and she was seen bidding her farm a tearful goodbye.

Hannah Hauxwell moved to a cottage at Cotherstone, a nearby village, telling an interviewer that hot water and a flushing lavatory had come as something of a culture shock.

'I have a fridge that doesn't work,' she went on. 'And a telephone – but it's not always convenient, so I don't always answer it. There's also a washing machine. I don't know if it works, because I've never tried it. I do it by hand. It's not one of my favourite jobs, but that's how I've always done it.'

In 1991 Barry Cockcroft made *Innocent Abroad*, a six-part series following Hannah Hauxwell, by now 65, on a trip to continental Europe. 'It is totally unsexy and there is not a young person in sight anywhere,' observed the Canadian *Globe and Mail*. 'The main character speaks with a thick regional accent, may not be in possession of her own teeth and has lived her entire life in a British backwater communing more with cows than humans. Yet *Innocent Abroad* has more charm, exquisite scenery and wit than most of what passes for entertainment on this side of the Atlantic Ocean.'

The series was followed by another trip, to America, in 1993.

Asked whether she would have liked to join the modern world sooner, she admitted that she had not enjoyed 'the really hard bits' of her life, but added: 'I liked the farming and I loved my beasties and I had the countryside, and nature all around me, and books and music and good friends. You really don't need much more than that.'

Hannah Hauxwell spent her final years in a nursing home, where she listened constantly to the radio.

She never married, explaining that she had never met anyone she felt 'special' about.

Hannah Hauxwell, born August 1 1926, died January 30 2018

Emma Smith

Award-winning novelist whose writing career
flourished again after half a century in obscurity

EMMA SMITH, who has died aged 94, looked set fair in the
late 1940s to become one of Britain's leading novelists after
publishing two highly successful books in her early twenties; in
the event she virtually stopped writing, but in old age she saw her
early works republished to renewed acclaim, and resumed her
career with two highly praised volumes of autobiography.

She was able, in her early fiction, to draw on a range of
unusually adventurous experiences for a young middle-class
woman of her generation, having been spared the expected life
of secretarial drudgery by the intervention of the Second World
War.

She was born Elspeth Hallsmith in Newquay on August 21
1923, into what she called 'a deeply unhappy, dysfunctional
family'. Her father Guthrie, a bank clerk who had been badly

affected by his service in the Great War, 'overshadowed our family like a black cloud', she said.

He was prone to terrifying outbursts and when she was 12, not long after the family had moved from Cornwall to Dartmoor, she felt relief when he abandoned his wife Janet and their children to pursue a career as a painter. In later life, though, she came to appreciate how much he had done, despite his other shortcomings, to stimulate her love of literature.

Early in the war she went to do clerical work for a branch of the War Office – or MI5, as she admitted in later life – in Blenheim Palace, but although glad to have escaped home she was bored stiff, and answered an advertisement for women to work on canal narrowboats that had been grounded since their male crews had been called up. Aged 19 she found herself working with other young women from all social backgrounds on three-week round-trips ferrying steel to Birmingham and coal back to London.

It was physically demanding work and lavatory facilities were rudimentary – it was 'bucket and chuck it', she recalled – but she was proud to earn the respect of bargemen and dockers, and found the experience hugely liberating.

In 1948 she published *Maidens' Trip*, a lightly fictionalised account of her adventures, which won the John Llewellyn Rhys Prize and was a bestseller. 'It was what people wanted, something light-hearted about the war,' she reflected in old age.

In the meantime she had met the film-maker Raymond 'Bunny' Keene when he asked her to dance at the Gargoyle Club, and in 1946 she agreed to accompany him as a gofer on a trip to India to make a documentary about tea plantations.

The scriptwriter accompanying the party was Laurie Lee, who encouraged her early attempts at writing (as she encouraged his) and suggested that she take 'Emma Smith' as a pseudonym. 'People always tried to make me say I had a love affair with Laurie,' she said in 2009. 'But he was just a very good friend. I went off [him], though – he needed so much adulation.'

The contrast between drab wartime London and the colour of Bombay and Calcutta hit her 'like an explosion', she said, and she kept a detailed diary of her trip; on her return she went to live in Paris and started to write another novel based on her experiences.

One day while working on her typewriter by the Seine she was unwittingly snapped by the photographer Robert Doisneau. The picture became one of the most famous examples of his work, but it was not until 2013 that Emma Smith revealed herself to be its subject.

Her second novel, *The Far Cry*, was published in 1949; the story of an English girl spirited off to India by her neurotic father to escape the clutches of his loathed ex-wife, her mother, it proved to be Emma Smith's masterpiece. It was another popular and critical success, and won the James Tait Black Memorial Prize. Elizabeth Bowen hailed 'a savage comedy with a vicious streak ... She brings to English fiction something too often lacking: a superabundant vitality.'

In 1951 Emma Smith married Richard Stewart-Jones, an architectural conservationist who had once been the lover of James Lees-Milne, a month after she had met him at a new year ball. She enjoyed a smart social life unlike anything she had known before, and lost interest in writing.

In 1957 her husband died of a heart attack, leaving considerable debts, and Emma Smith went to live with her son and daughter in a cottage with no electricity or running water in Wales; she occupied her time by writing children's books. She published another novel for adults, *The Opportunity of a Lifetime*, in 1978, and the following year *Maidens' Trip* was dramatised on BBC Two, but it was not until 2002, when Persephone Books reissued *The Far Cry* as part of a series of neglected classics by women, that her work again received serious attention.

Emma Smith, who wore bright colours and even as an octogenarian had an air of 1930s Bohemia, was delighted to receive praise from writers such as Michael Ondaatje. She decided to return to writing for a wider audience, keen to record her experiences for her grandchildren.

Her two volumes of memoirs were *The Great Western Beach* (2008), describing her childhood in Cornwall, and *As Green As*

Grass (2013), which dealt with her life up to her marriage; it was typical of her determined personality that she finished the latter book despite having broken her back. Her publisher noted that she had 'total recall' and, unlike many memoirists, invented nothing.

Emma Smith is survived by her son and daughter.

Emma Smith, born August 21 1923, died April 24 2018

Maurizio 'Zanza' Zanfanti

Lothario from Rimini whose fame mirrored the seaside resort's expansion as a citadel of hedonism

Zanza in the mid-1980s, by which time the Italian Adriatic had reached the peak of its popularity as a package holiday destination for northern Europeans

MAURIZIO 'ZANZA' ZANFANTI, who has died aged 62 while *in flagrante*, was the most famous Latin lover of the package holiday boom in Italy, of which the epicentre was his home town Rimini.

In his prime, women queued up to be seduced by him and according to legend he slept with thousands.

He died of a heart attack at around two in the morning in his Mitsubishi Pajero 4x4, parked in a small peach grove owned by his family, seconds after making love with a 25-year-old Romanian woman, who raised the alarm.

Maurizio Zanfanti was born on October 20 1955 into a family of poor peasant farmers who lived near Rimini on the Adriatic coast. Italy was still a largely agricultural country, devastated by the Fascist period and the Second World War but on the brink of the 1960s economic miracle which would see its GDP briefly overtake Britain's.

Young Maurizio left school at 16 with no qualifications and in 1972 became a *buttadentro* (thrower-in, literally) at a notorious discotheque called Blow Up. His job was to search for women on the beach and in bars and entice them with free tickets and smooth talk to go with him to Blow Up.

The work paid him a pittance, but gave him carte blanche to accost young women at will and engage them in conversation.

His rise to fame as a seaside end-of-the-pier version of Casanova was as rapid as the rise to fame of Rimini as a citadel of hedonism. So effective was he that he quickly earned the nickname 'Zanza', short for *zanzara* – the Italian word for mosquito.

In those years, mass tourism transformed the Adriatic coast into one long, endless line of brutally ugly hotels, apartment blocks, bars, restaurants and discotheques, and the sandy shore in front into a forest of beach umbrellas.

Federico Fellini was also born in Rimini and his Oscar-winning 1973 masterpiece *Amarcord* ('I remember' in local dialect) is about a year in the life of this small coastal town before mass tourism stole its soul. He wrote in a 1976 memoir: 'I don't like going back to Rimini.'

Nevertheless, few Italians cared enough to stop the desecration, since most cared more about the money it brought to their economy. Least of all the young Zanfanti. For him, this desecration was not just a means of making a living: it was paradise on earth.

Such was his status as a serial seducer of the tourists from northern Europe who flocked to the Adriatic in the 1970s and 1980s in search of sun, sea and sex that he was often front-page news in Germany and Scandinavia.

In 1984 the German tabloid *Bild* dedicated two pages to him, calling him the 'Sex Bomber Der Nation'. A pop song he and staff at Blow Up made reached No 2 in the Swedish charts.

Short and swarthy, he had dense caveman-style hair which he dyed golden brown. He wore his shirts unbuttoned to the waist or, better still, just a skimpy leather waistcoat, to display to full advantage his chunky gold chains, tanned torso and hairy chest. He invariably wore platform heels and had a fondness for tight leather trousers.

But he was blessed with innate charm and it was this – they say – that bowled over the women. A Norwegian, Mette Homburg, now 50, told the *Corriere della Sera* after his death that when she met him at Blow Up in 1984 his first words to her were 'Ciao, bella'.

'But they were enough,' she explained, 'to make me fall in love with him, and I was so in love. He had the air of being a macho man but he was so nice, and so funny.' For three years, Mette returned each summer to Rimini just for Zanza, and they remained friends until his death. 'I knew he had loads of women, but it didn't matter.'

Many other old flames kept in touch down the years and some even organised group trips decades later to see him in Rimini for reunion parties.

In a typical three-month summer season, he used to say, his average tally was 200 women, roughly two a day, rising to four a day in the infernal heat of August. He knew how many there were because he recorded each one, with brief details, in notebooks which rapidly filled up and had to be replaced. But he always declined to reveal the grand total, which is reckoned to be 6,000.

'They were nearly all foreign women,' he said. 'The Italians had to make do with my brother.'

After his death, Walter Lanzetti, who owned the now long gone Blow Up discotheque, told the Bologna-based daily *Il Resto del Carlino* that he took him on as a *buttadentro* all those years ago, and then as artistic director, because he knew a bit of Swedish, which no one else did, and he always had a smile on his face.

And what drove his passion to seduce women – insisted Signor Lanzetti, however unlikely it may seem – was an altruistic sense of duty. 'He didn't do it for fame, or to be top of the *cucadores*

(Latin lover) league tables which existed in those days,' Lanzetti said, 'He just wanted to make women happy. Zanza was a romantic.'

However, the arrival of AIDS in the 1980s, combined with a growing awareness of feminism, began to curtail his activities. These developments coincided with the decline of the Italian Adriatic as the package holiday destination of choice for northern Europeans. '1988 was a lean summer,' Zanza conceded. 'Only 120 women.'

When in 1993 *Bild* warned female readers to beware Italian philanderers brandishing forged medical certificates on the beach or in the disco to 'prove' that they did not have HIV, Zanza was swift to leap to his own defence.

'Me, I keep my certificate signed and countersigned by the doctor in my wallet,' he told *la Repubblica*. 'But I've yet to meet a girl who has ever wanted to see it.'

In 2015, by now 60, Zanza announced his retirement in *il Resto del Carlino*, insisting that he had 'done more for the promotion of tourism in Rimini than 100 travel agencies'.

He never married but is thought to have fathered nine children dotted about Scandinavia and Germany.

Asked once if he had ever been in love, he replied: 'I cannot allow myself to do it. I cannot allow myself to stop ... Work is work.'

His family's parish priest refused to allow his funeral in their local church, not because in canon law Zanza was a *peccator manifestus* ('notorious sinner'), but because the priest did not want – or so he said – a media scrum in his church.

Instead, the funeral took place, regardless of canon law, in the chapel at the cemetery in Rimini in which Zanza was afterwards buried – a stone's throw from Fellini's grave.

Hundreds of people, including the mayor, were present. Many said that Zanza deserved if not a street in his name, then at least a medal.

Throughout his life as a *tombeur de femmes* Zanza lived on the first floor of the family farmhouse above his mother Teresa, who is 80 and still owns a small fishmonger's nearby, his brother Loris and sister Mara, neither of whom is married. They all survive him.

Though his mother was 'not happy' (as he once put it) with the life he had led, he did his bit each day at the family fish shop and on their farm. After his death, she told the press: 'He was a good boy, who always helped me.'

Maurizio Zanfanti, born October 20 1955, died September 26 2018

Nigel Morgan

Adventurer dubbed 'Nosher' who was embroiled in the abortive 'Wonga' coup in Equatorial Guinea

Morgan: he suggested that Stephen Fry could play him in a docudrama

NIGEL MORGAN, who has died aged 64, was an adventurer and bon viveur with a hatred of authority and convention and a tendency to depression; he attracted enemies as easily as he did friends.

Barrel-shaped, orange-haired and with a bright red swollen face, Morgan was affectionately known as Football Face, Nosher or Captain Pig (the last two on account of his mammoth appetite for rich food and pints of pink gin). As a young man he spent a few years in the Irish Guards when he was, by his own account, 'the only officer not allowed to carry a gun for his own safety', then worked at the Thatcherite think tank, the Centre for Policy Studies, for a couple of years under its equally pugnacious ex-communist director Sir Alfred Sherman, resigning in 1983.

In the late 1980s Morgan rescued an old farmhouse in Herefordshire and embraced the life of an 18th century squire, riding a terrifying 17-hand bolter called Fred, and holding debauched parties dedicated to the notorious rake 'Mad Jack' Mytton in his barn. Then, apparently tiring of a life of excess, he decided to train as a Jesuit priest in Birmingham and stuck it out for almost a year before departing in high dudgeon after a row with his superior about the involvement of order members in Leftist 'liberation theology'.

He then tried the life of a gold prospector in the Yukon, and later a disastrous alluvial gold-buying venture in Liberia in which he lost $1 million of investors' money buying gold-coated brass. In the 1990s he moved, as a freelance security consultant, to South Africa, where he spent his last 25 years and where, in 2004, he was one of the colourful cast of assorted renegades, chancers, politicians and shady businessmen named in connection with the so-called 'Wonga' plot – a botched coup against the dictator of oil-rich Equatorial Guinea.

The plot was nipped in the bud in March 2004 when police in the Zimbabwean capital, Harare, probably tipped off by the intelligence authorities in South Africa, impounded a plane which had flown in from Pretoria and arrested Simon Mann, an Old Etonian ex-SAS officer, and more than 60 others, amid suspicions that they were mercenaries.

Mann was eventually jailed in Equatorial Guinea (he eventually served 15 months of a 34-year sentence) after admitting conspiring to oust the president. The incident received international media attention after the reported involvement of Lady Thatcher's son, Sir Mark Thatcher, in funding the coup.

Morgan was a close friend of both Mann and Thatcher, and his name first appeared in the press as one of the addressees on a desperate letter, written by Mann in Zimbabwe's Chikurubi Prison shortly after his arrest, appealing to his friends for 'splodges of wonga' to bribe his way out of jail. The letter, which was leaked, implicated Mark Thatcher – referred to as 'Scratcher' – and Morgan (described in press reports of the time as a

187

specialist in security services for the Democratic Republic of Congo's mining industry) in activities linked to the planned coup.

As Morgan was known to be close to certain people in the South African government for whom he had written risk analyses, those involved in the plot apparently thought that they had the support, or at least tacit backing, of lower-level sources in the administration.

But Morgan's involvement was not all it seemed. As it emerged later in leaked intelligence reports, he had been regularly passing reports on the 'Wonga' operation to the South African secret services. He had also, allegedly, planted a mole to work as one of Mann's assistants.

In his book *The Wonga Coup* (2006), Adam Roberts portrayed Morgan as an enigmatic and ambivalent individual; both a keen participant in the plot and yet also an agent for the South African government, though Roberts was unclear about whether Morgan could be described as a double agent, suggesting that Mann might have known Morgan was informing the authorities about the planned coup to get their feedback.

In an article in 2009 in the *Daily Mail*, however, Andrew Malone reported that Morgan had admitted to him that he had been a double agent, taking $10,000 from Mann for his help in the plot but then tipping off South African intelligence. Mann's mood, the journalist reported, had not been helped by learning that someone he considered a close friend had betrayed him for a 'pot of gold'. Morgan, though, was unrepentant: 'I warned Simon not to do it, but he wouldn't listen,' he told Malone. 'So he shouldn't whinge now. What he was doing was amoral.'

Morgan was also reported to be on 'non-speakers' with Mark Thatcher having, according to Malone, promised him it was safe to return to South Africa after the coup was smashed, only for the Iron Lady's son to be seized by the country's elite Scorpions crime squad. In January 2005 Thatcher was fined the equivalent of £265,000 for breaking South Africa's anti-mercenary laws by providing funds for a helicopter for the operation. He denied knowing about the plot but was given a four-year suspended jail sentence in a plea bargain.

When in 2005 the BBC was reported to be busy preparing a docudrama based on the story, the consultant for it was none other than Morgan, who suggested Hugh Laurie for the part of Mann and Stephen Fry for himself.

Nigel Morgan was born on September 25 1954, in Woking, Surrey, the son of Ronan Morgan, a hard-drinking publisher who was a familiar figure in the Fleet Street wine bar, El Vino, and who treated his son robustly. When Nigel ran away from prep school, which he hated, his father always took him back, despite promises not to, shaking Nigel's faith in the adult world. An uncle was Cliff Morgan, the former rugby player and television sports commentator.

Nigel's mother Pamela was a loving but depressive woman who abandoned her family soon after the death in a motorcycle accident of Nigel's older brother, Malcolm, in 1970. Nigel was 16 and the tragedy – and his mother's departure – affected him deeply.

From Cranleigh School, Nigel joined the Irish Guards, the regiment of his idolised older brother, and went on an Army bursary to Durham University, where he read Politics and became president of the Union. Hoping to get out of the five-year service commitment that went with the bursary, he informed his CO that he 'couldn't command a tea trolley' and made himself determinedly objectionable – all to no avail.

Leaving the Army, he went to work at the Centre for Policy Studies under Sir Alfred Sherman. History does not relate the reasons for his resignation in 1983, but the pair were said to have matched each other in certainty and belligerence. He then worked for a time for David Hart, the millionaire businessman and freelance adviser to Margaret Thatcher known to friends as 'Spiv'.

After moving to South Africa in 1992, Morgan set himself up as an expert in sub-Saharan affairs, writing trenchant political and commercial analysis for multinationals and risk management companies in London. He started a specialist security company and became involved in advising companies with mining interests in the Congo. On one outing to a diamond mine in the country, he claimed to have been poisoned, almost fatally, with a rare lizard saliva by local chiefs and ministers. He had to be airlifted to Johannesburg, spent several days in an induced coma, but somehow recovered.

According to friends, Morgan's company was eventually 'stolen' from him by a fraudulent employee, leaving him penniless. Nothing if not resilient, he built a second security company. When he was ousted from this firm, too, he went on a massive bender which resulted in him being put into an induced coma for a second time.

He resurfaced sufficiently to leave hospital, but in the end was unable to recover from the accumulated toll of a life of excess which finally destroyed his liver.

Morgan did not marry. Though he had several glamorous and aristocratic girlfriends over the years he never really understood women, treating them with a combination of affection and what a friend described as 'bantering hostility, often disguised as real hostility'.

He is survived by his sister Nicky.

Nigel Morgan, born September 25 1954, died November 17 2018

Baroness Trumpington

Former Bletchley Park cipher clerk who became a
much-loved institution in the House of Lords

BARONESS
TRUMPINGTON,
who has died
aged 96, was a
former mayor
of Cambridge
and became
the oldest and
second longest-
serving member
of John Major's
administration;
she was also
by far the most
popular.

Built to last,
forthright and formidable, Jean Trumpington made up for any
lack of intellectual brilliance with a capacity for hard work
combined with down-to-earth common sense and an engaging
habit of telling jokes against herself.

First recruited into Government ranks in 1983 as a Lords
whip, her first job was to act as 'keeper of the gate' by placing her
imposing form next to the most popular exit to persuade errant
Conservative peers to vote. But in fact she became far more
effective in this role as a government minister; the prospect of a
vintage performance by Jean Trumpington was usually enough to
pack the chamber.

In 1987, as a minister at the Department of Health and Social
Security, in answer to a question about whether AIDS could be
transmitted by insects, she replied: 'I have replies to questions on
bed bugs and monkeys, but I regret that I do not have fleas.'

In 1992, as an agriculture minister, she gave an answer to a question in which she referred to 'the Commission's proposals for reforming the CAP would replace existing support arrangements by a system of compensatory aid, linked directly or indirectly to the cultivated area or the number of animals kept by each farmer,' ending with: 'And if you understand that, you're a better man than I, Gunga Din.'

In October 1993, shortly after her appointment as a spokesman at the Department of National Heritage, she confessed to finding it difficult to master her brief and during one flustering question session she admitted: 'I had been worried I might get my knickers in a twist.'

The following year, wearing a stout woollen suit that evoked her career in naval intelligence, she struck an incongruous figure as the department's representative at rock music awards: 'I am here to collect autographs for my secretary,' she announced. 'Is Elton John here?'

'I seem fated,' she protested unconvincingly. 'When I'm trying very hard to be dignified, something always goes hideously wrong.'

In 2011 she was captured on camera giving a V-sign to Lord King of Bridgwater (Tom King) when he referred to her as looking 'pretty old' during a Remembrance debate. 'It was entirely between him and me – I thought,' she told *The Daily Telegraph*'s Elizabeth Grice. 'I wasn't conscious of there being television [cameras there]. I did that [she repeats the gesture with faux innocence] to his face. His family say he is famous now.' She repeated the two-fingered salute at Ken Clarke when they both won Oldie of the Year awards in 2012.

There were few members of either house who did not have a stock of Jean Trumpington stories, for she was a factory of self-mocking jokes. Once, when asked about her wardrobe, she confessed to having three, labelled 'outsize', 'fat' and 'obese'.

In 1980, when she was created a life peer, she told Garter King of Arms that she wished to become Baroness Trumpington, after the Cambridge ward she had represented. But apparently the title belonged to somebody else. 'Is there not another place near Cambridge you would like?' he asked.

'You don't think I'm going to call myself Lady Six Mile Bottom, do you?' she demanded. She emerged as Baroness Trumpington.

Nevertheless, she had a serious side. As a junior minister at the Department of Health, she was responsible for its public campaign against AIDS, a problem she confronted with characteristic robustness: 'Children must learn the facts properly,' she argued in 1986, 'instead of getting behind the bicycle shed to pick up bits and pieces.'

Jean Trumpington was born Jean Alys Campbell-Harris on October 23 1922. Her father, Arthur, was a Bengal Lancer who had been ADC to the Viceroy of India. Her American mother, Doris, was an heiress of a Chicago paint manufacturer, and the family lived in a Georgian town house with 10 servants in Great Cumberland Place, just north of Hyde Park.

Her parents, Jean recalled, 'brought me up much as they had been brought up: young children led a nursery life, with mother and father sweeping in to say goodnight, all dressed up for the evening with their friends in the Prince of Wales's set'. After the family money vanished in the Wall Street Crash, they moved to a smaller place in Kent.

As a child, she recalled: 'I wavered between wanting to be a vet and a ballet dancer,' and she was briefly dispatched by her mother to train at the Ballet Rambert. Aged 11, she was sent to Princess Helena College, Ealing, which she hated, leaving aged 15 with no qualifications. She was then sent to study art and literature at a finishing school in Paris, where she also played a lot of tennis, recalling that 'there was serious talk of junior Wimbledon'.

During the Second World War she worked as a Land Girl on Lloyd George's estate at Churt and then took a secretarial course before being recruited to work on naval intelligence at Bletchley Park. She was selected to work at Bletchley because of her family ties. There was a general belief at the time that people from the upper classes were less likely to betray their country.

'They were really frightfully snobbish about the girls who worked there,' she recalled. 'A friend of my father's said: "Maybe when Jean's finished her secretarial course she would like to go to a place called Bletchley."'

Frank Birch, the head of Hut 4, the German naval section, interviewed her over tea in the Lyons Corner House at the Trafalgar Square end of Whitehall. Birch, a famous actor and producer, had been a codebreaker during the First World War.

Once the naval Enigma ciphers were broken, she and a number of other young women selected for their knowledge of German typed the intercepted German messages into British Typex cipher machines modified to work like the Enigma machine.

The deciphered messages came out on streams of sticky tape like that used for telegrams, which was stuck to the back of the original messages and sent into the 'Z Watch' next door where the intelligence reports were compiled.

She became very friendly with two of the debs working in Hut 4, Osla Benning, whose boyfriend when Jean and she first met was Prince Philip of Greece, and Sarah Norton (later Sarah Baring), whose godfather was Lord Mountbatten. On their days off, they rushed up to London on the train to sample a bit of nightlife. They were young women who, despite the awful backdrop of the war, were determined to enjoy their time off.

One afternoon, when their watch was over, Osla Benning and Sarah Norton decided to propel Jean Harris down a long, sloping corridor in one of the wheeled laundry baskets in which the decoded messages were delivered.

'We launched it down the corridor, where it gathered momentum by the second,' Sarah Norton recalled. 'To our horror, at the T-junction, Jean suddenly disappeared, basket and all, through some double swing doors.'

Sarah Norton would subsequently dine out on the claim that the basket carrying a giggling Jean careered into the gents' loo, but in fact it burst into the office of Commander Geoffrey Tandy, the head of technical intelligence.

The middle-aged Tandy was a very serious academic who had already shown his irritation at the girls' willingness to enjoy themselves when there was a lull in the work. Jean took the brunt of his anger.

'Geoffrey Tandy had already decided he did not like me and now he was absolutely furious. As a punishment the three of us were taken off the same shift and it took us three weeks to get back together again.'

After the War Jean Harris was sent by the Foreign Office to Paris to help set up the European Central Inland Transport Organisation. From 1950 she worked as secretary to Viscount Hinchingbrooke – Victor 'Hinch' Montagu MP.

In 1952 she moved to work for an advertising agency in New York, where she lived above the Stork Club on East 52nd Street, off Park Avenue, and threw herself into the glamorous social whirl of Manhattan and the Hamptons.

There she met a young Cambridge don, Alan Barker, a former cavalry officer who had been wounded in Normandy and was there on a Yale fellowship. They married in 1954 and returned to England, living first at Eton, where he taught history, then at Cambridge, where he became headmaster of the Leys School in 1958.

She soon established herself in the affections of boys at the school, who remembered her for the hearty Sunday lunches to which they were often invited at the headmaster's house.

'I like my beef bloody and my lamb pink,' she once said. 'I think summer pudding is the greatest British pudding that ever happened. I love good sausages and there's an awful lot you can do with mince.'

Once, when reading a lesson at the King's College carol service, the passage 'a little lamb shall lead them' came out as 'a little lamb shall feed them'. She did not realise her mistake until her son said: 'Trust you, Mum, to think of food.'

She stood no nonsense. Once, brought in by her husband to talk to a group of boys who had grown their hair long, defying school regulations, 'I said, "In my day, hair like yours was known as buggers' grips." And I walked out again. The next morning, in chapel, I looked over and saw that every single one of them had had his hair cut.'

She celebrated her husband's retirement in 1975 by leaping fully clothed into the swimming pool in front of the entire pupil body and their astonished parents.

It was at Cambridge that Jean Barker began her long career in the Conservative Party. She became the first woman to be elected president of the Cambridge Conservative Association and tried twice to be selected for a Commons seat, but encountered hostility to women MPs. Instead she threw herself into local government.

She served for 13 years as a Conservative councillor on Cambridge City and later on Cambridgeshire County councils. As Mayor of Cambridge in 1971–72, she became known as 'the Swinging Mayor' for giving a discotheque as a civic reception.

In 1972, on a visit to a Newmarket stud, as she approached the box of an inmate called Hopeful Venture, the stallion began to show every sign of excitement. The director of the stud suggested it might be the scent she was wearing. 'When stallions are not interested, we put scent on the mares,' he explained. 'I am not only wearing scent,' she replied, 'I am also an ex-mayor.'

Also in the early 1970s she became a magistrate at the time when Peter Cook, otherwise known as 'the Cambridge Rapist', was terrorising women in the city. In 1975 Cook, who would later be convicted of six rapes and a string of other offences, was charged and brought before her at an early hearing.

She recognised him as her friendly delivery man from Mac Fisheries. 'He would drop off my groceries and I would always say: "Must lock the door after you've gone in case the Cambridge Rapist comes",' she recalled. 'I had to leave the bench straight away, of course.'

Created a life peer in 1980, Lady Trumpington made her mark as the Lords' secret weapon in the annual tug-of-war contest with the Commons. In 1982 she introduced a Shops Bill to liberalise

196

the laws on Sunday trading. The bill was passed by the Lords but talked out in the Commons.

In 1983 she caused controversy when she suggested that minefields on the Falklands should be cleared by driving flocks of sheep across them. Thousands of furious animal lovers wrote her abusive letters; one correspondent called her a 'fat old scrubber', she recalled. She remained completely unmoved: 'I have received a very rude letter from the RSPCA to which I replied that sheep were replaceable and limbs and men were not,' she said.

She served as Government Whip in the House of Lords between 1983 and 1985, and again between 1992 to 1997 (when she was successively spokesman at the Foreign Office and at the Department of National Heritage). She served as Parliamentary Under-Secretary of State at the Department of Health and Social Security between 1985 and 1987 and at the Ministry of Agriculture, Fisheries and Food from 1987 to 1992. She was promoted to Minister of State in 1989.

In 1982 Lady Trumpington's husband Alan Barker, by then headmaster of University College School, Hampstead, had suffered a debilitating stroke and had to retire. Thereafter, Jean Trumpington combined her work as a Government minister with the devoted care of her husband. He remained an invalid until his death in 1988.

Her title as a whip was Baroness-in-Waiting to the Queen, a job that involved greeting overseas visitors on behalf of the monarch. In 1998, in recognition of her experience at court, the Labour government appointed her an Extraordinary Baroness-in-Waiting. She was appointed DCVO in 2005.

As a castaway on *Desert Island Discs* in 1990 she had chosen as her luxury item the Crown Jewels, to maximise her chances of being rescued.

The publication, in 2011, of her jaunty memoir, *Coming Up Trumps*, brought her invitations to appear on television. In 2012 the chain-smoking peer appeared on the BBC's satirical show *Have I Got News For You*, becoming its oldest ever guest and joking about smoking cigars after sex.

She also appeared on the *Great British Menu* and on a television documentary, *Fabulous Fashionistas*, about older women and fashion, and in December 2017 she was a guest editor for the BBC's *Today* programme. Topics she chose to explore included her long-standing campaign to legalise brothels, and living with incurable diseases.

She retired from the House of Lords on October 24 2017, the day after she turned 95.

She is survived by her son.

Baroness Trumpington, born October 23 1922, died November 26 2018

Sister Wendy Beckett

Nun who became a much-loved champion of fine
art thanks to her popular television programmes

Sister Wendy Beckett: her series of weekly columns on art for *The Catholic
Herald* led to her reincarnation as a television personality

SISTER WENDY BECKETT, who has died aged 88, was the Roman
Catholic nun who acquired unexpected fame late in life after she
presented a succession of popular fine art television programmes.

Sister Wendy, as she was known to her viewers, was a nun
who for two decades before becoming a television presenter had
lived a contemplative life in a caravan parked in the grounds of a
monastery. It was this apparent incongruity, allied to her love of
painting, her refusal to indulge in the esoteric jargon and remote
theories of art criticism, and the obvious reverence in which she
held her subject, that transformed Sister Wendy into one of the
more unlikely icons of 1990s television.

With her traditional Catholic habit, her protruding teeth,
large glasses and inability to pronounce her Rs, Sister Wendy

swiftly became both a cult figure and one capable of reaching a wide audience. Her popularity, alongside her simple articulation of ideas, inevitably led to accusations from critics that she was 'dumbing down' her subject.

She denied this, claiming that she was 'not educated enough to speak to people in elitist languages'. This was at best disingenuous, for she had been awarded a Congratulatory First in English Literature at Oxford and was capable of translating medieval Latin into English. Sister Wendy was shrewder than she may have appeared, and was intensely aware of the differing requirements of appearing on primetime television and writing learned articles in fine art quarterlies.

Wendy Beckett was born in South Africa on February 25 1930. She said later that she had always disliked the name Wendy because it sounded 'trivial'. Her father was a banker who became a doctor and moved the family to Edinburgh when Wendy was two. She attended a Catholic convent in Edinburgh where, from an early age, she knew she wanted to be a nun. She later said that she had never experienced doubt, that she had always had 'an abiding and constant sense of what God is'.

In 1945 she left school and joined the Sisters of Notre Dame de Namur, a teaching order, taking the name Sister Michael. She had intended to lead a contemplative life – and took her solemn vows in 1947, aged 16 – but her request not to teach was declined.

After four years' teaching, the Sisters sent her to Oxford University in 1950, where she studied in a nuns' hostel with a strict rule of silence that even forbade her to converse with her fellow students. Despite – or because of – this restriction, Wendy Beckett came top of her year. J. R. R. Tolkien, the Oxford don and author, attempted to persuade her to pursue a career in academia, but she returned to the Sisters of Notre Dame, teaching initially in Liverpool before returning to South Africa in 1954.

Sister Wendy taught in South Africa until 1970, when she started suffering epileptic fits. She returned to England as a Reverend Mother, and the Vatican finally sanctioned her desire to live a contemplative existence, devoted to solitude and prayer. She bought a small, leaky, uninsulated trailer for £50 and parked it in the grounds of Quidenham, a Carmelite monastery in Norfolk.

For almost 20 years Sister Wendy lived an austere life in the caravan. She had no telephone, no television and no radio. Her day commenced at 1am and included seven hours of prayer. Each day a nun from the monastery brought her meals and took her laundry; it was her only social contact.

During the 1970s she translated the sermons of John of Ford, a medieval prelate, from Latin into English, but in 1980 she was given permission to study fine art. She immersed herself in books and photographic reproductions before deciding to help the monastery by making money from her knowledge.

In 1988 she published *Contemporary Women Artists*. The modest earnings from the book were put towards the hospice for children that the monastery ran in its grounds, but the publication also brought her publicity and led to a variety of freelance work for art magazines and newspapers. Thanks to the enthusiasm of her friend, the television cook and devout Catholic, Delia Smith, she began writing a weekly series on art for *The Catholic Herald*.

This in turn brought her to the attention of a BBC producer, Nick Rossiter, who commissioned a documentary about the National Gallery, in which she appeared. The programme was an unexpected triumph, launching Sister Wendy's third incarnation, as art critic and television personality.

She was an unusual presenter. Passionate about her subject, Sister Wendy worked without script or teleprompter and displayed a love of painting and an utter lack of inhibition when discussing the sexual subtext of a chosen work. Her comment on Stanley Spencer's *Self-portrait with Patricia Preece* ('I love all those glistening strands of his hair, and her pubic hair is so soft and fluffy') may have made the Carmelite sisterhood blanch, but it transfixed viewers.

In 1992 she published her second book, *Art and the Sacred*, an extended essay in which she revealed the core of her artistic beliefs; she argued that the sacred was not synonymous with the religious; rather, it involved the intense communication of a personal truth through which the viewer received a direct experience of God.

She analysed works by artists as diverse as Kim Lim, Winifred Nicholson and Picasso, and included paintings that, to the casual viewer, were not religious at all, such as Frank Auerbach's *Head of JYM*. It was the inclusion of paintings that had no obvious theological significance that demonstrated Sister Wendy's belief that it was contemplation that led to a greater understanding of God.

In the same year she produced *Sister Wendy's Odyssey*, a series of 10-minute analyses of paintings which attracted 3.5 million viewers and was the most successful BBC arts programme since Kenneth Clark's *Civilisation*. The public warmed to her gifts as a storyteller as much as to her enthusiasm.

The programme was repackaged as a book in 1993, as was her next venture, *Sister Wendy's Grand Tour* (1994). This 10-part series – also presented in 10-minute slots – featured the great museums and churches of Europe, and allowed Sister Wendy actually to see these treasures for the first time.

With her fame now reflected in a tenfold increase in her fees, her next series, *Sister Wendy's Story of Painting*, based on a 1994 book of the same name, required her to travel 30,000 miles in 12 countries during 100 days of filming, throughout which she was contractually entitled to attend mass each morning. She guided viewers through the history of Western art, from the cave paintings of Lascaux (where she memorably described male bison as being like 'great balls of male erotic fury') to Picasso.

The programme was shown to critical acclaim in the US. It also became a successful market for her books, which eventually numbered more than 25. She was the author of *The Mystery of Love: Saints in Art Through the Centuries* (1996); *Sister Wendy's Book of Saints* (1998); and an entertaining monograph on the German Expressionist painter and printmaker, Max Beckmann, entitled *Max Beckmann and the Self* (1997). Her final series was made for US viewers in 2001, after which she declined all further on-screen offers, though she continued to write, notably about Orthodox icons, another great enthusiasm.

When she was not performing before the cameras Sister Wendy returned to her caravan and lived a life of contemplation and prayer. When the caravan decayed her Carmelite sisters moved her into a well-insulated prefabricated hut, and in her final years she lived in the monastery itself. She devoured art magazines and enjoyed walks in the woods, listening to birdsong and observing the squirrels. She marked her 70th jubilee as a nun in 2017 by donating £3,000 to the Catholic charity Aid to the Church in Need, which supports persecuted Christians around the world.

Sister Wendy Beckett, born February 25 1930, died December 26 2018

Clem Tompsett

'Carrot King' of East Anglia who promoted his favourite veg with purple varieties and carrot whistles

CLEM TOMPSETT, who has died aged 84, was affectionately known as the 'Carrot King' of East Anglia and headed a root vegetable empire producing 65,000 tons of carrots, 16,000 tons of parsnips, 1,000 tons of red onions and 1,000 tons of shallots a year, supplying retailers such as Waitrose, Sainsbury's, Morrison's, Asda and Lidl.

'Mention Tompsett's name in vegetable circles,' wrote Carolyn Hart in *The Daily Telegraph* in 2011, 'and the response is always the same: "Quite a character," they say, with varying degrees of awe.' His company, now known as Tompsett Burgess Growers, based at Whitehall Farm, Isleham, near Ely in the Cambridgeshire Fens, is famous in farming circles, but was

Tompsett and his prize-winning purple carrots

always somewhat overshadowed by its founder, a sort of carrot evangelist who also had a parallel existence in the equine world.

As well as being the longest serving district commissioner in the Pony Club, he founded the annual Isleham Horse Trials, one of the chief horse trials on the eventing calendar. In 2010 thousands turned out to watch as Zara Phillips took to the saddle for the first time at the event, coming first and third in the intermediate section on two separate horses.

Tompsett claimed to eat carrots almost every day, and as chairman for many years of the British Carrot Grower's

Association launched several ingenious initiatives to try and persuade others to follow his example.

In 2004 he was the inaugural winner of the National Farmers' Union Best Innovation in the Food Chain Award, sponsored by Marks and Spencer, after being the first to grow purple carrots commercially as a way of tempting children to eat his favourite veg. Carrots, he explained, were originally purple until Dutch growers patriotically developed an orange variety – which soon took over.

In 2012, inspired by the Vienna Vegetable Orchestra, whose players perform on homemade edible instruments, Tompsett got together with the Great British Carrots group to launch a Great British Carrot Whistle Olympics, with the aim of finding Britain's best player of a carrot transformed into a whistle by being drilled with a series of holes.

Clements Harry Tompsett was born on June 28 1934 at the family 140-acre dairy farm near Soham where his grandparents ran the milk round. During the Second World War his father served in the RAF and his mother worked for the Ministry of Agriculture; she was one of the first people to enter Hamburg in 1945, sent there to advise on farming. After the war, however, they did not get back together again, so Clem was largely brought up by his grandparents.

He bought his first field, nine and a half acres, in 1948, and when his grandfather became ill the following year, he left Norwich High School for Boys aged 15 and was given 80 acres of the family farm to manage himself. When his grandfather died two years later, he took over the whole enterprise.

As well as the dairy operation, the farm had a small amount of arable land and Tompsett soon decided to get rid of the cows and switch the whole farm to arable and vegetable production, on the grounds that cows meant a seven-day working week, made no money and did not fit in with his passion for playing cricket.

The availability of good irrigation gave him the idea of growing carrots and the first crop was sown after lifting early potatoes, then covered up over the winter with soil to protect from frosts, and sold in March. Tompsett always said that the first crop made a fortune and he refused to be put off when the crop failed the second year.

Over the years he expanded his operation, buying land and taking on extra acreage on contract agreements from other farmers in East Anglia and as far afield as Perthshire. He built packing facilities and established strong links with the major supermarkets, supplying Waitrose with all of its British parsnips from 1985.

At the end of the 1980s, after having major heart surgery, he sold the company to Unigate, only to buy it back two years later. Around 2000 he merged with Russell Burgess, another family-run vegetable company. The companies later split, though they continued to work closely together.

Tompsett was dedicated to preserving and restoring the Cambridgeshire countryside, replanting hedges which had been removed earlier, establishing a tree planting programme and creating areas of natural beauty, including woodland and reservoirs which have become a haven for wildlife.

In 1959 he married Mary Leverington, whom he had met while playing for his cricket team at Worlington, near Mildenhall, Suffolk, where she was working as a barmaid at the local pub.

The couple had two daughters, who got the riding bug and joined the Pony Club. When the branch at Soham needed better facilities, Tompsett offered the family fields and was persuaded to become district commissioner – a post he held for more than 40 years.

In 1991 he organised a committee to hold the first Isleham Horse Trials, which has raised some £200,000 for charities including the East Anglian Air Ambulance and Papworth Hospital.

In 2006 Tompsett was appointed MBE for his services to agriculture and charities.

His wife and daughters survive him.

Clem Tompsett, born June 28 1934, died March 22 2019

Edda Tasiemka

Archivist upon whom generations of researchers
relied thanks to the vast store of cuttings she built up

Edda Tasiemka at home: she lived in terror that she might be closed down as a
fire risk and listed herself on official forms as a 'researcher' rather than 'librarian'

EDDA TASIEMKA, who has died aged 96, was a German émigré
revered as the owner of the best cuttings library in Britain.

It was unique in that it included articles cut from magazines
as well as newspapers, and from German, French and Swiss
publications. She also owned a fine archive of historic cuttings –
contemporary accounts of the American Civil War, the opening of
the Great Exhibition, the death of Queen Victoria and so on.

This treasure trove was housed in her own home in
Hampstead Garden Suburb, north London, and largely hidden
away in beautiful antique chests and cupboards – nothing so
vulgar as a filing cabinet was allowed to intrude, though even her

kitchen, bathroom and garage were stuffed with cuttings. Those on international football, one of the few subjects which held little interest for her, were stored in the first-floor lavatory.

She was born Edda Hoppe in Hamburg on August 5 1922. Her father was Paul Frolich, a well-known Communist leader and biographer of Rosa Luxemburg, but he never married her mother, and was expelled from the Communist Party and forced into political exile in the US when Edda was still a baby.

She was brought up in a village outside Hamburg but, even as a child, was keenly aware of political events: she remembered that when the Nazis came to power in 1933 many of her mother's friends were arrested and disappeared. Consequently she refused to join the Hitler Youth, which meant that she was disbarred from her local secondary school and had to commute many hours a day to attend one in Hamburg.

Her mother was arrested on New Year's Eve 1938, and imprisoned for six months, during which time the 15-year-old Edda had to fend for herself. She was unable to fulfil her dream of becoming a civil engineer, though she trained as a technical draughtswoman.

Postwar, Edda worked as a secretary for the British Army of occupation in Hamburg, and always said she learnt her (excellent) English by taking dictation from 'my Major Holt' of the Royal Engineers. In 1949 she met Hans Tasiemka, who was also working for the British Army, as an interpreter at the War Crimes Trials Centre.

He was a left-wing Jewish journalist who had fled to Paris at the outbreak of war and joined the French Foreign Legion and, eventually, the British Army. He was in the habit of carrying around pieces of paper which tended to overflow from his pockets and fall to the ground. 'When I asked him what they were,' she told *Vice* in 2016, 'he said "they are cuttings". That's how it all started.'

He was 17 years older than Edda but, according to her, 'politically on the same level'. They moved to London together and married in Hampstead register office – Tasiemka's friend Peter

Lorre, the film actor, stood them lunch at the Dorchester and Mrs Lorre gave Edda a pair of camiknickers as a wedding present.

The couple lived first in a north London boarding house run by a Mrs Beasley, where their nascent archive was stored in boxes hidden under the bed. Hans Tasiemka collected them as reference material for his articles and also went round antiques shops buying up old magazines. It was a source of sadness that Edda proved unable to have children, but cats – and cuttings – filled the gap.

She had a lifelong fear of dogs, dating back to her childhood memories of being taunted by German shepherds which the Nazis used to let loose in her home, but in later life, to the irritation of some of her neighbours, she befriended the neighbourhood fox, whose typical menu would include chicken and beef.

The Tasiemkas moved in 1962 to the house in Hampstead Garden Suburb that would be fondly remembered by generations of journalists and researchers. Edda, meanwhile, had become a successful journalist, writing for many German magazines.

Hans Tasiemka died in 1979 but Edda carried on cutting, and registered the library as The Hans Tasiemka Archives in his memory. For some years the Tasiemkas had allowed friends and friends of friends to use the library – Robert Lacey started using it in 1974 to research his book *Majesty* and recalled: 'After five years of dealing with *The Sunday Times* cuttings library, who said things like: "Why would we cut *Woman's Own*?" it was just wonderful to find these massive folders drawn from the most esoteric sources – American and European magazines, clearly clipped with love and fascination.'

As word spread, more and more journalists started using the archive and Edda Tasiemka invested in photocopiers and fax machines. She never advertised, and lived in terror that the authorities might close her down as a fire risk – on official forms, she called herself a 'researcher' rather than a librarian.

After Hans Tasiemka's death, Edda found happiness with Peter Knight, a literary agent and former syndication director of Express Newspapers, whom she referred to as her 'young man', he being four years younger. They were fond of going to dinner-dances ('smoochy dancing', Edda insisted) and to the theatre and opera, and they dined by candlelight twice a week.

Edda was a brilliant cook by all accounts – 'The only woman,' according to John Pearson, 'who really knew how to bone a chicken.' But Edda always refused to marry Peter Knight and said it was 'much more harmonious' that way.

She was an obsessive collector, not only of newspaper cuttings, but of Meissen china, Georgian salt cellars, knife rests, Staffordshire figurines of Queen Victoria's children, Louis Wain cat paintings, Victorian fairings and Regency tea sets with Adam Buck mother-and-child decorations.

She also had a most peculiar collection of china figurines of women suckling animals, mainly sheep. 'I do like sheep,' she explained, and indeed, she had two life-size model sheep in her drawing-room.

Into her eighties, she retained her puckish sense of humour: journalists who only dealt with her by phone used to be surprised by her Christmas cards, in which she posed sitting on Father Christmas's lap or frolicking on the lawn with her sheep. She remained fiercely Left-wing to the end of her life, and went on the two big anti-Iraq war marches when she was 80.

Successive attempts to house the cuttings collection with British academic institutions came to nothing. Last year, when she was 96 and felt too frail to carry on, she handed the archive over to a former DJ and documentary producer, James Hyman, who entered *Guinness World Records* for owning the world's largest magazine collection. He installed it in a temperature-controlled warehouse in Woolwich and plans eventually to put it all online.

Edda Tasiemka, born August 5 1922, died March 30 2019

The Reverend Angus Smith

'Wee Free' minister who made headlines in 1965 trying to stop a Sunday ferry service to Skye

The 'Ferry Reverend' in 1980 outside his kirk on the Isle of Lewis: he later joined the Free Presbyterian Church – aka the 'Wee Wee Frees'

THE REVEREND ANGUS SMITH, who has died aged 90, was a minister in the fundamentalist Free Church of Scotland – the 'Wee Frees' – who made headlines in 1965 when he lay down on a road leading to the slipway at Kyleakin on the east coast of Skye to prevent cars coming off the ferry from the mainland.

The protest was the culmination of a nine-month campaign by islanders against proposals by the Caledonian Steam Packet Co, a subsidiary of British Rail (now Caledonian MacBrayne or CalMac), to introduce a Sunday ferry service to the island.

In the run up to Smith's protest, a petition sponsored by the Church of Scotland, the Free Church of Scotland and the Free Presbyterian Church of Scotland was signed by 3,883 people out of Skye's population of 7,400. The service, it declared, was a 'desecration of the Biblical Sabbath'.

But their pleas fell on deaf ears.

On Sunday June 6 Smith and another minister led protesters at Kyleakin Free Church in a Gaelic prayer service, then Smith marched them out to the narrow road leading to the slipway as the first Sunday ferry arrived. As police asked them to move, Smith told his followers in Gaelic, 'Seas eir an toiseach!' – 'stand fast before them' – then lay down in front of the first car.

After a 25 minute struggle, more than 30 policemen managed to clear some 50 islanders, mostly crofters, off the road, lifting some bodily, including Smith. 'It took seven constables to move one 20-stone crofter,' reported *The Daily Telegraph*.

Then the demonstrators held an open-air Gaelic prayer meeting and sang the 40th Psalm: 'I waited patiently for the Lord and he inclined unto me and heard my calling.'

Fourteen, Smith included, were hauled away and charged with breach of the peace.

But not all Smith's fellow Sabbatarians supported the demonstration. After all, by demonstrating on a Sunday the protesters themselves were breaking the Sabbath. The Rev Archibald MacVicar, clerk to the Church of Scotland, described the occasion as 'the most massive breach of the Lord's Day that Skye has ever known', while a Free Church elder accused the demonstrators of making an 'exhibition of themselves and the island', adding: 'It was sad to see them following each other like sheep.'

Inevitably, perhaps, Smith became known as the 'Ferry Reverend'.

Angus Smith was born in Govan, Glasgow in 1928 to parents from the Isle of Lewis. Ordained in 1958 into the Free Church of Scotland, he served as minister at the Snizort Free Church in Skye, before moving in 1968 to Lewis, one of the last bastions of Sabbatarianism, as minister of Cross Free Church, Ness. In 1986 he was appointed Moderator of the Free Church General Assembly.

He retired as minister of Cross Free Church in 1997 but remained steeped in controversy to the last.

In 1996 he was named in court as one of several accusers during the trial, on four charges of sexual assault, of the Free Church theologian Donald Macleod, a professor of systematic theology at the Free Church College in Edinburgh, whose comparatively liberal and reformist views, including his tolerant approach towards the rights of Roman Catholics, brought him controversy and enemies.

Macleod was cleared of all charges, the court finding that his female accusers 'had all lied in the witness box to further the ends of [his] enemies in the Free Church of Scotland'. During the hearing it was alleged that he had been the victim of a conspiracy involving ministers from within the church, including Smith, who also happened to be his brother-in-law.

The revelation prompted Smith to issue a statement denying the claims and accusing Macleod of describing fellow ministers as 'Nazis' and 'ayatollahs' and putting 'blasphemy in the *West Highland Free Press*'. 'I am loath to say anything about the Donald Macleod affair and I have carefully kept these matters from my pulpit, but deliberate distortion, untruth, and confusion in the minds of people force me to act,' the statement read.

But the row continued. After being cleared, Macleod was the subject of moves to have him removed from the church on charges of heresy, and there were accusations that the church had failed to investigate more allegations about his private life.

Meanwhile Macleod's claims that Smith and other church figures had conspired against him were subsequently dismissed by a Free Church committee, only for the decision to be later overturned, prompting Smith, in 1999, to petition the Isle of Lewis presbytery, challenging it find out which one was lying: 'Either there was a conspiracy against Prof Macleod by us, or there wasn't. If Macleod is right, then I am a liar. If I am right, he is a liar. If the presbytery finds there was no conspiracy, then it must clear my name.'

Macleod described the petition as 'a piece of nonsense' and dismissed it as part of the campaign against him. Subsequently, a number of Macleod's critics formed a new denomination, the Free Church of Scotland (Continuing).

Smith went even further, leaving the Free Church for the ultra-Calvinist Free Presbyterian Church – also known as the 'Wee Wee Frees'.

He continued to thunder from the pulpit until earlier this year. In 2006 he laid part of the blame for the decline of the Sabbath on the royal family, politicians and television soaps, 'which portray an immoral culture involving drink and drugs'. In 2009 he protested when Caledonian MacBrayne proposed a new Sunday ferry service between Lewis and Ullapool, predicting that crime would rise on Lewis as a result and the services would bring 'things that terrified parents'.

When the vessel due to make the first Sunday crossing broke down due to a faulty exhaust the day before, Smith hailed it as a reminder of 'God's providence', though in the event another ferry was drafted in for the inaugural Sunday sailing.

'Neither CalMac nor its managing director understand that the God of the Sabbath was speaking to them,' Smith protested. 'It means nothing to them. If they do not have a heart or an ear to hear, they may as well be pagans. CalMac is fighting God – not the people of these islands.'

Asked if the breakdown was divine intervention, a spokesman for Caledonian MacBrayne said: 'I really do not think there is anyone here qualified to comment on that one.'

Smith was married and had four children.

The Reverend Angus Smith, born 1928, died August 28 2019

The Marquess of Bath

Britain's most flamboyant and eccentric aristocrat, known as 'the Loins of Longleat', whose rooms he covered in his erotic paintings

Lord Bath: with a loose marital arrangement, he always had three or four 'wifelets' on the go, some of them living on the Longleat estate

THE 7th MARQUESS OF BATH, who has died of Covid-19 aged 87, was the proprietor of Longleat, his family's magnificent Tudor seat in Wiltshire, and the most flamboyant and eccentric member of Britain's aristocracy.

A large, long-haired and straggle-bearded bohemian, Lord Bath pursued a colourful career as an artist, novelist and sexual libertine; he painted garish erotic murals all over the walls of Longleat's west wing, and stood as parliamentary candidate for the Wessex Regionalist Party, which believed in a world government based on the Sinai peninsula.

'Alexander,' wrote Gyles Brandreth, 'has the jut-jaw and fierce nose that you see in all the family portraits; but his blue eyes are hazy-soft, and underneath his leopard-print poncho is a belly the size of a flour bag. The family has a long tradition of enmity between fathers and sons, and of mild eccentricity, but it has come to full flower in the 7th Marquess.'

Lord Bath's father, the 6th Marquess, opened Longleat to the public on a commercial basis after the Second World War in an attempt to pay off death duties. Known as the 'father of the stately home industry', he did so with panache, populating the park with lion 'extras' purchased from the film *Born Free*, then adding tigers, baboons, chimpanzees, giraffes, zebras, hippos and sea-lions – not to mention a funfair, pleasure boats, a putting green and tea rooms.

The 7th Marquess adopted his unorthodox lifestyle in reaction against the equally unorthodox views of his father who, unusually for a decorated British war hero, had been a fervent admirer of Hitler. The Nazi leader was, he claimed, 'a helluva fella', and he showed his admiration by amassing a formidable collection of Hitleriana, before switching his interest to Margaret Thatcher.

Notwithstanding a difficult relationship with his father, the 7th Lord Bath inherited his commitment to Longleat – adding the Center Parcs Holiday Village, a version of Stonehenge and no fewer than seven mazes, including the longest hedge labyrinth in the world, to Longleat's other attractions. He raised large sums of money from the sale of artworks and other valuables for a Longleat conservation fund.

He also fully exploited the commercial value of his own personality; many visitors to Longleat came not to see the lions, let alone the house, but to glimpse the man they called 'the Loins of Longleat'.

Lord Bath was mainly known for his interest in pantheism and sex. He had studied painting in Paris, and from 1969 the covering of Longleat's walls with his murals was one of his most publicised obsessions. These ranged from the 'Paranoia Murals' (which include an autobiographical scene featuring a wolf-like father-figure battling it out with a dragon-like mother over an unborn foetus) to the erotic fantasies of the 'Kama Sutra room', featuring depictions of a variety of sexual couplings, triplings and quadruplings. Lord Bath liked to show visitors around these himself.

Lord Bath was also a collector of women. Downstairs, visitors could marvel at 'Bluebeard's Gallery', a spiral staircase on whose walls he had mounted a series of three-dimensional portraits in oil and sawdust of all the women he had known (in the biblical sense), with the date of first meeting to the left of each face and the date of painting to the right.

Popular legend had him spending his days *in flagrante* with a resident harem of young beauties. The reality was rather different, though no less remarkable. Throughout his life, Lord Bath had three or four mistresses – or what he called 'wifelets' – at any one time.

They came in all shapes and sizes, including a black model, a Chinese artist, a 17-year-old from Sri Lanka, a Wessex housewife and Jo-Jo Laine, former wife of the pop musician Denny Laine. Some lived in cottages on the estate; none ever sued him and only one ever bore him a child.

There was also an official wife, Anna Gael, a Hungarian model whom he had picked up outside a Paris cinema when she was just 15. She lived in Paris and visited Longleat once a month.

Despite all these distractions, Lord Bath himself lived rather a lonely existence in a bachelor penthouse in the attics. The only permanent residents of Longleat, apart from himself, were a kindly married couple who looked after him and his beloved labradors. It would have been nice to have found a soulmate, he admitted, 'but I haven't. And it's too late now.'

Alexander George Thynne was born on May 6 1932, the second son of Viscount Weymouth, eldest son of the 5th Marquess of Bath. An elder brother had died in infancy.

He would change the spelling of his name to Thynn in 1976, believing it to be more authentic.

He traced his bloodline to Tacitus and Charlemagne, but his direct family tree was stranger still. The founder of the family fortunes, Sir John Thynne, a fiercely ambitious Tudor apparatchik, got his hands on a dissolved Augustinian priory, built Longleat and was nearly executed for embezzlement.

He founded a dynasty that included the first marquess, who, as George III's Secretary of State, lost the American colonies; a marquess in Victorian times whose servants were instructed to scrub his wife's small change every morning; a great-grandfather who once forced two prostitutes at gunpoint to share his wife's bed; a maternal grandmother whose five marriages and several illegitimate children made her the model for Nancy Mitford's character 'the Bolter'; and an aunt who hoarded food in her cheeks like a hamster.

Alexander's father Henry, Viscount Weymouth, had been described by his headmaster at Harrow as 'moronic beyond reach', yet got into Oxford, where he was a contemporary of Evelyn Waugh. Alexander's mother, Daphne Vivian, was a spirited girl who had been 'removed' from two schools, once for spearing a geometry mistress in the backside with a compass. As their respective parents disapproved of the relationship, they married in secret in 1926.

As might be expected, their children had an unconventional upbringing. 'Frightfully noisy and drunken,' Waugh reported after a weekend at Longleat in 1948. 'Daphne keeping me up until 3.30 every night, and the children riding bicycles round the house with loud cries from 6.30. No sleep. Jazz all day. Henry at meals reading the most disgusting parts of Malinowski's *Sexual Life of the Savages* (and goodness they are disgusting) aloud to his 18-year-old daughter.'

But young Alexander was not a happy child. As a small boy, he was close to his mother but, after she deserted her husband for the travel writer Xan Fielding, a man 15 years her junior, in the early 1950s, he felt she stopped defending him against his authoritarian father.

It seems that he felt in some way responsible for the break-up of his parents' marriage: 'During the war, when my father was away, my mother was unfaithful, repeatedly,' he recalled. 'I did this terrible thing when he came home on leave. I don't think I meant to be malicious. I was just mischievous. I said to him, "Papa, there's an awful lot of new men you've got to meet." He wasn't amused. And after that he started having girlfriends.'

At prep school, Alexander tried to please his father by emulating Hitler. As a prefect, he punished some boys by trapping them under the floorboards. When he wrote to his father boasting of what he had done, the Marquess reported him to the headmaster. On another occasion, he beat Alexander with a riding crop for spilling some water while washing his dog.

Yet at first Alexander seemed destined to follow a well-trodden aristocratic path. At Eton he was a member of Pop and Keeper of Boxing. Contemporaries recalled him as 'tall, handsome, athletic ... something of a school hero ... totally straight up and down'.

He went on to do National Service in the Life Guards, winning an officers' welterweight boxing title. He did the society balls, lost his virginity to a prostitute, then went up to Christ Church, Oxford, where he read PPE and was president of the Bullingdon. When the 5th Lord Bath died in 1946, Alexander Thynne became heir to the marquessate as Viscount Weymouth.

But somewhere along the way he rejected his father's ambitions for him and developed a philosophy of his own based on free love and pantheism. He grew pigtails and, though in possession of a trust fund, pretended to be impoverished. Having decided that he wanted to become an artist and aesthete, he wrote a novel, which was rejected, left Oxford with a Third and went to Paris to study painting. It was there that he developed his distinctive sartorial style, favouring floral waistcoats, purple velvet caps and bare feet.

In 1964 the 10,000-acre Longleat estate was made over to him by his father, who had moved to another house on the estate with his second wife and daughter. As soon as he moved into the big house, Lord Weymouth set to work on his artistic *grand projet*, beginning with the Victorian drawing-room used by his grandmother. Eventually, his efforts would cover about a third of the walls of Longleat.

In the mid-1970s the 6th Marquess, alarmed by his heir's increasingly disreputable lifestyle, decided to split the responsibilities of running the estate, giving his favourite second son Christopher the job of running the house and attractions, leaving Alexander to run the estate.

The two boys had never got on – the more conventional Christopher described his brother's daubings as 'pornographic pizza'. The 7th Marquess's first act on inheriting the title in 1992 was to sack Christopher as Longleat's manager and to order his family out of their estate house.

Also in the 1970s, Lord Weymouth founded the Wessex Regionalist Party, unsuccessfully contesting the seats of Westbury in the February 1974 general election and Wells in the 1979 election. He also failed to win the Wessex Euro-seat in 1979. The party was wound up and he joined the Social Democrats in the 1980s.

After succeeding as the 7th Marquess of Bath – 'The causes which I advocate are Individualism, Pantheism, Wessex Regionalism and Polygamy and Polyandry within a Polymorphous Society' – he found a home on the Liberal Democrat benches of the House of Lords until the Labour government removed most of the hereditary peers.

For some years before inheriting the title Lord Bath had been beavering away on a 25-volume autobiography. By 2002, when he published volume one (which ends while he was still at prep school), he was said to have written five million words. The series continued with *Top Hat and Tails* (2003), *Two Bites of the Apple* (2003) and *A Degree of Instability* (2005).

Other publications include three novels and a work of philosophy, *The World View of Alexander Thynn* (2000). He also made a record of his own songs, *I Play the Host*.

In 1969 he married Anna Gael (whose real name was Anne Abigail Gyarmathy), in an arrangement whereby both were free to take lovers and mostly lived apart. They had a daughter, Lenka, and a son, Ceawlin, pronounced 'See-aw-lin', after the 6th King of Wessex.

Ceawlin Henry Laszlo Thynn, Viscount Weymouth, who was born in 1974, succeeds as the 8th Marquess of Bath.

The 7th Marquess of Bath, born May 6 1932, died April 4 2020

Roy Kerridge

Writer with an eye for the ridiculous who chronicled
the colourful and eccentric byways of British life

Kerridge on a visit to Eynsham Hall where he was born

ROY KERRIDGE, who has died aged 78, was a lover of lost causes
who immersed himself in and chronicled parts of British society
which were beyond the reach of more conventional writers.

His most successful decade began in 1979, when *The Daily
Telegraph* published an article he had sent in about a friend
of his, a tramp called Commander Williams who, after being
'returned to the community' by a mental hospital, was found
frozen to death in a lavatory cubicle.

In the early 1980s Kerridge, a small, friendly man with a
round face and an innocent expression, became a familiar figure
in Fleet Street, dressed in a sheepskin coat over a Dunn & Co
jacket, pastel shirt and nondescript tie, walking from newspaper

office to newspaper office with a carrier bag containing the articles he hoped to place.

Alexander Chancellor, editor of *The Spectator*, was among those who recognised his gift for talking to anyone, catching their tone of voice and, with a mixture of naivety, generosity and irony, conveying their essential nature, and it was in that magazine that much of his best work appeared.

On his journeys through the British Isles Kerridge was able at the same time to see what was good in people and to hint at their ridiculous side. It was not always clear who he was sending up, but his targets generally included himself.

His friends included Irish tinkers, English aristocrats, Japanese artists, members of various bizarre religious cults, and Caribbean church members at whose services he was usually the only white person present and was fondly addressed as 'Brother Roy'.

Kerridge himself was an Anglican, with a profound attachment to the King James Bible, which he was delighted to find in general use when he went on a journey through the Deep South of the United States.

He had a total distrust of technology, did not own a car, television, mobile phone or computer, and on being given an iPad by his brother, refused to touch it, denouncing it as the work of the devil. Even more unusually for an aspiring writer, he never learnt to type, and throughout his life had to pay from his own scanty resources for his manuscripts, written in neat blue biro, to be typed out.

Roy Kerridge was born on September 8 1941 at Eynsham Hall, a mansion in Oxfordshire used during the Second World War as a maternity home for evacuees from the East End of London. He attributed to the circumstances of his birth his feeling that he was a working-class duke.

His father, Eric Kerridge, a historian, and his mother, born Blanche Gerson, were devout Communists, and strove to bring him up in that faith, but divorced when he was 10. Blanche contracted a second marriage, to John Wellings-Longmore, a fiery Nigerian politician who fascinated and frightened Roy, and prompted his lifelong interest in and friendship with immigrants from Africa and the West Indies.

Kerridge, who did not drink, lived frugally as a young man on an allowance of £7 a week from his grandfather, Adolph Gerson, a Polish-Jewish friend of Trotsky.

His career as a writer got off to a flying start as the 'Voice of Youth', the title conferred on him in 1959 by Kingsley Martin, veteran editor of the *New Statesman*. Kerridge had just left Brighton, Hove and Sussex Grammar School with two O-levels, and submitted a piece which appeared under the headline 'A Teenager in Brighton'.

He was anxious to get to know the local rogues, possessed a comprehensive knowledge of skiffle music, could remember the words of any song after hearing it once, and was a great admirer of Lonnie Donegan, precursor of the Beatles and the Rolling Stones. On the threshold of the 1960s, a career as a fashionable journalist beckoned.

But at about that time he discovered, as he later related, that he was a 'Romantic Conservative', who believed in 'hopelessly innocent ideals of chivalry, kindness and Christianity', and could not bear the drug-fuelled decadence of the Sixties: 'All England's noble history seemed to have come to an end in the squalid corruption and diseased minds of the hippies.'

Taking his stand against the spirit of the age, he entered a long period of obscurity as an anti-careerist who found in *The Telegraph*'s 'Way of the World' column – written by Michael Wharton, with whom at the end of the 1970s he became friends – 'a never-failing source of comfort, reassurance and strength'.

While still a teenager, Kerridge had conceived an intense admiration for the novels of Colin MacInnes, received encouragement from that author, and resolved that he too would write novels, a vocation to which he devoted most of his time after his early journalistic career had petered out.

In his delightful memoir, *The Lone Conformist*, published in 1984, which includes his account of life as a lavatory cleaner, Kerridge observed that in the early Sixties, for a writer to become a Conservative was equivalent to taking 'a Vow of Poverty ... recognition and a successful career could never be yours'.

By 1977 his grandfather's money had run out, and he was reduced to attending his local Job Centre, where he was asked what job he would like, and what sort he expected to get. He answered 'novelist' and 'lavatory attendant', and a post for him in the second of these roles was arranged.

The material he gathered from the tramps he woke in the morning from their slumbers in the public conveniences he had to clean helped him to relaunch his career as a journalist.

Several of his novels were at length published, including *Subjects of the Queen*, a remarkable portrait of immigrant London written in the 1960s and brought out by Duckworth in 2002. But it is for his utterly original journalism that he will be chiefly remembered.

Kerridge had an encyclopaedic knowledge of animals, folk songs and folklore, and enjoyed charming children and adults by whipping out his pen and drawing cartoons with startling alacrity.

He never married, but continued to live with his mother, first at her bungalow in the village of Ferring in Sussex, and then for many years in her small terraced house in Kensal Rise, London. After her death on March 19 at the age of 99, he said the world had stopped making sense, stopped eating, and in the view of his sister, the writer Zenga Longmore, died of a broken heart.

Roy Kerridge, born September 8 1941, died April 6 2020

The Reverend David Johnson

High Church eccentric whose practical joking
included guying senior prelates with spoof letters

Johnson with Doreen and Florence, two goats employed by the parish of
Whiston, Northants, to trim the grass in the graveyards when he was rector

THE REVEREND DAVID JOHNSON, who has died aged 66, was a
priest of the Church of England the like of whom may never be
seen again. He was keen of mind and sharp of wit; but he was
also possessed of an eccentricity which led some to revere him as
an institution and others to opine that he ought to be confined to
one.

Johnson's gifts as public speaker and raconteur were evident
in adolescence when he was one of a team which won a national
schools' debating competition. On going up to Cambridge he set
his sights on becoming president of the Cambridge Union debating
society, an ambition he achieved for the Easter Term of 1976.

He used his time at Cambridge to hone his skills as a prankster,
or at least to persuade others to put his ideas into effect. These
included marking the visit of Archbishop Coggan to Selwyn College
by hanging the organ scholar's underwear on a washing line
between the west towers of the chapel; and, more memorably, a
mock academic procession through the streets of the city for 'The
Immersion of the High Professor' in the River Cam.

Publicised on posters replicating official proctorial notices, the exercise achieved Johnson's aim of persuading a significant number of tourists to stand on one leg as the 'High Professor' (alias Father James Owen of Little St Mary's Church) dipped his toe ceremoniously in the water.

Johnson's fondness for practical jokes attracted national attention with the one-off publication in September 1981 of 'Not The Church Times', a facsimile of the Anglican newspaper, complete with almost credible advertisements and errata.

The front page reported on the enthronement of the new Bishop of London, Graham Leonard, as though the event was on a scale akin to the wedding of Prince Charles and Lady Diana Spencer.

In 1994 Johnson collaborated with the priest-author Toby Forward to send spoof letters to church dignitaries on a variety of subjects, ranging from requests for tickets to the races or the details of the recipient's toupee makers, to the possibility of installing a monument to the Cumberland sausage in Carlisle Cathedral.

Their targets included the Rt Rev Alec Graham, then Bishop of Newcastle, whom the pair had heard was 'a first-rate Tory'. Perhaps, they suggested, he might lead a new Right-wing leather-clad boys' group 'liberated from the restricted old-fashioned sexual morality which causes such unnecessary gossip'.

The Bishop replied that, alas, he did not have much to do with youth organisations and suggested they try someone with a more popular image: 'But you are certainly right about my political views.'

The letters of inquiry and replies were published in a book, *The Spiritual Quest of Francis Wagstaffe*. It was described by Johnson's own bishop as 'contemptible', but the profits were shared with a charity for the young homeless.

David William Johnson was born on December 5 1953, the son of a civil servant. Educated locally at Ponteland on the outskirts of Newcastle upon Tyne, Johnson proudly claimed that his greatest childhood achievement was winning the Ponteland

Sunday School's Twist-and-Shout competition, more by virtue of his ability to shout rather than to twist.

He went up to read Theology at Selwyn College, Cambridge, before training for Holy Orders at Ripon College, Cuddesdon. It was typical of his style as a bon viveur that he arranged for the ordinands' bar, hitherto a beer barrel on a trolley, to be replaced by a cocktail cabinet in the college common room.

He was ordained in 1978 to a curacy at St Etheldreda's, Fulham, where it soon became apparent that all was not well. Following his ordination to the priesthood a year later, Johnson presided at Holy Communion for the first time, an occasion which he choreographed with ceremonial and vestments so ornate as to make the Vatican seem low church by comparison. Significantly, his training incumbent did not attend the occasion.

Nevertheless Johnson remained in Fulham until 1982, when he took up a five-year post as Communications Secretary of the Church of England Board of Mission and Unity.

Based in Church House, Westminster, Johnson, who was always generous in sharing his talents, made good use of his networking abilities. Ecumenical dignitaries visiting from abroad were charmed to be greeted with a hamper from Fortnum & Mason. It is said that on one occasion, when a French Catholic bishop needed to return home in a hurry, Johnson used his contacts in the military to fly him back.

During this time, he also served for three years as a Priest-Vicar (Honorary Minor Canon) at Westminster Abbey. Life in central London offered Johnson many opportunities for socialising, which he took up with alacrity. He frequented, among other venues, the Chelsea Arts Club, where he staged what he publicised as 'A Fathers' Day Fuddle'. Chaired by Bishop Bill Westwood, the cabaret was performed entirely by Fathers in the ecclesiastical sense.

As the television critic of the *Church Times*, Johnson ranged further than one might have expected for that newspaper, but his comments were always sharp and entertaining. On the occasions when he failed to submit copy, the *Church Times* explained to its readers that 'David Johnson is unwell.'

In 1987 Johnson left London to become Rector of Gilmorton with Peatling Parva in the diocese of Leicester. Unfortunately, while Johnson's ability to reduce an argument and its proponent to the ridiculous within a couple of sentences might have enhanced his performance in the debating chamber and amused his peers, he did not always find it easy to summon the pastoral tact and patience required in rural ministry.

Deeply unhappy, he was rescued after four years by Bill Westwood, by now Bishop of Peterborough, and installed as Rector of Cogenhoe and other villages in Northamptonshire.

Sadly, this move to another rural benefice proved if anything even more disastrous, leading to a severe breakdown of pastoral relationships in the villages. Johnson even found himself banned from a village pub which he had patronised assiduously. His mental and physical condition was in decline to the point where Bishop Westwood arranged for him to retire early on health grounds.

Johnson settled in Oxford. With typical perversity he named his house 'Seaview Cottage'. His telephone answering machine would inform callers that he was either all at sea or out with the tide.

Pottering about in a Latin cassock and shovel hat, he became a familiar feature of life in the city and, for a while, at the Oxford Union, of which, by virtue of his past role at Cambridge, he was an honorary member.

A frequent writer of letters to newspapers, in 2005, apropos a *Telegraph* reader's observation that 'giving gin to wasps causes them to take off in ever-decreasing circles before collapsing in a flower bed', he wrote: 'I have found the same treatment works equally well on Oxford undergraduates.'

But as Johnson's health further deteriorated, with one or more strokes, he had to move into residential care.

David Johnson was unmarried.

The Reverend David Johnson, born December 5 1953, died April 22 2020

David Twiston Davies

Telegraph veteran and champion of Empire who established a close rapport with traditionalist readers

Twiston Davies in 2011: his enthusiasms included the novels of P. G. Wodehouse and he was devoted to Canada and the Roman Catholic Church

DAVID TWISTON DAVIES, who has died aged 75, spent 40 years of his working life in journalism on *The Daily Telegraph*, where he was held in great affection and to which, as to the Roman Catholic Church and to Canada, the land of his birth, he was devoted.

Having joined *The Telegraph* as a news sub-editor in 1970, in 2010, aged 65, he put on a brave face and retired after almost a decade spent on the obituaries desk with the designation of Chief Obituary Writer. His heyday, however, undoubtedly came during the long spell he spent as the newspaper's letters editor, from 1989 to 2001.

While responsible directly to the newspaper's editor, the letters editor enjoyed much latitude in his choice of correspondence for the daily column. During Twiston Davies's tenure, no *Telegraph* editor could have had a more loyal foot soldier, or a letters editor more in tune with the attitudes of the paper's more traditionalist readers.

Letters, 350 or more of them each day, still came mostly by post or fax. The letters desk staff comprised Twiston Davies and his secretary Dorothy Brown, facing one another across a cluttered workstation on the edge of the open-plan floor of the paper's offices. Twice a day, Dorothy opened the pile of post for her principal to peruse.

Thirty or so letters concerned with the issues of the moment or judged to be of interest to, or likely to amuse, the readers would be typed into the computer system in the course of the day, and from these 11 to 20 items chosen to fill the column. A proof would go to *The Telegraph* editor's office and final revisions were made. Twiston Davies's work was not made easier by the fact that he struggled all his life with dyslexia.

The commotion of his daily routine, the sound of his voice on the telephone, the banter passing between him and Dorothy, and the bluff conservatism of his old-school opinions broadcast at full volume made Twiston Davies a character impossible to ignore, unique on the newspaper's staff, but also helped to foster a sense of corporate camaraderie.

He was a one-off, his eccentricities bolstered by an underlying conviction that things would work out. He liked to quote a remark by his English master at school that the young David 'was like a character in a novel', and at times it even seemed as if 'The Twister' or 'Twisters', as all knew him, was taking part in a theatrical production; there was always a strong element of self-parody in his performance and he took the joshing of colleagues in good part.

Telegraph journalists pinched themselves as they heard him opine sagely into the telephone on some matter of grave consequence – the value of birching, perhaps, or National Service – long since consigned to history. (In his entry in *Debrett's* he listed his recreation as 'defending the reputation of the British Empire'.)

Having picked out a letter for publication, Twiston Davies would punch out the author's number emphatically on his telephone keypad, announce himself in the manner of a master of ceremonies, explain the reason for his call, and then go through the letter, querying points and suggesting cuts or revisions that he considered desirable.

The letter would then be read aloud in full, slowly, with stops and starts as he lost his place and found it again. There would then be a further reading, and thereafter as many more as it took to produce a text acceptable to both author and editor.

With the telephone receiver clamped between chin and shoulder and a pair of metal-rimmed glasses perched on the tip of his nose, Twiston Davies would look up and down rapidly from computer screen to keyboard as he talked and typed, with now and then – being a slave to a print deadline – a quick glance at the clock on the wall.

A call to the author of a letter who was unknown to Twiston Davies would nearly always conclude with the businesslike formula: 'We must have a telephone number for you where you can be contacted day or night. And my name is David Twiston Davies. Twiston, T-w-i-s-t-o-n; Davies spelt in the conventional way with an "e".'

When conversing with a man of rank or title, the tone was more that of the gentlemen's club. A series of comments, interspersed by snorts of approval, would typically run, 'Quite ... Indeed ... Admirable ... Absolutely ... Very good ... Egg-zactly'. Longer remarks opened time and again with 'Quite frankly' and 'I have to say'.

A valued correspondent of 'sound' views might be invited to 'a spot of lunch'. While lunch in a pub might brighten a slow day, and sandwiches and 'a sticky bun' from the staff canteen suffice on a busy day, lunch out with a guest on expenses – 'Colonel, can I interest you in a bottle of bubbly?' – was an event to be savoured.

In lulls during the lively dispatch of letters business, there were no longueurs. A regular contributor to *The Catholic Herald*, Twiston Davies had telephone calls to make to Father This and

Monsignor That to ensure that he kept abreast of developments in Rome and the wider Catholic world.

As the New World woke up, there were calls to make to contacts in Canada. Twiston Davies had a deep knowledge of Canadian politics and constitutional history; the proprietor of *The Telegraph* at the time, Conrad Black, a Canadian and a Catholic convert, was sympathetic to this.

There were visits from retired *Telegraph* colleagues, old comrades to be greeted warmly by nickname. 'Chunky! Come into my office. Have a seat. Dorothy, you remember Chunky?' A chance to reminisce about bygone Fleet Street and old times at *The Telegraph*, or even just to say the words 'hot metal printing', was prized.

To stretch his legs, Twiston Davies, always clad in a sombre suit and tie (or corduroys and cravat at the weekend), would hurry off to collect the office gossip. News of any staff dismissal put him in a state of high nervous excitement. '*Sacked!*' he would bellow.

Work done, he left to catch his train back to Tunbridge Wells, home also to that famous letter-writer 'Disgusted'. 'Another day, another dollar,' he would exclaim. 'Time to draw stumps and head back to the Royal Borough.' He would then rush off, clutching an ancient leather briefcase full of papers and coming apart at the seams.

David James Twiston Davies was born in Montreal on March 23 1945. Although he thus started out in life in the French-speaking Canadian province of Quebec, as an adult he was to display scant enthusiasm for anything French – wine, war cemeteries and the Bourbons' support for the Jacobite cause excepted.

Descended from Samuel Davies (born 1788), Welshman and Wesleyan minister, David was the eldest of the two sons and two daughters of (Mervyn) Peter Twiston Davies, who converted to Roman Catholicism, and his Canadian wife Isabel, née Fox, from a Catholic family which had emigrated from Co Tipperary in the early 19th century. His great-uncle, Sir Leonard Davies, a noted civic figure in Monmouth, added Twiston to the family surname by deed poll in 1939.

Taken to Britain as an infant, at the age of four David contracted tuberculosis and for a time returned to Montreal for treatment with streptomycin, a drug which was not at the time readily available in Britain. He was later sent to prep school at All Hallows, Cranmore, in Somerset, and then to Downside.

Having cut his teeth in journalism with two years (1966–68) on the *East Anglian Daily Times* at Ipswich, he returned again to Canada (nearly all his life he travelled on a Canadian passport), and for two happy years – having hitch-hiked from Montreal to Winnipeg – worked for the *Winnipeg Free Press* in Manitoba.

He joined *The Telegraph* as a news sub in 1970, and was assistant to the paper's literary editor from 1977 to the mid-1980s, when he had a stint on the desk dealing with the Manchester edition.

Then in 1986 he was assigned to work for the new obituaries editor, Hugh Massingberd, who had been recruited to launch *The Telegraph*'s first separate, daily obits column and to create a new style of less stuffy obituary.

Twiston Davies helped to familiarise Massingberd with the way things worked at the newspaper, and to find specialist contributors to write obits of people in their fields of expertise, such as the RAF and the Church. He also wrote obituaries, often of characters with links to Canada ('the senior dominion') or to Britain's former empire.

He liked the work, but in 1987 was made letters editor, and then in 1988 editor of the Peterborough column. In that role, in 1989, he was proud to report his telephone call to a retired manual worker in Australia to break the news that, following the death in England of a remote cousin, he was now the 18th Earl of Lincoln.

On Peterborough he nurtured a string of talented young journalists (among them Damian Thompson and James Delingpole) and served as an avuncular and much-loved mentor to them.

There followed his long spell on Letters up to 2001, by which time some views which continued to be aired regularly on the letters page – views, for example, in vigorous opposition to homosexuals in the Armed Forces – were becoming out of step with the times. A fresh approach was sought, and Twiston Davies returned to Obituaries.

He wrote obits with brio, sharing Hugh Massingberd's belief that in an obituary, as in a memorial service address, laughter provoked by feelings of exasperated affection for the deceased's shortcomings had its place, and that, as Twiston Davies himself once put it, the subject should be 'shown as the person the reader would have encountered'.

Having already produced in 1996 *Canada from Afar: The Daily Telegraph Book of Canadian Obituaries*, as well as a book of letters two years later, he edited four books of Armed Forces obituaries and *The Daily Telegraph Book of Imperial and Commonwealth Obituaries*. The word 'imperial' was ever a favourite in his vocabulary.

In retirement, he wrote the odd article for *The Telegraph*, for example about the sale of a large collection of antiquarian books he had inherited from an old colleague, Baron Seymour de Spon, and which on moving house he was obliged to sell. He continued also to contribute thoughtfully to *The Catholic Herald*.

He never forgot his Welsh heritage, and when in the home circle needed little prompting to break into song with *O Canada!*

He never learnt to drive, and had a tendency to clumsiness – his wife Rita would caution the children: 'If you see your father with an electric drill in his hands, remove it painlessly.'

He loved books, enjoyed the novels of P. G. Wodehouse and Robertson Davies, and had the greatest respect for the monarchy.

Strong in his Catholic faith, with his family he attended the Easter retreat at Downside each year.

He married, in 1970, Margaret Anne (Rita) Montgomery; she survives him, with their daughter, Bess, and sons, Benedict, James and Huw.

David Twiston Davies, born March 23 1945, died May 3 2020

Gwenda Wilkin

Accordion virtuoso who entertained the troops and trained her dog Danny to bark in time to Liszt

GWENDA WILKIN, who has died aged 86, was billed in the 1950s as 'Britain's leading lady accordioniste'; while still in her teens she established herself as a virtuoso performer and toured widely in Europe, Africa and the Far East to entertain British troops.

Gwenda Wilkin: she made her clothes herself, wore heavy make-up and dyed her hair pink

Confounding those who looked down on the 'squeeze-box', her performances of music specially written for the accordion – such as Pietro Deiro's Concerto in D, at the Royal Festival Hall in 1951 – were breathtaking. And yet she seemed just as comfortable fooling around in a double act with her dog Danny, whom she taught to bark in time to one of Liszt's Hungarian rhapsodies.

She often performed on *Workers' Playtime*, the BBC radio variety series broadcast from factory canteens, and spent a decade providing music for Wilfred Pickles's phenomenally popular quiz show, *Have a Go*.

Her radio work was her bread and butter, she recalled, while 'all the other jobs were the jam': these included tours of the Moss and Stoll Empires, cabaret, Sunday concerts, and seaside variety shows.

Gwenda Wilkin always cut a glamorous figure, making her colourful clothes herself, and did not let standards slip on her tours abroad, even if high heels turned out not to be always appropriate for the makeshift stages she had to play on.

She was 16 when she began to travel abroad performing for the troops, having probably lied about her real age. There were rarely more than two female artists on the bill: among those she toured with were Vera Lynn and Gracie Fields, who both looked after her and taught her how to hold her drink – or how to get away with not drinking.

She was in Egypt at the time of the Suez Crisis, in Cyprus during the Emergency – when the car she was travelling in was shot up – and found an audience of soldiers in Malaysia too busy looking out for snipers to concentrate on her performance.

She contracted dysentery in Cyprus and, because it was thought she would not survive the journey to the hospital in Larnaca, she was taken in desperation to an old healing woman in the nearby Troodos Mountains, who restored her to health with boiled tree bark.

Even in her youth, Gwenda Wilkin was a formidable character who defied convention. She wore heavy make-up, dyed her hair pink, and befriended black performers such as the variety duo Harriott & Evans.

She learnt to drive so that she could travel more easily abroad and, when told that it was dangerous for a young woman to drive great distances on her own, she secured a gun licence and bought herself a weapon.

Gwenda Wilkin was born in London on May 20 1933, the only child of Frederick Wilkin, a farrier, and his wife Lillian (née Leith). Educated in Walthamstow, she first showed musical promise on the violin, but found that it made her neck and wrist ache. The accordion proved to be a more natural fit. Her first show was in a local bus depot in 1946, and in 1948 she won the All England Accordion Championship.

When Gwenda was 15 she was interviewed on the television programme *Picture Page*, her parents having defied the headmistress's injunction that she should not be allowed a day off school for such frivolity; branded a subversive influence, she was expelled.

She went to work for the great Italian accordion-maker Bruno Allodi, who built an instrument specially for her. When, some years later on a tour of Tripoli her accordion was left out in the sun by careless baggage handlers, and fell apart, hollering at the airport staff to fetch beeswax, she was able to strip it down and rebuild it.

In 1948 she came sixth in the World Accordion Championship, held in Belgium, and the following year she came third, in Milan. The same year she played on the inaugural radio run of Hughie Green's *Opportunity Knocks*.

She served an arduous apprenticeship in front of tough audiences at working men's clubs and football clubs. In 1950 she spent the summer in an orchestra in Felixstowe, but did not enjoy it: 'I was not a team player.'

By the time she married and had children in the 1960s, she was hugely successful. Her baby daughter would sleep in the accordion box backstage while she was performing.

Her fans included Princess Margaret and Princess Alice, and she performed at the Queen's garden parties at Buckingham Palace. But the heavy instrument was taking its toll and she was eventually told to give it up or end up in a wheelchair. She was devastated, and had her husband secrete her accordion in a hidden compartment in the spare bedroom that she could not reach.

She did not repine, however, and, in pursuit of a new career, decided to study animal husbandry; she was several decades older than the other students, to whom she played agony aunt. She went on to work in various veterinary establishments until she was 72. She also gained a private pilot's licence in her sixties.

Gwenda Wilkin married, in 1961, Anthony Mulvaney; he died in 1985, and their son and daughter survive her.

Gwenda Wilkin, born May 20 1933, died May 6 2020

Naim Attallah

Flamboyant Palestinian-born businessman and memoirist who 'ran Quartet Books like a sultan'

NAIM ATTALLAH, who has died aged 89, was a Palestinian-born entrepreneur who enjoyed a lucrative business career, notably with the luxury jeweller Asprey of Bond Street, but was better-known for his rather less financially rewarding role as proprietor of Quartet Books – a publishing company that he boasted had 'employed more pretty girls than MGM and 20th Century Fox put together'.

Attallah in 2007: his parties earned him one of his nicknames, 'Attallah the Fun'

'Naim ... made a name as the most exotic bird in the publishing aviary,' the former publisher Jeremy Lewis observed. 'Clad in red lizardskin shoes and different-coloured socks, one red, the other green, his jacket linings an iridescent flash, he ran Quartet Books like a sultan, buying books on a whim while a bevy of aristocratic beauties manicured his nails.'

Attallah explained his publishing philosophy thus: 'Suppose I meet you at a party and I like you a lot. I might create a project, just to see you again. The project would come second, the person first.'

This meant that Quartet, which Attallah purchased in 1976, published a great deal of dross, including an illustrated study of breasts called *Domes of Fortune*, and a collection of Arabella McNair-Wilson's photographs of her friends that one reviewer said ought to have been called *Sloanies and Their Cronies*. But there were also many distinguished works, including Julian Barnes's first novel, Ryszard Kapuściński's *The Emperor* and the memoirs of Brian Sewell.

Not the least admired of Quartet's publications were the many books written by its proprietor. His first, *Women* (1987), was the fruit of interviews with more than 300 female high-achievers and was one of Quartet's bestsellers, as well as being critically acclaimed. Attallah explained that his interviewees were forthcoming because, unlike British men, he actually liked women and displayed a genuine interest in what made them tick. There followed several more volumes of his interviews with the great and the good – John Updike, W. F. Deedes, Enoch Powell, Diana Mosley and Tony Benn among them.

There were also two well-received novels and several volumes of autobiography. But what really established Attallah as a central figure in literary London were his extravagant parties – which brought unwonted glamour to the publishing scene and earned him the sobriquet 'Attallah the Fun' – and his willingness to employ the daughters of eminent figures.

He found a job for Richard Ingrams's free-spirited daughter Jubby, who possessed no formal qualifications but turned out to be a great asset. Attallah hoped the arrangement would lead to less mockery from Ingrams's *Private Eye* (which nicknamed him Naim Attallah-Disgusting on account of Quartet's more dubious publications) although the attacks increased as Jubby ingenuously shared gossip about her employer with her father.

Attallah gave Nigella Lawson her first job and also counted Virginia Bonham-Carter, Sophia Sackville-West, Rebecca Fraser, Emma Soames, Arabella Pollen and Anna Pasternak among his stable of pedigree beauties at Quartet.

Attallah was married for nearly 60 years and told journalists that he was never unfaithful. But he expected flattery and adoration from his staff and although most of them seemed happy to grant his wish, there were reports that those who discouraged his flirting were made to feel so uncomfortable that they had to leave.

Although he seemed an unlikely ally of the sisterhood, in 1977 he established The Women's Press, which specialised in radical feminist literature. The star author was Alice Walker, author of *The Color Purple*, who eventually defected over late payments.

Attallah made little enough money from his publishing imprints, but some of his other ventures were so unremunerative as to be purely philanthropic. In 1981 he purchased the magazine *Literary Review*, installing Auberon Waugh as editor in 1986, and sank some £2 million into it with no hope of return, while Waugh drew a minimal salary and often paid contributors out of his own pocket. The two men admired each other's commitment to producing a first-class magazine (although it was too unpretentious to become fashionable) and in 2019, nearly two decades after Waugh's death, Attallah edited *A Scribbler in Soho*, a tribute volume.

In 1992 he became the proprietor of another fledgling magazine, which aimed for a similar combination of intelligence and lack of stuffiness – *The Oldie*. It was edited by his old foe Richard Ingrams, and they too became friends, Ingrams describing him as 'the first rich person I've met whom I like'. But by the time *The Oldie* finally began to flourish in the new millennium, Attallah had sold it on to John Paul Getty for a minimal profit.

Naim Ibrahim Attallah was born in Haifa, then in Palestine, on May 1 1931. His father Ibrahim was a bank cashier with Barclays bank who 'was inclined to violence and pushed my mother Genevieve around, then regretted it and cried'.

Naim longed to be a journalist, but his family felt the profession was too dangerous owing to the turmoil that followed the creation of Israel, and he studied engineering at Battersea

240

polytechnic. He did not complete the course and spent several years in manual jobs, including a spell as a steeplejack, before becoming a foreign exchange dealer for a French bank.

He then fell in with Yousef Beidas and worked for him at Intra Bank in London; in 1966 the bank collapsed and Beidas fled to Brazil before being arrested in Switzerland, but Attallah emerged from the debacle wealthy.

He became friends with John Asprey, the jewellery heir, and as joint managing and financial director of Asprey from 1979 he pursued an ambitious programme of acquisitions and oversaw a big increase in turnover.

Meanwhile, he set his sights on becoming a cultural impresario. As a film producer he backed the cinematic version of Dennis Potter's banned television play *Brimstone and Treacle* (1982) and, in partnership with his friend David Frost, the fluffy Cinderella musical *The Slipper and the Rose* (1976); there was also a disastrous attempt to stage a musical, *The Arabian Fantasy*, at the Albert Hall. He dabbled in perfumery, fashion and art dealing, but publishing was the only one of his extracurricular activities in which he made an enduring impact.

He was appointed chief executive of Asprey in 1992 and the following year was voted Retail Personality of the Year. But in 1996 he was ousted after the company reported its first ever annual loss.

He raged in the press against what he saw as the disloyalty of the Asprey family. But an even more humiliating betrayal followed in 2004 when one of his former Quartet employees, Jennie Erdal, published a memoir in which she revealed that she was Attallah's ghost writer, the true author not just of his books and articles but also his business letters and even love letters to his wife.

Jennie Erdal had begun by researching the questions for Attallah's interviews and ended up writing his novels; the putative author's contributions were limited to enquiries as to how much sex had been included: 'Beloved, we need the jig-jig!'

In fact, *Private Eye* had long questioned how somebody with Attallah's tortured command of spoken English could write so well, but the literary establishment, in deference to a much-loved benefactor, had blithely blinded itself to the issue.

To compound Attallah's fury at this spilling of the beans, Jennie Erdal's book, *Ghosting*, was hailed as a comic classic, with its central character expatiating on the unknowability of women ('So much mystique. You know, even their sexual organs are on the inside') and forbidding his staff from defecating on the premises. Attallah pulped the unsold stock of the books she had worked on.

In 2007 he told *The Telegraph* that he had divested himself of all his business interests except Quartet and was so impoverished that he was down to buying three or four bespoke suits a year instead of one a month.

Attallah was a doughty campaigner for Palestinian causes but rarely courted controversy on the issue, although he was excoriated in the press when he allowed an anti-Semitic article by Roald Dahl to be published in the *Literary Review*.

In *The Spectator* Jeffrey Bernard called for him to be whipped and added that Attallah was the ugliest man he had ever met, although Attallah insisted that the ferocity of the attack was due to his having made Bernard pay back the advance for an unwritten book on racing.

Although his application to join the House of Lords was turned down, Attallah was appointed CBE in 2017.

He married, in 1957, Maria Nykolyn, whom in the 1980s he set up as proprietress of the erotic Mayfair boutique Aphrodisia. She died in 2016 and their son survives him.

Naim Attallah, born May 1 1931, died February 2 2021

Clive Murphy

Writer whose 'Ordinary Lives' series gave voice to
pigmen, mantle-pressers and lavatory attendants

CLIVE MURPHY,
who has died
aged 85, was a
colourful writer
and historian best
known for his
'Ordinary Lives'
series of books,
for which he
interviewed modest
but eloquent
individuals who
had lived through
the upheavals and
social changes of
the first three-
quarters of the
20th century, and
edited their taped

reminiscences into compelling memoirs.

Murphy, who also published several novels and volumes of
what he called 'ribald rhymes' (titles such as *Sodomy is not
enough!* and *Gay Abandon* indicate their general drift), lived
for more than 40 years in bachelor chaos above the Aladin [sic]
curry house in Brick Lane, East London, in a two-room flat so
chock-a-block with decades of accretions as to delight some
future archaeologist with an interest in middens.

'I collect all the things and people that interest me, either
because they attract me or because I dislike them,' he explained.
'I also keep all correspondence and note all phone calls.'

It was amazing that he managed to publish anything at all.

It was shortly after he arrived in London from Ireland in the late 1950s, renting a bedsit in Pimlico, that Murphy got the idea for his series on 'ordinary lives'.

'There was a retired lavatory attendant and his wife who lived down below, and they invited me down for supper,' he told the anonymous 'Gentle Author' of the online magazine *Spitalfields Life*. 'He had such a natural gift for language and a quaint way of expressing himself, so I said, "Let's do a book!" and that was *Four Acres and a Donkey*.'

Other 'ordinary' people whose lives he recorded included a gamekeeper, a pigman, an East End Salvation Army hostel dweller, a river-keeper, a struggling poet, a failed tenor turned Jewish mantle presser, and Marjorie Graham, who had been a flapper, actress and chorus girl of the Roaring Twenties before falling on hard times and becoming a lavatory attendant at the Metropole Cinema in Victoria.

The series of memoirs was praised by Ronald Blythe as 'a marriage of art and artlessness', but when Murphy first tried to interest publishers in his 'brace' of lavatory attendants to 'make a fortune for all concerned', he received a pile of rejection slips, one editor advising him to apply again 'when you've recorded an attendant that's a hermaphrodite'.

Eventually Marjorie Graham and her male counterpart were taken on, along with other 'lives', by Dennis Dobson, founder of an eponymous publishing house, acquiring a select but enthusiastic following. Later they became available through Murphy's own publishing company Brick Lane Books.

Marjorie's memoir *Love, Dears!* (1980), republished in 2013 by Pan Macmillan as *Up in Lights*, was described by John Betjeman as 'deeply moving and authentic and compulsive reading. Her story has the full gloom of Tottenham Court Rd Underground Station and the precariousness of being alive. The lady is lovable indeed. My word what a good book.'

The 'Gentle Author' of *Spitalfields Life* observed that Murphy chose his subjects 'because he saw the poetry in them when no one else did'. But there was also a magpie fascination with the forgotten backwaters of human experience: 'The gamekeeper said to me, "You mean you don't know how to skin a mole?" I am amazed that we are all stuck in our little worlds – he really thought everyone would know that.'

Murphy claimed that his original aim had been to begin with the humblest 'and then work my way up in the world until I got to Princess Margaret'. But he abandoned the project as his subjects began to rise up the income scale, finding that members of the middle classes 'had an image of themselves they wanted to project' and insisted on being able to 'correct' what they had said before Murphy translated their words into published 'memoir'.

Clive Murphy was born in Liverpool to Irish parents on November 28 1935. The family returned to Ireland when he was a small child and he was brought up in Dún Laoghaire, a suburban coastal town near Dublin which, as it is pronounced 'Dun Leary', he would take pleasure in challenging people to spell. His mother wanted him to become a lawyer, and he qualified as a solicitor. But two holidays in London left him with a longing for the 'bright lights', and in 1958 he left Dublin for London bedsit-land and got a job as a liftman at a Lyons Corner House for £8 a week. Later, he taught primary schoolchildren in Islington, then children with special needs in the East End, while trying to make his name as a writer.

From his first bedsit in Pimlico, Murphy lived in rented rooms in various insalubrious parts of the capital, including the headmaster's study of a meths drinker-haunted derelict school in the East End, with cold water on tap but no electricity, from which he was flooded out, before moving into his flat in Brick Lane in 1974.

There, as the area became gentrified and his landlord wanted to charge a higher rent, Murphy, a rotund figure with a voice said to resemble that of the artist Francis Bacon, saw him off by inviting the rent officers to see his bathroom – a tin tub on top of his wardrobe: 'That brought my rent down.'

He had his first literary success with *Summer Overtures*, a novel featuring four young Irishmen (including a male prostitute and a writer manqué) making their way in London, which was joint winner in 1972 of the First Novel Award of *ADAM International Review*, the judges describing it as consisting of 'sulphurous sketches of life at several different levels of decay – personal, social, even in a sense political'.

It was followed by two novellas, *Freedom for Mr Mildew* and *Nigel Someone*, published as one volume in 1975. As with *Summer Overtures* they drew on Murphy's own experiences (*Nigel Someone* concerns a primary schoolteacher determined to make something of a pupil who has no interest in being made something of), and after that he concentrated on his oral history project.

His 10 collections of 'ribald rhymes' were described by one blogger as 'not for the faint-hearted' although they would be ideal presents for an in-law. The last of the series, *To Hell with Thomas Bowdler, Mrs Grundy and Mary Whitehouse!*, was published in 2015.

Though bedridden in his final years, Murphy retained his sense of humour. Mishearing an interviewer who asked him whether he minded being recorded with a Dictaphone, he replied: 'I thought you said with your d---, and I thought, here is an eccentric young man.'

Clive Murphy, born November 28 1935, died June 17 2021

The Alaafin of Oyo

Monarch of an ancient African kingdom who
became the most senior of Yoruba traditional rulers

The Alaafin of Oyo at the World Sango Festival, a celebration of a Yoruban deity

LAMIDI ADEYEMI, THE ALAAFIN OF OYO, who has died aged 83,
was the traditional ruler of the ancient Oyo kingdom in Nigeria.
As occupant of a seat that had survived for centuries into the
modern republic of Nigeria, he wielded great influence as an
authoritative representative of the interests and culture of the
Yoruba people.

Adeyemi held the position of Alaafin of Oyo for 51 years, longer
than any of his predecessors. By the time of his death, he was
recognised as the most senior of Yoruba traditional rulers in a
vast region in which almost every town has its own *oba*, or king.

He achieved this status by his sheer longevity (he outlived his main rival, Okunade Sijuwade, the Ooni of Ife), and by adroit political manoeuvring, safeguarded his position as chairman of the Oyo State Council of Obas and Chiefs (defying a civilian governor of Oyo State who tried to unseat him in 2011 for not supporting his re-election).

The Alaafin's palace in the city of Oyo – today, a sprawling town of about 500,000 people – is said to be the largest in the Yoruba heartland in south-western Nigeria. Here, the Alaafin lived and maintained a tradition of kingship which held that, as the Yoruba historian the Reverend Samuel Johnson wrote in his *The History of the Yorubas* (1921), the Alaafin 'is more dreaded than even the gods'.

Like his predecessors, the Alaafin had numerous wives (his father was said to have had 200), and a court of office holders and servants whose duties included singing panegyrics, playing trumpets and unfurling the royal umbrella. His fleet of cars bore licence plates that read IKU BABA YEYE – 'Master of Life and Death'.

Under British imperial rule, which lasted from 1901 until Nigeria's independence in 1960, the country was governed indirectly, with the minimum of resident officials from London. To achieve this, local traditional rulers were given official status and authority within the British protectorate.

The abundance of Yoruba rulers led to a system of ranking in which the Alaafin of Oyo was given first place, in recognition of the history and prestige of the Oyo empire and the Alaafin's willingness to work with the British.

In the years after independence, the Alaafin of Oyo found his status as the first among Yoruba kings slipping in favour of the Ooni of Ife, traditional ruler of a neighbouring land that claims not only to be the cradle of the Yoruba people but also the birthplace of mankind.

The rivalry of the Ooni and the Alaafin, played out in contention for chairmanship of the Oyo Council of Obas and Chiefs, reflected two different aspects of Yoruba kingship: the